GREENBERG'S® GUIDE TO

LIONEL® HO
Volume II • 1974-1977

George J. Horan

A Greenberg Publication

Lionel® and American Flyer® are the registered trademarks of Lionel Trains, Inc., Chesterfield, Michigan.

Copyright © 1993
by Greenberg Publishing Company, Inc.

Greenberg Book Division
Kalmbach Publishing Company
21027 Crossroads Circle
Waukesha, Wisconsin 53187
(414) 796-8776

First Edition

Manufactured in the United States of America

Greenberg Publishing Company, Inc. publishes the world's largest selection of Lionel, American Flyer, LGB, Marx, Ives, and other toy train publications as well as a selection of books on model and prototype railroading, dollhouse building, and collectible toys. For a complete listing of current Greenberg publications, please call 1-800-533-6644 or write to Kalmbach Publishing, 21027 Crossroads Circle, Waukesha, Wisconsin 53187.

Greenberg Shows, Inc. sponsors *Greenberg's Great Train, Dollhouse and Toy Shows*, the world's largest of its kind. The shows feature extravagant operating train layouts, and a display of magnificent dollhouses. The shows also present a huge marketplace of model and toy trains, for HO, N, and Z Scales; Lionel O and Standard Gauges; S and 1 Gauges; plus layout accessories and railroadiana. They also offer a large selection of dollhouse miniatures and building materials, and collectible toys. Shows are scheduled along the East Coast each year from Massachusetts to Florida. For a list of our current shows please call (410) 795-7447 or write to Greenberg Shows, Inc., 7566 Main Street, Sykesville, Maryland 21784 and request a show brochure.

Greenberg Auctions, a division of Greenberg Shows, Inc., offers nationally advertised auctions of toy trains and toys. Please contact our auction manager at (410) 795-7447 for further information.

ISBN 0-89778-359-X (Hardback)

Library of Congress Cataloging-in- Publication Data

Horan, George J.
  Greenberg's guide to Lionel HO.

  Vol. 2 by George J. Horan.
  Vol. 1 by Vincent Rosa and George J. Horan, c1986.
  —Vol. 2 t.p. verso.
  Includes indexes.
  Contents: vol. 1. 1957-1966 — v. 2. 1974-1977
  1. Railroads—Models. 2. Lionel Corporation.
  I. Rosa, Vincent. II. Rosa, Vincent. Greenberg's
  guide to Lionel HO trains. III. Title.
  TF197.R67 1993   625.1'9   92-38714
  ISBN 0-89778-359-X (v. 1)
  ISBN 0-89778-339-5 (v. 2)

CONTENTS

PREFACE

Sometime near the end of 1985, and a few months before *Greenberg's Guide to Lionel HO Trains*, which I had the pleasure of coauthoring, was to be published, one question kept coming to mind. Should the General Mills Fundimensions HO line of the 1970s be included in this first book on Lionel HO products? That first book covered the period from 1957 to 1966 and told of the development of Lionel HO from the original manufacture of items by Rivarossi, a leading manufacturer in Italy, through the period when Athearn supplied Lionel with HO models, to the eventual manufacture by Lionel Corporation itself. (An entirely revised and expanded edition of that publication, now entitled *Greenberg's Guide to Lionel HO, Volume I: 1957–1966*, has just been published as I write this introduction to Volume II.)

It had been a big job in itself, and I rationalized that more than 75 percent of the items produced in the 1970s — when General Mills owned Lionel train manufacture, under the Model Products Corp. (MPC) — were really not Lionel-made items. (The Introduction, Chapter I, explains in detail the sources of later Lionel HO items, manufactured by five companies in seven different countries, and how collectors can identify which manufacturer produced a specific item.)

I realized that it took me six years to finish coverage of just the early production items and to satisfy myself that the information given was fairly accurate. I rationalized further: if I waited to include the 1970s production items (what collectors generally call the MPC era, since the Model Products Corp. division of General Mills had produced Lionel trains from 1969 until 1973, when the Fundimensions division took over), it could very well take another two or three years. I also told myself that no one ever asked much about these later items at the meets I attended. Rarely did the items come up in conversation. Maybe there was no interest in these models as collectibles.

On the other hand, I did have a sizable collection of everything Lionel sold, with the exception of a few of the Canadian items and three of the building kits that had been offered. Thus I also knew that instead of dealing with three manufacturers, as was the case with the 1957–1966 lines, I would have to sort out five manufacturers to complete the Lionel HO story.

Maybe just a listing of the items that were available for the four additional years would do. No, I told myself. A listing of numbers would simply cause confusion. It would not provide enough information to properly identify the items. The Fundimensions end of the collection was packed up and put away. I would not take the time to include it. The written text was sent on to Bruce Greenberg less the General Mills-era production.

It was not long after the book appeared that the letters, phone calls, and conversations started. The talk at meets, the calls and letters that came through the Greenberg offices and to my home were always the same. "The book is great," I heard. . . . "It's something that we really needed! The information given is right on. But where are the 1970s items?". . . "I know Lionel remade their HO line when General Mills took over; I have some of the items, but not much information on just what was available. . . ." At the meets I attended it was much the same: "I have lots of original boxed Lionel that is not covered in your book. I must have some really rare stuff. Any idea of what this is worth?"

Well, friends, I had made a Giant Mistake back in 1985. In fact, I should title this Preface "Apology." The interest *was* there. If it was sold by Lionel, it was collectible — no matter how poorly made. Information was needed and wanted by the HO collector.

By the end of 1986 I had made a number of promises that the General Mills production of Lionel HO would be added to any new edition of the book. If not, then it would be a separate book.

A short conversation with my coauthor of the first volume, Vincent Rosa, revealed that he would not have the time available to get involved this time around. After a second conversation with Bruce Greenberg, I found myself unpacking my MPC collection. And here, six years later, the information-gathering is finished. I hope readers find the wait was worth it.

HOW TO USE THIS BOOK

This book first looks at the U.S. Lionel HO line — that is, those products that were marketed as Lionel in this country. After a survey of the complicated history of later Lionel HO, and illustrated explanations of how to identify the products of each of the manufacturers involved, two separate chapters study the lines of locomotives, the freights, and the few passenger cars. The scenic accessories and handsome building kits are described and illustrated next, followed by full coverage of MPC Lionel HO sets, catalogued and all authenticated uncatalogued. Chapter VI covers all items that were marketed in Canada, and then Chapter VII describes catalogues, packaging, and paper items found in the U.S. and Canadian markets. The last chapter illustrates the various motive parts, track, couplers, etc. used with Lionel HO during 1974–1977. A factory parts list is included.

Discussion of frames, trucks, couplers, and other car details are provided in the appropriate chapters, right before each group of listings using the specific types. For your convenience these types are summarized in Chapter VIII, following which you will find selected instructional sheets and a Glossary of terms used in this book.

The listings in this volume are organized by Lionel catalogue number. In most cases at least the last four digits of the catalogue number appears on the car. Anything that does not appear on the car is placed in parentheses. If the side-of-car number differs only by the prefix number we run that full car number after the catalogue number that appears in parentheses. If a side-of-car number varies greatly from the catalogue number, this number is also listed within the coverage of that particular type of car, and you are referred to the full descriptive listing under the catalogue number. In other words, if you are trying to identify a car, ignore the prefix on the car and in listings and look first under the last four digits. If it is not there, look for side-of-car numbers cited in the Index or at the beginning or end of the specific listings to see if you are referred to a catalogue number.

The first information given in any listing covers the often complex cataloguing and availability matters. Each listing concludes with suggested values, and any relevant comments as to an item's changing position in the marketplace.

Values

Values are reported for each item where there have been reported sales. I have kept a constant watch on the asking prices at meets in all six states within four hours driving time of my home, and I have analyzed sales lists from across the U.S. and conferred with other HO collectors. The information gathered reflects the asking price only, as most dealers will not reveal the actual selling price.

Toy train values vary for a number of reasons. First, consider the **relative knowledge** of the buyer and seller. A seller may be unaware that he has a rare variation and sell it for the price of a common piece. Another source of price variation is **short-term fluctuation** that depends on what is being offered at a given train meet on a given day. If four examples of the same locomotive are for sale at a small meet, we would expect that supply would outpace demand and lead to a reduction in price. A related source of variation is the **season of the year**. The train market is slower in the summer, and sellers may at that time be more inclined to reduce prices if they really want to move an item. There is also the matter of **regional differences**; certain gauges and/or road names are more popular in some areas of the country than others, and thus the relative value of HO items can vary from one region to another. Another important source of price variation is the relative strength of the seller's **desire to sell** and the buyer's **eagerness to buy**. Clearly a seller in economic distress will be more eager to strike a bargain. A final source of variation is **the personalities** of the seller and buyer. Some sellers like to quickly turn over items and, therefore, price their items to move; others seek a higher price and will bring an item to meet after meet until they find a willing buyer.

A number of times in the last year, I found myself in a situation similar to one at a 1988 TCA meet at York, Pennsylvania, where I witnessed the sale of the pre-1966 5711 set for an unheard-of price. Recent situations also involve prices I thought quite high, but the sales were made. One event in Philadelphia saw the sale of the two-piece 5-8422 UP crane car set for $75; the same dealer sold two U-18-B diesels for $125. As was the case with the buyer at the York meet, this buyer came from an area with few train meets and was willing to pay more to add the models to his collection.

Overall, the last few years have in most cases shown a steady increase in prices, with the Lionel-made later HO items leading. But the Roco-made models in many cases are just as sought after. A complete reverse appears to have taken place with the new Lionel-made items of the 1970s. They are now commanding the higher prices, as contrasted to the trend of the pre-1966 models (there Lionel-made models demand comparatively low prices and seem to be more plentiful at meets). I do feel that the very short two-year period during which the Kader-made models were available will be in itself the reason all Kader production will become the most sought after and the most challenging; their prices, fairly low at present, will steadily rise.

Condition

For each item, we provide three categories: **Good**, **Excellent**, and **Mint**. The Train Collectors Association (TCA) defines conditions as:

Good: Scratches, small dents, dirty

Excellent: Minute scratches or nicks, no dents or rust

Mint: Brand new, absolutely unmarred, all original and unused, in original box.

In the toy train collecting field there is a great deal of concern with exterior appearance and less concern with operation. If operation is important to you, then ask the seller whether the train runs. If the seller indicates that he does not know whether the equipment operates, you should test it. Most train meets have test tracks provided for that purpose.

We include "Mint" in this edition because of the important trade in Lionel HO items. However there is substantial confusion in the minds of both sellers and buyers as to what constitutes mint condition. How do we define mint? Among very experienced train enthusiasts, a mint piece means that it is brand new, in its original box, never run, and extremely bright and clean (and the box is, too). An item may have been removed from the box and replaced in it but it should show no evidence of handling. A piece is not mint if it shows any scratches, fingerprints, or evidence of discoloration. It is the nature of a market for the seller to see his item in a very positive light and to seek to obtain a mint price for an excellent piece. In contrast, a buyer will see the same item in a less favorable light and will attempt to buy a mint piece for the price of one in excellent condition. It is our responsibility to point out this difference in perspective *and* the difference in value implicit in each perspective, and to then let the buyer and seller settle or negotiate their different perspectives.

We receive many inquiries as to whether or not a particular piece is a "good value." This book will help answer that question, but there is NO substitute for experience in the marketplace. WE STRONGLY RECOMMEND THAT NOVICES DO NOT MAKE MAJOR PURCHASES WITHOUT THE ASSISTANCE OF FRIENDS WHO HAVE EXPERIENCE IN BUYING AND SELLING TRAINS. If you are buying a train and do not know whom to ask about its value, look for the people running the meet or show and discuss with them your need for assistance. Usually they can refer you to an experienced collector who will be willing to examine the piece and offer his opinion.

No Reported Sales: In the few cases where there is insufficient information upon which to determine the value of a given item, we indicate that in the price column. Here again we recommend that you rely on your experience, or on the assistance of an experienced collector to determine what price you should pay for any of these items.

ACKNOWLEDGMENTS

Once again I find myself in the situation of picking and choosing words to thank people whom in many cases I have never even met. To those listed here my debt cannot be repaid. A simple thank you seems to be so little for all the help received.

First I must thank **Bruce** and **Linda Greenberg** for their patience and support during the past few years, as usual. They were both right there when needed. A project like this can be very stressful at times without the proper backing. Thank you both. A very special thank you is also in order for **Elsa van Bergen**, member of the Greenberg staff and editor of this publication. Her many long hours of work, including our weekend telephone conferences, were contributed enthusiastically, and her publishing expertise is plainly seen on these pages. I thank her for her time, patience, and understanding.

And to my daughter **Stacy** and son **Mark**, special thanks with much love for all the gentle pushes during the hard times these last two years.

Also I must thank my many old friends who always had an eye out for the models I was still searching for and which were always found by one of them. Regarding the items marketed in this country, these friends include **Ed DeVincentis**, **Mike Nechapor**, and **Joe Otterbein**, all of Philadelphia. I thank my nephew **Fred Coppola**, for the many pieces he located, and his sister, **Cathy**, for the many hours she spent typing some of the notes appearing here.

To my brother-in-law **Tom Armenti** and his son **Kent**, for the use of their collection, special thanks. This book benefitted from the knowledge of **Charles Sommer**, who thoroughly checked for accuracy and pointed out details and uncatalogued sets I did not have. To **Paul Besser, Dr. Geoffrey Bunza, Ken Fairchild, Wally Krocsko, Ron Mapps, Matt Padgett, Ronald Pelletier, Ken Rosenberger, Paul Summers**, and to any I may have forgotten, sincere thanks for assistance — apart from that specifically acknowledged below — with the preparation of this volume. Thanks to my neighbor and good friend, **Dick Wegner**, who spent long hours building the different scale buildings Lionel offered, which appear in this book.

Letters to and phone calls from **Lee Riley**, Bachmann's director of product development, with whom I spent many hours in the 1970s, when he was affiliated with AHM, was a great help in sorting out the Kader-made models sold as Lionel. Lee has certainly made a name for himself in the model train world in recent years, and I venture to say he is a great asset to the Kader-Bachmann Corporation. I remember him as a collector with remarkable knowledge, not limited to any one scale or prototype of train model. In the early 1970s his comments on which of the GG-1s AHM was introducing to the HO market would probably become collectible turned out to be very reliable, and his information on items sold by both Bachmann and Lionel in the 1970s made the job of noting differences in these items far easier.

To **Dan Johns** of Craft House Corporation my sincere thanks for the letters and the time spent helping me sort through so many interesting questions from his perspective as former Director of Product Integrity and Consumer Services at Lionel.

I thank **Elke Krug**, my first Pola contact, and **Dr. Rene F. Wilfer**, of Pola Corporation, for their help in identifying Pola products and in learning more about the company; and **H. Adlgasser**, and the people of Roco International of Austria, for the helpful information concerning their fine products. Thanks go to the people of **Anheuser Busch, Coors Beer, General Mills, Heinz Foods, Railway Express Corporation, Redco Foods, Salada Tea, Spalding Sports, Stroh Brewery, Sun Maid Growers, Tropicana Products**, and **Voit Sports Equipment**, for their time in producing information on the use of their logos and names by Lionel on their HO line of cars. Thanks also to **Don Simonini** for information on the Salada boxcar and to the people of **Bev-Bel Custom Painters** of Cresskill, New Jersey, especially **Irv Belkin**, owner; to **Steve Young** of Cudec, Inc.; and to **Ray Thrayfell** of C.M. Shops, both of northern New Jersey, for help in sorting out the custom-painted items available in the late 1970s.

Chapter VI, on the models sold in Canada under the Lionel name, could never have been written without the help given freely by both old and recently found friends in Canada — some of whom I have not yet met. Sincere thanks to all those listed below, and to those who asked that their names not be given.

First, my friend **Paul Besser** and his son **Kevin** were responsible for letting me know there were indeed models specially made for the Canadian market and for their time in helping me acquire many of the items pictured in this book. To say they are both knowledgeable on this subject is quite an understatement. I've learned that if Paul says it was made, it was. **Jim Walther** of Mount Albert Junction, Ontario, although not into HO himself, took the time to put me in contact with **Mike Tibando**, who was most helpful. Thank you both.

Thanks to **Bill Jamieson**, my first contact with George's Trains of Ontario, for help back in 1980, and to owner **George Olieux**, who was generous with his time and knowledge, which helped me to compile accurate information. The people of **Windsor Hobbies**, Ontario; **Lark Spur Line**, Ontario; **Golden Spike Models**, Winnipeg; and **Van Hobbies**, Vancouver, all took the time to answer my inquiries, whether they had models for sale or not.

I am grateful to **Don Taylor**, of Manitoba, who provided a second mint Confederation Flyer set, with cars having construction different from that in the ones I had already written up. And, once again, Dan Johns of Lionel is thanked here, for his expert help in identifying both U.S. and Canadian-offered models.

To my very special friend, **Ann Polito**, who spent many hours typing notes and who was always there with her support, thank you. In addition to Bruce and Linda Greenberg and Elsa van Bergen, many at Greenberg Publishing contributed to this volume. A special thank to **Norm Myers** for his expert art direction, particularly of the covers that enhance both this volume and the first. Photographer **Al Fiterman** took the photographs for these volumes with both skill and good humor, which were both appreciated. **Donna Price** once again proofread carefully several versions of this text as well as its illustrative materials and helped assure accuracy and consistency. The volume was designed and pasted up by **Wendy Burgio**, with the assistance of **Maureen Crum**. **Kevin Stansbury** and **Bill Wantz** did the printing and statting of illustrations that document my text. Support was also provided by Greenberg managers **Allan Miller, Sam Baum**, and **Cindy Lee Floyd**.

G. J. H.

This book is dedicated to the memory of my beloved mother Catherine and of my oldest sister, Elizabeth — both passed away during the preparation of this book. Their continuing support made its publication possible.

CHAPTER I
Introduction to Lionel Fundimensions HO Line

When it was announced that the Fundimensions Division of General Mills had been licensed to make Lionel trains again, I was overjoyed. Surely they would also remake the HO line, too. Lionel had not done too well in the 1960s with their HO products. By now they must have learned that any HO model would have to be at least as good as what was already available to the HO operator and collector. Now they would be up against companies like AHM (Associated Hobby Manufacturers) of Philadelphia, who were marketing outstanding steam locomotives and cars and had been importing Rivarossi models since the early 1970s. New engines and cars not being sold by other manufacturers at this time were what would be needed. Lionel's gimmick cars of the 1950s and 1960s were not well received by HO enthusiasts. However, the passenger cars from the early HO line were fine models; surely these cars would be a part of any new line Lionel introduced.

The year 1970 came and went, but there was no HO line from Lionel. Three years of waiting produced only more rumors that Lionel would again make a line of HO. Following a year more of waiting, 1974 saw Lionel finally reentering the HO marketplace.

As I considered myself something of a collector with a fair amount of knowledge about their past production in HO, I looked forward to once again having the chance to add a few more rectifiers to my pre-1966 collection. Possibly they would reintroduce them in different road names. That would be wonderful. As things turned out, however, that was not to be. The new HO models — with the exception of the reworked shells of the Alcos, the GP-9s, and the box, stock, and flatcars offered, and a few of the accessories — showed that Lionel had not learned much about the market.

None of the older line items were to be remade, as they were in the 1960s. In the late 1950s, Lionel first entered the HO field with foreign-made models and after three years introduced their own models to the marketplace; some of them were quite good. But in the 1970s just the opposite was true. They started out with their own models and within four short years ended up with 85 percent of what was offered being made outside the United States.

Only five different types of power units were offered in the entire HO line of the 1970s, with twenty-three different road names being used. In the 1950s and 1960s they had offered sixteen different power units with over thirty road names available.

The same holds true for the rolling stock. The first few Lionel-made items were fairly good models, with Austrian-made items a close second. Then the more poorly made freight cars showed up in Lionel cartons and at a slightly higher price. This demonstrates that once again Lionel, as a company, was not committed to the HO enthusiasts. Take the U-18-B diesel of 1976 as an example. It was a great piece of motive power. Everyone liked it, and it was the only one available on the market at the time. Still, it was dropped from the catalogue the very next year (which also just happened to be Lionel's last year in HO).

ANTICIPATING THE RETURN OF LIONEL HO

The first official word of Lionel's reentry into HO appeared in the *Model Railroader* column "Off the Train Wire," in May 1974. The short six-line announcement stated only that Lionel was back in HO with a special new GE-made motor. The announcement also stated that the new line would be available only in sets the first year. It left the reader to wonder if Lionel would do a better job at a second attempt to take its place in the HO marketplace. The fact that Lionel would use other manufacturers as suppliers was not mentioned.

A second bit of information appeared in the *Model Railroader* column in September 1974: it merely stated that a catalogue was now available for 50 cents from Lionel in Mount Clemens, Michigan. Finally, in the November 1974 issue of the same magazine, the first Lionel ad appeared, on pages 40 and 41, to introduce their new HO line. The caption "THE GRAND OLD NAME IN TRAINS IS NOW THE GREAT NEW NAME IN HO" appeared below a picture of the gold Chessie GP-9 in both O and HO Gauges. Totally in black and white, the ad was not much of an investment in dollars, nor much in the way of fanfare — especially from an outfit as large as Lionel, and in this prime vehicle to HO operators. The second page of that first ad was devoted to information on the special new GE motor, on the painting and lettering of the new line, and on the drive train. The pulling power of the new locomotives was also mentioned. Overall, it was not the kind of ad to turn you on, or to make you want to run out to see these new trains. Nothing was said about which items were to be available or in which road names.

One collector, Charles Sommer, stated he found it ironic that page 2 of this first catalogue clearly showed a Santa Fe FA-1 with a pre-1966 shell and the number 0595 with its truck side frames also missing, while pages 5 and 6 showed the UP set of 5-1481 with the locomotive carrying a triple 000 mockup number, while the SF and GN on page 3 show no catalogue numbers at all. These mistakes demonstrate the haste with which the first catalogue was issued.

I made up my mind to pick up these new items as they became available. I had the feeling the line would not last, but the very short period of only four years shocked me nevertheless.

After examining the first two sets I purchased, I was *sure* the line would not sell well. There was simply nothing new. As things turned out, the 1974–1975 Lionel-made items were the best Lionel offered during the full four years the line was available.

1974: THE DEBUT OF MPC LIONEL HO

The first catalogue offered by Lionel was an eight-page color folder with a solid blue cover, which carried the year "1974" and nine

THE NEW LIONEL HO MOTOR

The very heart of a train is the motor and Lionel engineers, after more than a year of testing every motor available, have chosen the finest. It is the all American-made General Electric motor built to Lionel specifications. It is the motor that has proven its reliability through actual daily use in American homes in millions of electrical products. It is a motor that offers extremely long-lasting performance, an efficient, quiet operation, plus instant starting.

TOTALLY NEW HO DURABILITY

Around the GE motor, Lionel engineers designed a new drive train, one that was performance-tested for thousands of hours under the harshest conditions to assure durability, efficiency, and trouble-free operation. It is a drive train that combines the right design with the right materials . . . die cast metal, and the most exotic engineering plastics . . . offering heavy weight, exceptionally smooth acceleration and realistic operation at both low and high speeds.

TOTALLY NEW HO PULLING POWER

Lionel HO engines provide heavy-duty pulling power, a result of extended testing for just the right combination of design, materials, and weight, to pull a number of cars that far exceeds the most ardent enthusiast's requirements. This superior pulling power allowed Lionel to heavily weight every car for the added feature of stability and realistic railroading. And Lionel's needlepoint bearings and acetal resin-nylon trucks provide jewel-type free wheeling action for virtually friction-free operation.

TOTALLY NEW ATTENTION TO DETAIL

Every Lionel HO locomotive and car is painted, sometimes three and four times. And as with Lionel 'O', the Lionel HO line features markings unmatched for clarity, crispness, depth of color, and attention to detail. This is due to the technical advances and equipment used exclusively by Lionel. Over every inch of the train, Lionel has strived meticulously to duplicate the real world of railroading . . . a Lionel tradition for 17 years.

This page from the 1974 catalogue announces all the new features of Lionel HO.

small photos of items offered — which made it useful though deceiving to the novice collector. The inside cover featured the same picture of the gold Chessie that appeared in the first ad in *Model Railroader,* but the caption now made reference to the new HO locomotive being as powerful as its O Gauge counterpart. The trouble with that kind of thinking was that most operators in HO at that time never ran an O Gauge layout and did not know what an O Gauge locomotive could pull or how it performed; the smaller HO is what they understood and cared about. Give them a good-looking model, as close to scale as possible, with fine details and dependability in operation, and HO people will buy it.

This booklet was devoted to the full "new" line — a total of four sets. No items were catalogued for separate sale, and none were available this first year.

The first "new" power units offered were a GP-9 and an Alco FA-1, both available in two road names. All four used the Lionel 5400-series catalogue numbers. The GP-9 in the B & O golden Chessie color scheme headed set number one — 5-1480. This first set contained nine freight cars, track and DC power pack, a signal and girder bridge, and a manual switch. It also held a set of twelve telephone poles, a bumper, and a set of twelve road signs. Made of plastic, the set was priced in the $40 range. The second catalogued set, 5-1481, was also headed by a GP-9 in the Union Pacific colors.

The first Alco FA-1 introduced came in the Great Northern colors and headed the third set (5-1482), and the second Alco FA-1 in the Santa Fe passenger colors headed the fourth set (5-1483).

Rolling stock, available only in these sets this first year, were a 40-foot boxcar in two road names — CP Rail and Grand Trunk. There were also three 40-foot flatcars, in two road names and one unmarked. These flats, the red Santa Fe and the yellow Union Pacific, came with twelve black plastic stakes but had no loads. The black unmarked flat had the same black stakes and a load of five brown plastic simulated steel I-beams.

Also available that year was a 40-foot gondola in three road names. The red Southern Pacific, the blue B & O Chessie, and the orange Rio Grande. This last gondola was available in two sets, with and without a load of three white plastic culvert pipes. One stock car, also a 40-footer, was also available; it came in the red MKT road name. One four-bay hopper came in the Burlington road name. Further available was a black three-dome tank car in the Dow Chemical markings. This was to be the only type of tank car Lionel offered in the 1974–1977 period. A 50-foot steel reefer was also shown in two names — the green Railway Express and the orange Pacific Fruit Express.

One manually operating crane car was also offered, the only operating car offered for the four-year period. It was available in the C & O road name. It was sold unpainted, in black plastic. The road name and number were added to the model as decals by the modeler; the decaled road name was the only change made to this car in the next three years.

The 1974 line finished up with a steel-sided Santa Fe–style caboose, offered in four road names. There was a Santa Fe in red, a yellow Union Pacific, a yellow and silver Chessie, and a red Great Northern. The four caboose road names offered matched the first four power units available in these sets.

All in all, it was not much of a first step for the biggest name in trains. Their new line of HO contained only two types of power units and ten different pieces of rolling stock. Not one item in the line was *really* new to the market (the one exception was the gold-painted Chessie: the paint scheme at least was new and not available elsewhere). All could be had elsewhere — and in most cases at a cheaper price in the production of other HO manufacturers of the day.

The two types of power units, the cabooses, the boxcars, and one stock car were all manufactured in Mount Clemens, Michigan, the new 1974 items made from Lionel pre-1966 reworked dies. The other types of catalogued rolling stock first offered in 1974 were all of foreign manufacture.

It also must be noted here that the design of the Fundimensions-built power units were prone to breakage. This problem existed in the truck side frames for the four years and on the black plastic U clamps that hold the metal weights in place, which were used from 1975 until the end of production. Many collectors have stated they were embarrassed to have sold a mint locomotive, only to have the wheels fall off when the buyer first opened the carton.

Before continuing the saga of later Lionel HO, we need to pause to explore the complicated matter of who actually produced the items of the MPC era.

SOURCES OF LIONEL HO, 1974–1977

In the four short years Fundimensions offered their Lionel HO line, the items — or parts of them — were manufactured in the United States (Lionel), England (Airfix), Canada (London Plastics), Austria (Roco), West Germany (Pola), Hong Kong (Kader), and Taiwan (Kader). The last two sources produced the poorest quality of items offered. What follows are profiles of the major producers of later Lionel HO — three manufacturers other than Lionel itself. (In addition, Airfix of England produced some accessories.)

The Roco-Lionel Connection

The Roco firm was founded in 1960 in Salzburg, Austria, by Mr. Heiz Rossler and his wife Elfriede. Known in 1960 as "Ing. Heiz

Rossler," it was to be a major part of the railroad hobby market, both in the United States and abroad, in just ten short years.

Like most new businesses, it started small, with a line of plastic toys such as sand buckets, assembly-type games, and toy automobiles, all for sale on the European market. Also produced during this first year was a line of military vehicles for export to the United States. It was a major success in a very short time. Marketed here under the trade name "Minitank," the vehicles had excellent detail, and they are still part of the Roco line today.

In 1963 Roco produced the first HO freight cars, using American prototypes for the U.S. market. They too were a great success. 1963 also saw the first of the new N Gauge trains, introduced by Roco — another hit. By the end of that year a large expansion program was in full swing to keep up with the demand from the United States market. One U.S. associate sent a note to Mr. Rossler stating: "Ship as much as you can, of anything you can." Soon half a million Minitank vehicles alone were rolling off the production line. Not bad for a three-year-old company. By 1967 the firm was ready to add a line of European prototype HO for its European customers. Needless to say, it was still another successful product, and these models remained in the line. By 1973 Roco introduced its new railway system at the Nuremburg Toy Fair, under the name Roco International. A close coupling system for HO and N Gauge was also introduced. Patented by Roco in 1967, it is still in use today.

The firm also acquired the tooling and diework from the now-bankrupt Rowa HO firm. Roco reworked the dies and increased its line of European-prototype HO models for its customers. Late 1973 saw the firm make the commitment to Lionel to produce rolling stock for Lionel's new line of HO trains to be marketed in 1974 in the United States. Some of these models were decorated exclusively for Lionel, utilizing both silk-screening and rubber-stamping methods. The Lionel HO collector of the 1990s will discover a real challenge in trying to acquire these models, due to the short four-year period of availability.

One wonders: if Lionel had made some sort of financial commitment to this fast-growing company, with its many innovations in the hobby field, would Lionel still have an HO line on the United States market. Then again, it did not appear that Roco needed outside help of any kind. Everything Roco introduced to the HO railroader was accepted and enjoyed. What was Lionel thinking when, in 1976, it moved most of the HO production to a Taiwan- and Hong Kong–based manufacturer? The quality of the new products was dramatically lower — as were Lionel HO sales. As we have seen, the following year, 1977, saw Lionel leaving the HO marketplace for the second time.

In 1977, the Roco firm also suffered a major loss in the passing of Mr. Rossler. But, in contrast to Lionel's decision to quit HO, Mrs. Rossler and her brother Walter Tschinkel took over the Roco operation and continued to move ahead.

The Pola-Lionel Connection

The building kits catalogued and sold as Lionel HO in the 1975–1977 time period were all manufactured by Horst Pollak under the Pola (of Rothhausen, West Germany) trade name. (The Pola company was founded in 1957 by Horst Pollak, who headed the firm until his passing in 1986; it was then purchased by "Pola Spiel-und Freizeitartikel GmbH" and continues to supply its products to our hobby.) The building kits sold as Lionel in the 1957–1966 HO line were manufactured by Bachmann of Philadelphia, Pennsylvania, and were part of their HO Plasticville line. These new Pola kits had excellent detail. All parts were multicolor and no painting was required. In almost all cases the parts fit together perfectly.

First catalogued in 1975, the kits used a 4500-series numbering system. The first kits included a pickle factory, water tower, engine house, and a large passenger station; these were available until the end of the Lionel HO line in 1977.

In 1976 new kits, which retained the 4500-series numbers, were added to the line with a stockyard that included three horses and a ranch hand figure. Also new was a boiler house and a rooming house. Both included figures and tools, boxes, and crates. The 1976 catalogue presented three other new kits that changed to a 4600-series number designation: a coaling tower, grain elevator, and ice station. Close inspection of the pictures in the catalogue shows a big difference in the detail present, along with the filled-in window areas of the three kits.

The 1976 catalogue presentation of the kits, shown in color on pages 58 and 59 of this book including, the ice station, coal tower, and grain elevator that were never made for Lionel.

After much hunting on my part, I finally decided to write Pola for some answers about these three newly advertised items. Pola spokesman Dr. Rene F. Wilfer informed me that I had wasted many hours and written many letters searching for items that did not exist. (Apparently I was not alone in my search, though; the kits were advertised by some of the leading hobby shops of the day, with model numbers and prices included, which led many collectors off on a wild goose chase.) According to Dr. Wilfer, these three new kits were illustrated in 1976, but the dies were never made for HO. A coaling tower *was* made at the time and is still in the line. However, this is not the tower shown in Lionel's catalogue. No Pola tower kit was ever sold as a Lionel product.

Almost all of the kits that were sold have both the Pola and Lionel names on their bases. Of the kits that were available as Lionel most are available today in the HO lines of Model Power, Tyco, Con Cor, and Oregon Supply Company.

All of the kits carrying the Lionel name — as opposed to the late 1970 kits with the Pola name only — are highly collectible and difficult to find. Glue was needed to assemble these kits, and this makes for a tougher job in finding a built-up kit in good shape. With their outstanding detail, they were right at home on modelers' layouts of the 1970s and 1980s. They add value to any collection and should be acquired while prices are still rather reasonable.

The early kits of 1975 came with a soft sheet of acetate plastic for use as window material to be cut to size, while the kits of 1976–1977 had hard preformed clear plastic panels that fit the window case. This is a very important point. It is the only known difference in construction of the Pola kits offered as Lionel in the last three years of MPC-era Lionel HO, 1975–1977. All assembly sheets carry the Fundimensions Division of General Mills name but none mention it was a Pola-manufactured kit.

The Lionel-Kader Connection

Of the foreign-made models sold as Lionel in the 1974–1977 HO line, the most difficult to sort out have to be those made by Kader Industries of Hong Kong. With factories located at that time in Taiwan and Hong Kong, where its main headquarters are also located, Kader was the largest manufacturer of toy trains in the Far East during the time period 1974–1977. In 1980 a new modern plant opened on mainland China, and the older Taiwan plant closed four years later.

Not much was known about Kader Industries until the end of 1989 when an excellent article written by Dick Christianson appeared in the October issue of *Model Railroader*. The eight-page article included a personal interview with Mr. Kenneth Ting, vice-chairman of Kader Industrial Co. Ltd., Hong Kong. Although the article does not mention the Lionel name nor the items supplied to them by Kader, it does provide a history of the company and the acquisition of Bachmann of Philadelphia in 1988, which gave Kader the inroads needed to grow in the United States HO market.

According to the article, Kader worked with the Bachmann Company as early as 1968, when Kader became the first manufacturer in the Far East to produce N Gauge trains for the worldwide market and Bachmann distributed them. Until that time Kader was not producing motive power. This may also help to explain some of the variations found on some of the 1976–1977 Lionel HO items. It can also help one to understand how tough it is to find some of this early equipment sold as Lionel.

One must also note the answer given to Dick Christianson by Mr. Ting when he was asked about the quality of items coming out of Hong Kong in the early 1970s. Mr. Ting stated that many small companies in Hong Kong were copying products and that there were and still are small manufacturers with only two or three machines: this contributes to the range of quality coming out of Hong Kong. It is my speculation that items from Hong Kong were produced by manufacturers other than Kader; in other words, I believe they subcontracted work. I remember the first time I saw the decoration applied to the 5-5610 tricolored Chessie GP-9 of 1976; I thought it was without question the worst paint job I had ever seen on a model and I knew it was not Lionel work. I was also sure it was too poor a model to be a Kader-decorated item. Some other

company had to be making some of these models. I found it impossible to prove my theory, but I do state that models will be found stamped "Hong Kong" and "Taiwan" but show no manufacturer's name. According to my information, if it had the pancake-type motor and one powered truck, it was a Kader product. (Additional information on identifying Kader products is provided on page 12.)

Light was also shed by Dan Johns, who was heavily involved with the Lionel HO line of the 1970s. Although Dan cautioned that his information was strictly from memory of events fifteen years ago, I found his information checked out pretty well with what I had learned from other sources in the United States and Canada over a period of years. Dan stated that as best he could remember, no Lionel diework was ever shipped outside the United States for another manufacturer to produce the Lionel HO line. The GS-4 of 1975 was a Kader-owned die, made to Lionel specifications, with the locomotive being exclusively a Lionel item until 1977 when Lionel left the HO market. The same locomotive was then sold as a Bachmann model and remains in their HO line, but it is not quite the same locomotive of 1975, having had four or five changes made to its diework since it was used for the first Lionel-sold model.

This was according to Lee Riley, who was involved with the development of the Kader-made GP-30 Lionel offered; the tooling had been made and owned by Kader from the beginning. This diework became the well-known Spectrum Series GP-30 sold by Bachmann in 1988, with its highly detailed shell surpassing the model sold as Lionel a dozen years before. The modified die cannot now be used to remake the Lionel shell, reports Lee.

Lee and Dan agreed that Kader also produced an array of rolling stock for Lionel which included models for the Canadian line sold by Parker and the special Parker Brothers sets sold in Canada (these special sets were exclusive to the Canadian market and command extremely high prices today; they are covered later in this book). In a few cases these Kader-made models were the very same items offered in the U.S. line of Lionel HO.

Dan Johns and Lee Riley did not agree on the items shipped from Kader, however, with Dan unable to recall decorated rolling stock being part of the Kader program. Lee recalls that London Plastics, of Ontario, Canada, did the molding of the 1974–1975 power units for Lionel before shipping them in bulk to Mt. Clemens for assembly and decoration. Lionel was literally going in all directions as far as HO was concerned.

Lee also stated that he remembers the tooling used on the GP-9s of 1976–1977 was a Lionel tool reworked by Kader and returned to the United States after Lionel left the HO market. This move would help explain the GP-9s of 1976–1977 and the differences found on these shells, such as the roof-mounted tabs to which the clear light shaft was glued, and the thicker side area to support the new plastic handrails. He also remembers RailScope as the last HO model produced, in the late 1980s (see page 31). Lionel tooling was used for the two A shells that made up the model, while Kader produced the frame with its two motors and eight-wheel direct drive. The electronic components were produced in the United States, with all parts then shipped to Mt. Clemens, Michigan, for assembly.

A point of disagreement with many collectors is the gantry crane, catalogued in 1975, with Dan remembering it was never put into production, while other ex-employees remember that its base was made with original Lionel tooling ("the base was made for the beacon"), with the Roco-made crane attached to it. I must lean towards Dan's memory in this case, as I have only seen the crane once, pictured with accessories, and it was certainly not factory-made. (Some information is, however, given in Chapter IV on accessories.) One thing is for sure: Kader was Lionel's biggest supplier of HO products.

Surely all HOers today recognize the quality of the current Kader Bachmann line, with the new Spectrum Series N, HO, and G-scale train line. Once again you could ask: why didn't Lionel make some kind of move toward Kader? They seem to have had little difficulty improving, enlarging, and selling their HO products year after year.

IDENTIFYING SUPPLIERS OF LIONEL HO, 1974–1977

Note: Several comparative close-up photographs are included in this chapter; there are additional illustrations with the relevant discussion of car differences in Chapters II and III.

The matter of exactly what lettering appears on frames made by the several manufacturers (especially Kader) is a very complicated one. It is also an important one, since it is another way of identifying manufacturer. Instead of repeating the exact wording within each and every descriptive listing in the chapters that follow, we summarize the frame markings before each group of listings. All the possible Kader markings are provided in the box on page 12.

Each of the **Lionel-made items** carried the catalogue number on its side and "LIONEL" molded into the frame, except for the first Lionel-made Santa Fe-style cabooses, offered in 1974–1975, which did not have the Lionel name — an oversight on Lionel's part, I am sure. The first boxcars appeared very much like their 1965–1966 counterparts (see Volume I). They had the three-piece floor with metal weight and claw foot-type doors. They were reproductions of the Boston and Maine and New York Central–type boxcars introduced in 1965 and were made from original Lionel tooling. All of the rolling stock made in Austria carried the Lionel catalogue numbers on their sides but were not marked with the Lionel name, as all other power units and rolling stock produced outside the U.S. were.

The **rolling stock manufactured in Austria**, along with the tank and hopper of Kader Taiwan manufacture, were included in the first sets offered in 1974 and continued until the line was discontinued, although road names changed. The word "AUSTRIA" is visible on the frames of the gondola, 50- foot reefer, and marked flats; it appears to the right of the logo, a diamond (actually a turned square) with "RO / CO" within it. The Lionel catalogue number appears on the side of each unit but the Lionel name is not found. These cars were all produced with NMRA horn hook couplers and talgo-type trucks. The crane car has "MADE IN / AUSTRIA" but no logo.

The frames of the **cars and power units produced in Hong Kong and Taiwan** all bear the Lionel name and this helps to identify the items once they are out of their original box.

The models produced for Lionel by Kader Industries will be found with quite a variety of markings on their frames (see page 12); this also holds true for the Canadian line of models. With only one Kader plant in operation during the Lionel period, it is still unclear to me why the frame stampings on the models varied so greatly; they appear to change on almost every type of car produced in the Taiwan factory. The Kader-manufactured power units made in Hong Kong also carry variations of frame stamping, although nowhere as many. Some stamping is raised, and some is below the surface of the frame. Both factories use block-type capital printing in sizes ranging from very small (less than $\frac{1}{16}$ inch to $\frac{3}{16}$ inch). On the Taiwan-made rolling stock an oval gold paper sticker will also be found on *some* of the cars. In block capitals on the sticker is "MADE IN TAIWAN / REPUBLIC OF CHINA"; sometimes "R.O.C." or "ROC" is substituted for "Republic of China". One thing is for sure: the Kader name was never used on any model made for Lionel, whether it was made in Taiwan or in Hong Kong, and so the information that is on the frame is important to the HO collector. The green P & LE coil car is the only one known as bearing a white paper sticker.

Most of these models also carry part of the catalogue number on their sides. Many of the cars produced in Taiwan and Hong Kong were made not only for Lionel but for other HO companies selling in the United States at the very same time. Except for the style of lettering used, and some colors and numbers used on these cars, they are the very same car and can cause great confusion for collectors. (See the color photograph on page 55.) One must look for the Lionel name on the frame of each item in or out of a stamped carton. It also appears that many of the white individual cartons used for these items over the last two years were not always stamped with a catalogue number. Most cartons have no stamping at all when found in sets. The 40-foot three-dome Dow tank car and the first 40-foot Burlington hopper were both produced in Taiwan and were not Lionel diework. Both of these cars were also available for the full four-year period and were also produced with talgo-type trucks and horn hook couplers. The tank car will be found with the Lionel name on its frame and the catalogue number on its side, while the hopper only carries the catalogue number on its side and the word "Taiwan" on its frame. The Lionel catalogue number is used on both cartons.

Now having a sizable "duplicate" collection of the exact same Kader-made models stamped with either the Lionel or Bachmann names, I know that not *all* colors, road names, and numbers were duplicated, of course, but nevertheless the Lionel HO collector has to be careful in sorting through another manufacturer's items. Limit the sorting you need to do by looking for the Lionel name — then you will not be apt to accept a Bachmann-sold model as a Lionel item. More than once in the late 1970s I purchased a Bachmann model and, upon opening the package, found a car stamped with the Lionel name. I must admit it was just what I was hoping for, as the very same thing happened to me back in the late 1960s — when I bought Athearn models and found the Lionel logo as I opened the car carton.

It also appears that certain road names and colors were used strictly for the Lionel-stamped models and were not offered in the same road names in the Bachmann HO line until after Lionel had left the HO market in 1977. We now return to our chronological survey of Lionel HO; coverage of the years 1975–1977 follows.

1975

The only passenger cars offered for the full four years were the cars made for the Freedom Train sets, first shown in the 1975 catalogue in artwork that did little to show the cars as they were actually produced (see the illustration on page 14). When the sets were shown in the 1976 catalogue, photographs were used and so the sets were shown closer to the way they were actually produced. There is no question in the mind of this author that the two Bicentennial passenger sets will be the most difficult of the production items for the collector to find and will be highly valued. The cars became available separately in 1977 — but only because of dealer breakup of the sets. An extra number 105 display car was only available in the GS-4 steam set and will surely become the hardest of these cars for the collector to locate. This car was a short run of only 2500 pieces.

The 1975 catalogue saw the Alco FA-1 run again, in the Great Northern and Santa Fe road names. Both were now available for separate sale. While five new road names were also added to the catalogue, the numbers also changed to the 5-5500-series numbers on these new road names.

The first of the five new names was the red, white, and blue Freedom Train, shown for the first time in artwork that was fairly close to the produced reality. The second Alco was the red and yellow Rock Island. There was also a yellow Union Pacific, which was not catalogued in any of the last three years although it was available. The fourth locomotive in the tricolored Amtrak road name was also new, while the Southern Pacific, in Daylight colors, rounded out the new FA-1 line for 1975.

In 1975 collectors also saw the GP-9 return in the same road names as in 1974, with three new road names added. All were now eight-wheel drive units, as were the new Alcos for 1975 — all still made by Lionel. The newly added Geep road names included the red and white Frisco, the green and gold Southern, and the blue Grand Trunk. This was to be the last year the power units were entirely Lionel production, although nothing was mentioned about this in the catalogue.

The 1975 catalogue was the first to show items offered for separate sale. The rolling stock offered separately consisted of the same 40-foot stock car as appeared in 1974, with four new road names being added. The same four freight sets introduced in 1974 were still available with

MARKINGS ON KADER-MADE FRAMES

Kader Hong Kong Power Units
- GP-30s and FA-1 of 1976–1977
  Raised letters, "LIONEL" thicker, ⅛" capitals:

  "© 1976 FUNDIMENSIONS®
  LIONEL®
  Hong Kong"

  Note: "© 1976" does not appear on FA-1s.

- GS-4 (also on tender floor)
  3/16" capitals:
  "LIONEL®
  Hong Kong"

- GP-9s
  ⅛" capitals, "LIONEL" 3/16":

  "FUNDIMENSIONS
  LIONEL®
  Hong Kong"

- RailScope FA-1
  First letter capital:

  "©Lionel® Trains Inc.
  Mt. Clemens, MI 48045"

Kader Taiwan Rolling Stock
- Boxcars
  (a) ⅛" capitals for "LIONEL" and "TAIWAN"
      "MADE IN" smaller, in one line:
      "LIONEL   MADE IN TAIWAN"
  (b) Capitals all the same size

- Hi-cube Boxcars
  ⅛" capitals, two lines; periods in R.O.C.:

  "LIONEL   MADE IN TAIWAN
  R.O.C."

- Stock Cars
  ⅛" capitals, "LIONEL" in oval:

  "LIONEL   MADE IN
  TAIWAN ROC"

- 40-foot Reefers
  ⅛" capitals for "LIONEL",
  1/16" for rest:
  "LIONEL   MADE IN TAIWAN
  R.O.C."
  Gold sticker present with Republic of China spelled out.

- 50-foot Reefers
  ⅛" capitals
      "LIONEL   MADE IN TAIWAN
      ROC (for Republic of China)"

  Gold sticker present with:

      "MADE IN TAIWAN
      REPUBLIC OF CHINA"

- Cabooses
  (a) 1/16" capitals, "LIONEL" in oval:

      "LIONEL   MADE IN TAIWAN"
              s
  Gold sticker present with:

      "Made in Taiwan
      ROC"

  (b) Same as (a) but no oval around "LIONEL"
  (c) No oval, no gold sticker

- 48-foot Flatcars
  ⅛" letters:
      "LIONEL
      MADE IN TAIWAN"

- 50-foot Flatcars
  1/16" "LIONEL", rest 3/16":
      "MADE IN TAIWAN
      LIONEL"
  Gold sticker present on some with 1/16" lettering:
      "MADE IN TAIWAN
      REPUBLIC OF CHINA"

- Hoppers
  1/16" "LIONEL", ⅛" "TAIWAN":
      "LIONEL   TAIWAN"

- Coil Cars
  (a) ⅛" "LIONEL", 3/16" "TAIWAN":
      "LIONEL   TAIWAN   ROC"
  (b) Same as (a), but "R.O.C."
  (c) 1 x ¼" white sticker:
      "MADE IN TAIWAN
      REPUBLIC OF CHINA"

- Tanks
  (a) 3/16" "LIONEL":
      "LIONEL   Made in Taiwan
          Republic of China"
  (b) No Lionel name, otherwise as above, with catalogue
      number and gold paper sticker present
  (c) Same as (a), but with "ROC"

Closeup of the shells used on the 50-foot cars offered from 1974 to 1977. On the left: The Roco Austrian-made PFE reefer and the Kader-made Taiwanese Tropicana car; the only differences are in the steps and brakewheels. The third and fourth cars were offered in the Canadian line only and are models of 50-foot plug-door boxcars; both were produced by Kader with the white Confederation car made in Taiwan (with a separate roofwalk) and also in Hong Kong (with a cast-on roofwalk) and the green BC car only known to exist with Taiwan markings and separate roofwalk.

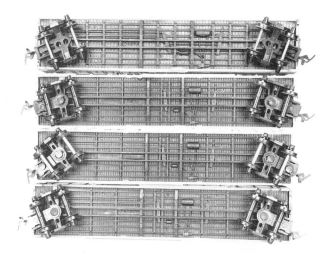

Underframes for 50 foot boxcars. The top car is the Roco-made reefer of 1974 marked with the company logo and name. It is followed by the Kader-made reefer and plug-door boxcar, both marked with the Lionel name and "MADE IN TAIWAN" as shown on page 12. The fourth frame shown, also Kader-made, was used in 1976 on some of the Confederation Flyer cars. A smooth steel-type frame was also used on the Confederation cars 1977 and not shown. It carries only the Hong Kong markings and is covered in Chapter VI.

The only two shells used on the gondolas offered, with the Roco-made car, 1974–1977, on the bottom and the 1976–1977 Kader-made car on top. Note the four-step ladder and black floor tab on the end of the Roco-made car; the top Kader-made car has the floor cast into the body and no tabs. The word "Austria" would be visible on the frame of the Roco model.

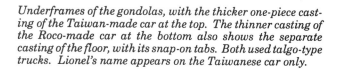

Underframes of the gondolas, with the thicker one-piece casting of the Taiwan-made car at the top. The thinner casting of the Roco-made car at the bottom also shows the separate casting of the floor, with its snap-on tabs. Both used talgo-type trucks. Lionel's name appears on the Taiwanese car only.

little change, and catalogue numbers remained the same as 1974 for these four sets. In 1975 all rolling stock catalogue numbers changed from the 8400 series to the 8500 series. They were the brown Rio Grande, the yellow Rath, the tuscan Northern Pacific, and the green P & LE. All were manufactured by Lionel. Six new names were also added to the 40-foot boxcar line, again of Lionel manufacture. These consisted of the Bangor and Aroostock, Spalding Sporting Goods, AMF Sporting Goods, Milwaukee Road, Union Pacific, and a silver feather Western Pacific. The CP Rail and Grand Trunk cars of 1974 returned without change.

The 50-foot reefer line, produced in Austria, was also expanded to include four new names. They were the white Gold Medal Flour, the white Schaefer Beer, red Heinz Foods, and tan Frisco. The Pacific Fruit and the Railway Express of 1974 were also still available. The C & O crane car was still available and the new road name of Union Pacific was introduced separately and in a special two-car set with a matching 50-foot work caboose. The caboose in this set was never available separately and the catalogue never mentioned the caboose was a new 50-foot model.

The last page of the catalogue introduced the new line of accessories along with four new building kits: a pickle factory, a water tower, an engine house, and a large passenger station. The kits were made for Lionel by Pola of West Germany. Great care was needed in the assembly of each kit, but the many colored parts required no painting. The frames of most kits had the Lionel name and Mt. Clemens, Michigan, along with the Pola name, molded into it. The engine, rooming, and boiler house kits issued in 1977 are without the Lionel name in the Lionel packaging.

The new accessories were made by Lionel, all produced from 1966 diework and were similar to the items sold in the 1960 HO line in terms of color and operation. They included an operating rotary light beacon, a manually operated gantry crane (shown but never made), a girder bridge, and a trestle set with arched bridge. With the exception of the ladders on the tower unit, all were made of plastic.

1976

The year 1976 was a major turning point for the Lionel HO line. That year's catalogue introduced one really new unit to the market. But the bad news was that from here on it would be downhill quality-wise, with few exceptions. Half of the power units were now being produced in Hong Kong — including the new GP-30 diesel and the GS-4 steam locomotive. The re-run gold Chessie and the Southern GP-9s were also switched to Hong Kong production. To HO operators, power units were of major importance, and many model railroaders turned away as 1976 unfolded. That Lionel had not given up altogether is attested to by the introduction of the U-18-B, a unit still made in the U.S.A. An ad in *Model Railroader* for December 1975 announces the four new diesels featuring double-drive eight-wheel traction, "rugged American-made GE motor, superb detailing, popular and colorful roadnames. . . ."

More rolling stock was added but this did not include anything not already available elsewhere, and some of it came from Hong Kong. Pages 1 and 2 of the 1976 catalogue presented three new freight sets, all now using 2600-series catalogue numbers.

The first set, catalogue number 5-2680, was headed by an Alco FA-1 in the new Santa Fe freight colors of blue and silver and was of Lionel manufacture. No change was made in the catalogue number of 5-5600 when the Alco was sold separately, or when it later appeared with a Hong Kong–made drive. The set contained a new UP boxcar, a flatcar, and a new Santa Fe caboose; track and transformer were also included. It was priced in the $25 range.

The second set was headed by a GP-9 in the tricolored Chessie. The shell and drive unit for this locomotive, including the decoration of the shell, were manufactured in Hong Kong. This set contained four freight cars, a new hi-cube UP boxcar, a new D & RGW gondola, a B & LE cable car (also new this year), and a caboose; track and DC power pack were also included. The set was dropped from the catalogue the following year.

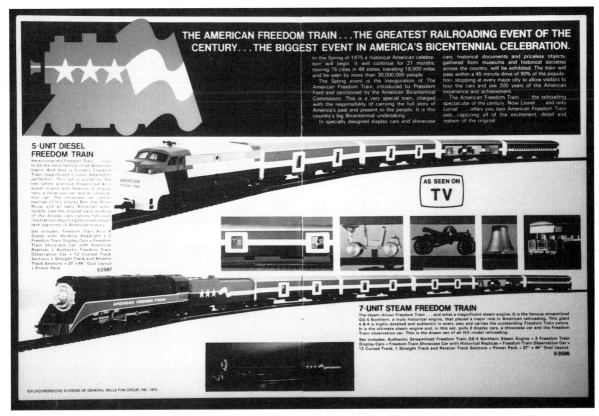

The misleading artwork of the American Freedom Train, in the 1975 catalogue; the cover of this book shows the actual locomotive and tender.

The third, more deluxe set was headed by the new Hong Kong–built GP-30 in the Burlington Northern road name. A caboose in a matching road name was also included, as in the first sets. This third set included five cars: a Dow tank, D & RGW gondola, BN hopper, B & LE cable car, and a GT boxcar; also included were track and DC power pack, with an over-and-under trestle set with bridge, as well as sets of twelve plastic telephone poles and road signs. This set was in the $40 range. With the exception of the trestle set and the locomotive, not one piece used in any of the three sets offered was a Lionel-made product; everything was from Hong Kong or Taiwan.

The only two road names shown for separate sale and also used in the sets were the two boxcars. The individual cars were shown still using the old 8400-series catalogue numbers, but the cars used in the sets had a number change. The 5-8514 UP boxcar became 5-8613 and the 5-8501 Grand Trunk car became 5-8614. Both cars carry these new catalogue numbers on their sides. Both were now made in Taiwan by Kader Industries.

All other cars shown in the 1976 sets were also available separately but were not catalogued that way. The nine-car gold Chessie set of 1975 was still available, with little change; extra tracks and switches were added, and the catalogue number changed from 5-1480 to 2683. This set also contained cars from Taiwan, Hong Kong, and Austria; only the white unmarked flatcar used in the set was manufactured by Lionel.

The gold Chessie GP-9 was now also a Hong Kong product. Its catalogue number changed to 5-5612. A Southern Pacific-type GS-4 steam engine was newly introduced in the SP daylight colors as well as still heading up one of the two Freedom Train sets of 1975, shown in the catalogue this time in photos illustrating the set close to the way it was actually sold (unlike the misleading artwork in the 1975 catalogue). The GS-4 in daylight colors was catalogued for separate sale and was also available in one uncatalogued set this same year.

The same locomotive in Freedom Train colors was catalogued as 5-6501 separately and in the seven-piece 5-2586 set. This, too, was a Hong Kong–made item produced by Kader Industries.

The Alco FA-1 set had four cars and the GS-4 steam set five cars, since it contained the extra number 105 display car (and this was the only way the car was available), which will surely become an increasingly difficult item to locate in the future. The passenger cars used in the two sets were of Lionel manufacture as were the new U-18-B diesels, available in three road names as well as unmarked. These new Lionel-made models retained the 5500-series numbers used in 1975, while other power units new this year and made in Hong Kong used the new 5600 numbers.

The catalogue made a point of the fact that the new Lionel-made locomotive was the only model of a U-18-B available on the market at the time. The new diesel units were catalogued in the red and white Soo Line, the red CP Rail, the orange and black Rio Grande, and an undecorated model. The second new kind of diesel model introduced in 1976 was a GP-30 in black and green with the Burlington Northern road name. It was produced in Hong Kong by Kader Industries. A second GP-30, uncatalogued, was also available separately in the red and silver Santa Fe passenger colors.

The two GP-30s and the two GP-9s, although they were not the only new locomotives this year, were the only ones to use the new 5600-series catalogue numbers, and all were Hong Kong–made products. Of the sets from 1975, the Union Pacific, Great Northern, and Santa Fe freight sets were all dropped from the catalogue in 1976. The Alcos introduced in 1975 were still available, along with the three GP-9s as separate-sale units.

The 50-foot reefers of 1975 remained unchanged, as did the stock cars. Only two changes, as stated earlier, were made to the boxcar line. The Union Pacific crane car and caboose set also reappeared, less a UP shield shown on the crane of 1975. The decal was still part of the set, however. The accessories line, with the exception of the gantry crane that was never made and dropped from the catalogue, remained unchanged.

The building kits from 1975 were joined by six more kits: the stockyard, boiler house, rooming house, coaling tower, icing station, and a grain elevator. All of these new kits came with extra detail, such as

tools, carts, people, or animals, and were made by Pola of West Germany. More than half of these kits were catalogued for only one year, and I have always believed that although shown in the 1976 catalogue, the last three kits were not actually made.

1977

The year 1977 was the last time Lionel offered an HO catalogue, although many items were still in stock and on dealers' shelves for at least two more years; some can still be found in shops today. The 1977 line of catalogued items consisted for the most part of carryovers from the previous year. The motive power did not change, but the U-18-B shown in 1976 was dropped from the catalogue. New road names were introduced in the Taiwan-manufactured boxcars, reefers, and hi-cube boxcars. The coaling tower, grain elevator, and ice station shown in 1976 were gone from the catalogue and would be extremely difficult to locate today. It is doubtful that these items were ever sold as Lionel.

Three more freight sets were introduced, all a little more deluxe than in previous years. All were headed by a GP-9 power unit and made in Hong Kong, as reflected in the use of the 5700-series numbers on these locomotives (all were available for separate sale although not catalogued that way). The set catalogue numbers also changed, to a 2700 series this last year.

The first set, headed by a black GP-9, with a new road name of Norfolk and Western, was shown with a red CP Rail hopper, a yellow Union Pacific hi-cube boxcar, and an orange Rio Grande gondola with three culvert pipes, as well as a black caboose with a road name matching the locomotive. Also included in the set was a metal tractor trailer that carried the same road name as the locomotive and caboose, along with sets of twelve plastic phone poles and a set of road signs, a railroad map, an information booklet, and an iron-on decal for a T-shirt. The same Hong Kong–made small power pack and track completed the set. It was priced in the $60 range. Note: Although the gondola car is shown with three white culvert pipes that came with the set, the car carried a simulated gray sand load.

The second set was headed by the green Southern GP-9. The catalogue showed the Lionel number "5514" on its side. However, the numbers did change to 5-5711 this last year, due to Hong Kong production. This set carried the exact same cars and accessories as did the first one, with the exception of the caboose road name and color in each set. The third set also contained the exact same components as the first and second sets, except for the caboose, and was headed by a yellow 5-5714 Union Pacific GP-9. One difference in this set is the unpainted Union Pacific caboose, the same car used in the special Sears sets of 1975; all other cars used in these sets were painted shells. The sets holding the unpainted caboose are thought to be the very last sets packaged in 1977 using existing parts inventory.

The metal tractor and trailer included in each set were also produced in Hong Kong. The three-piece castings were stamped with "Fundimensions", "Lionel", and "Hong Kong" on the outer trailer floor, while the cab held the Lionel name along with the number "2" and the Hong Kong name, both cast into its body. The trucks were riveted together and had black plastic wheels with metal axles. All carried a paper sticker on the trailer side with a name matching the locomotive road name found on the set.

Pages 4 and 5 of the 1977 catalogue showed three holdover sets from 1976, but the tricolored Chessie set was dropped. Also shown was the GS-4 in a new road name and heading set 5-2783. The Western Pacific road name was used in this set, which held five freight cars and a matching caboose. The yellow Union Pacific flatcar now held a load of stakes and plastic crates, while the blue Chessie gondola held the same three culvert pipes used in other cars. This set was in the $60 price range and also contained the road signs, phone poles, signals, and trestle bridges. The GS-4 was also catalogued in all three road names this last year for separate sale.

Four new 40-foot boxcars were also added, using the new 8700-series catalogue numbers: the blue Conrail, the red Southern, the blue

Chessie, and a yellow Rail-box, produced in Taiwan by Kader Industries. The yellow Union Pacific hi-cube boxcar of the previous year was joined by three new road names — the orange Illinois Central, the green Burlington Northern, and a blue Rock Island. These were produced in Taiwan.

Also added to the 50-foot reefer line were the names of Coors Beer, Budweiser, Tropicana Orange Juice, and Schlitz Beer. All these cars, with white sides and orange or green roofs, were new, made for Lionel in Taiwan; all were available for separate sale and were never catalogued in a set.

Two new names in the hopper car line were also introduced this last year: the red CP Rail, shown only in sets but available separately, and a light blue uncatalogued Boston and Maine. Both cars came with a plastic coal load and were also produced in Taiwan. The B & M car was sold separately and in one known uncatalogued set headed by the GP-30 in the Burlington Northern road name.

Three of the building kits introduced in 1976 — the coaling tower, ice station, and grain elevator — were not shown in the catalogue, and this reinforces my belief that they were never available as Lionel products.

The handwriting was on the wall. Lionel's four-year, half-hearted effort was over. The Lionel name was to disappear from HO once again.

SUMMING IT ALL UP

For some strange reason, more than half of the rolling stock offered over the four-year period never appeared in the *catalogues* for separate sale, although it does seem most of it was. Some items were never shown or listed — such as the Hong Kong–produced power units. I am quite certain there are more models that were uncatalogued and are still to be found; reader's descriptions are certainly welcome! It seems it was left to Lionel dealers to do as they saw fit to move the product. At least six of the sets in the possession of your author are marked "Dealers Special" and came from small hobby shops; others came from large department stores. The same pattern was followed in the Canadian end of the Lionel HO line, with United States items simply packed in the Canadian red and yellow boxes, with a change of model number on the carton, to be sold as uncatalogued items. The special Sears Simpson and Zeller Department Store sets sold in Canada contained an extra car as an incentive to buyers.

The foreign-made Lionel models were also sold in Canada and the United States by other HO dealers, with only a few of the road names used being strictly available as Lionel HO models. Instead of commiting to provide a really new line of models during the 1970s, Lionel chose to go in many different directions in search of suppliers. Often the result was that a "new" line was not something new and different after all.

Of all the Lionel HO offered in the 1970s, the pieces made by Lionel in the United States are of the best quality. The Austrian-made models run second in quality, with the Pola building kits next in line. The Taiwan and Hong Kong–made models are at the bottom of the list in terms of quality. They also present the biggest challenge to the collector, since they were available for such a short time.

In retrospect, one can say that Lionel generally repeated the mistakes made in their earlier attempt at gaining their place in the HO market. As a student of the company, having spent many hours examining their products, advertising, and sales methods, this author sees quite clearly that someone in their company had not done a very good job of letting HOers recognize that Lionel even had a new HO line in the 1970s.

The total advertising money spent in the model railroad magazines to inform HO operators could not have amounted to more than a few thousand dollars over the four years the line was available. The two-page *Model Railroader* ad in December 1975 for the U-18-Bs and the first and only color ad, appearing in November 1975 to announce the Bicentennial sets, seems to be the *total* advertising placed by Lionel itself.

On the other hand, in that same time period the dealers such as Murry Klein, H. O. Specialists, Hobbies for Men, Charles Ro, and Doug's Train World all ran ads that in some cases listed the entire line for that year and gave far more information than did any ad Lionel ever ran.

I believe this lack of promotional commitment by Lionel itself was the main reason the Lionel name once again left the world of HO trains.

One last observation has to do with the service offered for all these new products. Lionel always made a point in its ads that there were over seven hundred service stations available to customers. In reality few repair parts were available. A factory exchange program instituted for all service centers and individual customers no doubt caused more problems than it solved. As an example, the drive of a power unit would be returned to Lionel and simply replaced by the factory — but not always with the original type of drive issued. The program caused future collectors real headaches. When the Hong Kong power units showed up in 1976, the service centers became nightmares. Ironically, the exchange program is also the main reason why parts were never readily available. Some locomotive parts lists were issued in 1975 and appear in Chapter VIII of this book.

CHAPTER II
Locomotives

This chapter describes in detail the later HO line marketed in the United States and manufactured by Lionel and by Kader in either Hong Kong or Taiwan. After a capsule survey of the evolution of motive power in Lionel HO 1974–1977, the chapter illustrates the frame types and shells and then examines specific items offered, according to the producer and locomotive type:

- Lionel-produced FA-1s
- Lionel-produced GP-9s
- Hong Kong–produced FA-1s
- Hong Kong–produced GP-9s
- Lionel-produced U-18-Bs
- Hong Kong–produced GP-30s
- Hong Kong–produced GS-4s

The chapter concludes with descriptions of RailScope items and custom-painted units.

OVERVIEW OF PRODUCTION CHANGES

1974

The Alco FA-1 and EMD GP-9 offered in 1974 were single-drive units with only the rear truck powered. No dummy A or B Alco units were ever offered. These units were equipped with two traction tires each. They were all produced with a combination frame of cast metal and plastic, and all parts snapped in place; no screws were used in assembly. Both used worm and spur gears and were lighted with a single bulb that was held at the top of the front truck with a plastic clip. For added weight, the very first power units had a metal weight fastened to the inner roof of the shell. Two plastic rivets molded into the shell roof passed through the weight and were melted at the ends to hold the weight firmly in place. The weight's secondary job was to hold the motor to the frame itself. In late 1974 a heavier weight was introduced as part of the frame and held to it with two black plastic U-shaped clamps, new this year.

The GP-9 used the same type of frame and metal weight and was lighted in the same manner as the Alco. It had sheet-metal stanchions and wire handrails. Both units were equipped with two black plastic decorative horns and clear plastic headlights. The FA-1 and GP-9 units were each available in two road names the first year, and only in sets.

1975

The year 1975 saw major changes made to the drive units of both the Alco and the GP-9 power units. Both units were now dual drives with both trucks and all eight wheels powered. The rubber traction tires of 1974 were eliminated, and a slightly smaller metal weight was still a part of the frame. The single grain-of-wheat-type light bulb was still present but was now attached to the frame with a plastic pin that was pressed into a hole in the frame. The bulb and pin were removable for servicing.

More road names were added to the Alco and Geep roster with the first steam unit the new GS-4, also shown for the first time. All diesel power units offered in 1974–1975 were assembled by Lionel in Mt. Clemens, Michigan, with many components made from reworked original Lionel tooling from the earlier HO line and produced by London Plastics of Ontario, Canada, for Lionel. The locomotives can be found with the early and late types of frames described in the next section.

1976

Lionel's first really "new" locomotive in HO — the U-18-B — was introduced in 1976 and was available for separate sale in 1976 and 1977 (but only catalogued the first year). The frame and eight-wheel drive units introduced in 1975 were modified and used on these new units. It was an excellent-looking and -running engine. The locomotive had a lighted cab with plastic handrails. Also present were black decorative horns and a brakewheel. Clear window material was used in the cab area. The frames were stamped "Lionel Mt. Clemens, Molded in Canada", along with a zip code number, as were all the diesels Lionel built for the four-year period.

Unfortunately, the Hong Kong–built engines were also introduced this year, which showed Lionel was still following their 1960s thinking in some cases. They were already thinking about getting out, and efforts to lower costs showed up clearly when these Hong Kong engines were added to the line. It was exactly what they had done in their first attempt at HO: the more the line grew, the cheaper the item became, and the quality steadily fell. The magic of the Lionel name meant little to the HO operator of the 1970s, and sales fell off.

Even with the information received from Dan Johns and Lee Riley (see Chapter I), your author does not believe all the shells used on the new 1976 engines were made from original Lionel diework, nor that they were solely decorated by Lionel. The 5610 Chessie and the uncatalogued 5611 Illinois Central GP-9 introduced that year show a much thicker paint job and heavier lettering than what was used by Lionel. These units were decorated in Hong Kong. The same holds true for some of the rolling stock of 1976–1977.

All of the shells still carry the decorative horns, the two Geeps have the black plastic handrails, and all have the clear window material which carries the Lionel part number on it. A long, clear shaft runs from the headlight lens to just over the one light bulb located at the center of the frame. This shaft picks up the light from the bulb and lights the headlamp and cab area and is found on all Hong Kong–made Geeps.

The frames used on the 1976 and 1977 Hong Kong–made power units are all black unpainted plastic with little detail left below the floor line. All are weighted with either a center-located lead weight or seven sheets of metal fastened at the center of the frame. The light bulb is fastened in a small hole in the weight on the Geeps, just ahead of the motor on the Alco-type locomotives. All are powered with a cheap enclosed pancake-type motor, which is mounted on and is a part of the front truck. Only one rubber traction tire is used.

The dummy rear trucks on all Hong Kong–built units are used for electric pickup only and are held in place with a metal pin that passes through the truck and frame of the locomotive, allowing the truck to swivel freely. In 1977 this pin changed to plastic. Body-mounted couplers were used on all Hong Kong–built power units. Once again, no dummy units were ever available.

The new GS-4 of 1975 was now available in the Southern Pacific road name and made in Hong Kong. Both locomotive and tender carry the Lionel Hong Kong name on their frames. This Southern Pacific–type locomotive was to be the only steam engine Lionel offered. It was produced with a plastic and die-cast frame and boiler.

In the Lionel warranty program of 1976, the catalogue number 5-5612 was listed as a Great Northern GP-9 in orange and green, supposedly manufactured by Kader the same year. I have been assured that the road name was not used until after the Lionel period of 1974–1977. However, the premarked cartons using the same 5-5612 stamping were used on the gold Chessie GP-9 introduced new in 1976 and manufactured by Kader. Apparently the artwork for the Great Northern Geep prevented that road name from being part of the Lionel line.

1977

The GS-4 returned as a separate item and, in one set, with a new Western Pacific road name. The GP-9 also returned in three new road names — all now of Hong Kong manufacture. They were to be the last Hong Kong–made power units offered by Lionel. And they are all the most difficult GP-9s to find today.

LIONEL-PRODUCED FA-1s

Frames

Type I: Early 1974 Alco FA-1 Power Frame — Four-Wheel Drive

The frame of the early Alcos manufactured by Lionel is a cast-metal main frame with the upper portion of the coupler pocket and the center side tabs cast into it. Small center side tabs hold the shell to the frame. The metal coupler pocket has a black plastic cover with two pins pressed into it to hold the coupler firmly in place. The trucks used on the locomotive are also a combination of plastic and metal and have two rubber traction tires on the rear truck, the only one powered.

The truck is held to the metal frame by a separate plastic floor that snaps into a hole in the frame and is held at one end and both sides with small plastic tabs cast into the plastic floor (these tabs often break off, unfortunately). The front truck is made and held in place the same way, but it is nonpowered and only acts as a pickup for the power. A single grain-of-wheat-type light bulb is attached to the top of the truck with two plastic clips. Power is transmitted from the motor, a "new GE–built type" especially made for Lionel, by a single metal shaft to the rear truck.

The battery box area, found at the center of the frame, is also a black plastic casting and holds the only markings found on these frames. The stamping found on the bottom of the casting reads "Lionel, Mt. Clemens, Mich., Molded in Canada". A zip code number, 48043, is also present. The sides of this casting, which is seen with the shell in place, holds ladders, air tanks, vents, and battery box covers, all cast in place. A thin piece of sponge rubber at the top of the motor acts as insulation between it and the metal weight fastened to the roof of the shell. This sponge rubber was known to dry out from the heat generated by the motor. It would end up clogging the drive shaft, causing stoppage of the locomotive, and thus it was replaced in 1975 by a solid rubber pad.

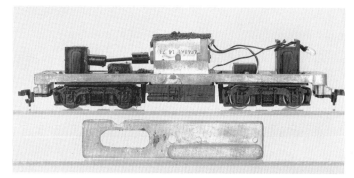

Type I: Early 1974 Alco FA-1. Note weight which was part of shell.

Type II: Late 1974 Alco FA-1 (bulb for headlight missing). Note new weight and new plastic clamps.

Type III: 1975 Alco FA-1. Note new double drive shaft.

Comparison of three Lionel FA-1 shells. Top: The special shell used for the RailScope model of the 1980s, with its special darkened window material and thinner walls. Middle: Early 1974 type with its two cast-on pegs to hold the metal weight used on these early shells. Bottom: The shell used from 1975 until the end of production in 1977, including the units with Kader-made drive. Note the clear window material with part number in lower two regular-run shells.

Type II: Late 1974 Alco FA-1 Power Frame — Four-Wheel Drive

In late 1974 some changes were made to the Alco frames. The weight is larger and now extends back over the rear truck. It is no longer part of the shell. The sponge rubber used for insulation was changed to a solid rubber pad and the weight is now held to the frame with two black plastic U-shaped clamps that run up over the weight through recesses at its top and down the sides to snap into the metal frame. These clamps are thin and easily broken. The light bulb was also changed and is now fastened to a plastic pin that is pushed down into a hole at the front of the metal frame. The two rubber traction tires are still present, but the locomotive's performance is not improved much. The notice of Canadian molding and the zip code number is found on the frame.

Type III: 1975 Alco FA-1 Power Frame — Eight-Wheel Drive

In 1975 the Alco frame changed again. The large weight of late 1974 was changed again and made smaller by more than an inch. It is still held to the frame with the two black plastic clamps and the single bulb remains on the pin at the front of the frame, but the locomotive was now eight-wheel drive, with the new 1974 single-shafted motor now having double-drive shafts to drive both front and rear trucks. No traction tires are used even though weight was removed from the frame. Its performance did improve. "Molded in Canada" and the zip code number is present on the frame.

Listings of Lionel-produced FA-1s

	Gd	Exc	Mt

(5-)5400 SANTA FE ("Passenger" Diesel): First catalogued 1974 in set 5-1483; returned 1975 in the same catalogued set before being replaced by the 5-5600 freight diesel of 1976; never shown as a separate sale item; was available that way in 1975. Although the engine was painted in the Santa Fe passenger colors, the only set it was available in was a freight.

Shell painted red and silver separated with thin black and yellow lines; two rear lower side panels hold the road name and "5400", both stamped in black; two decorative horns on cab roof; one clear plastic headlight lens and clear window material (marked part number 50-5400-20) in cab; "Santa Fe" also found on cab nose in black and yellow decal; 4" x ¾" metal weight fastened to shell roof with two plastic pegs; four open-type steps, grabirons, ladders, and rivet and roof detail cast into shell; Type I or II frame. **25 40 60**

(5-)5401 GREAT NORTHERN: First catalogued 1974 in set 5-1482; like Santa Fe, returned 1975 in same set, with same catalogue number; never catalogued as separate but available that way in 1975.

Similar to the 5400 shell, except for decoration; painted with roof, top row of side panels, and cab end finished in a very dark green color; pilot area and ¼" band running around body also dark green; orange nose and middle row of side panels, steps, and grabirons, with thin yellow line; "5401" and road name in yellow stamping on dark green lower side panels; decaled logo on nose below single headlight; decorative horns on roof; clear window material in cab; Type I or II frame. **25 40 60**

(5-)5504 AMERICAN FREEDOM TRAIN: First shown 1975 in set 5-2587; shown again in 1976 with erroneous catalogue number 5-3587 for Freedom set; never catalogued as separate but available, due to poor sales of set itself.

Shell painted red, white, and blue, with top row of side panels flat silver; middle row of white side panels stamped "AMERICAN FREEDOM TRAIN" and "5504" in red; two white stars below side cab windows; white nose bears red-stamped "AMERICAN FREEDOM

	Gd	Exc	Mt

TRAIN"; two decorative horns on roof; clear headlight and cab windows; can be found with Type II or III frame. **30 40 60**

(5-)5505 ROCK ISLAND: Introduced for separate sale 1975; catalogued again in 1976 separately before being dropped; first Alco-type diesel to have the new eight-wheel drive and use Type II frame only with shorter metal weight.

Shell painted flat red with bright flat yellow covering pilot and nose and continuing in ⅛" side stripe broken by road name and "5505" in white stamping; black decorative horn; headlight; clear window material; red and white decaled road name below headlight lens; shell can be found with two plastic pins protruding down from roof to secure weight to shell in early 1974. It is one of the more difficult Lionel-production Alcos to locate. **35 50 70**

(5-)5506 UNION PACIFIC: Introduced in 1975 but uncatalogued; engine as separate-sale item but also available in uncatalogued Sears sets in 1975, with slight changes to shell and with nose decal; available until 1976.

Medium yellow-painted body; "5506" on cab's floor line and road name in lower two side panels in high-gloss red stamping; black decorative horns; unlighted; Type II frame, with "Molded in Canada" present. Two versions, both hard to locate in any condition.
(A) Sears; dull yellow shell; decaled Union Pacific logo on nose.
 35 50 65
(B) Lionel; high-gloss yellow cab; no markings on nose.
 40 60 70

(5-)5507 AMTRAK: First catalogued 1975; returned 1976 unchanged; dropped in 1977.

Shell painted black, red, silver, and blue; lighted; "5507" on middle side panel at cab end and road name below cab windows, both in high-gloss blue stamping. Only known to exist with Type III frame but can be found with early or late shell (early had pegs cast into roof to hold early weight; front peg broken off in assembly so shell would fit over end of weight); second unit to use eight-wheel drive; "Molded in Canada" on frame. **35 50 70**

(5-)5509 SOUTHERN PACIFIC: First catalogued 1975, recatalogued 1976; available only separately.

Shell painted flat red; flat black roof; bright orange side panels extending across nose are separated from red with a thin white stripe; third white stripe at floor line extends across pilot; white-stamped road name in two lower side panels and "5509" in last panel; decaled logo in orange strip below headlight; black decorative horns on cab; clear headlight and clear window material; Type III frame. **35 50 60**

(5-)5600 SANTA FE (Freight): First catalogued 1976 in three-car set; completely Lionel-made model; not catalogued separately but available as such 1976-77, when the same catalogue number was still used and slight changes were made; second version of unit available 1977, as covered in section on Hong Kong production of FA-1s (see page 23).

Shell in blue and silver freight colors; black-stamped road name and "5600" in last two lower side panels; body colors separated by thin yellow and black strip; decaled road name below headlight; Type II frame with single power truck; frame carries Lionel name and "Molded in Canada" with a zip code number. Steadily escalating asking price. **25 35 45**

(5-5613) T-12001 CANADIAN NATIONAL: Uncatalogued; available 1976-77 as separate item. Causes great confusion because was packaged in both Canadian and U.S. cartons but carrying same number on its side — T-12001, which is Canadian catalogue number; U.S. catalogue number 5-5613 only on U.S. carton. Also available 1977 with Hong Kong drive unit as found on 5-5600 Santa Fe Alco.

	Gd	Exc	Mt

Shell painted semiflat black; orange nose; white diagonal stripes in two lower side panels; large white "CN" present on red nose; Type II frame; zip code number and "Molded in Canada" on frame.

(In U.S. box)   25   35   45

(5-5614) T-12002 GREAT NORTHERN: Last catalogued in 1975; found in both Canadian and U.S. packaging; Lionel catalogue number found on U.S. cartons only; also found in U.S cartons with Canadian number on its side and with Hong Kong frame and drive of 1977 as another attempt by Lionel to use up stock.

Shell decorated exactly the same as described in Chapter VI, including the Canadian T number. As in the case of 5-5613, only the Canadian number "T-12002" appears on the side along with road name. Type II frame with zip code number and "Molded in Canada".

                                       25   35   45

T-12001:   See (5-5613)
T-12002:   See (5-5614)

LIONEL-PRODUCED GP-9s

Frames

Type IV: Early 1974 Lionel GP-9

The frame used on the first Geeps followed the same pattern as did the Alco frame, with the same changes taking place in the four-year period, 1974–1977. The main difference of course was the length of the metal portion of the frame to accommodate the longer steps and platform area at each end of the shell. Lionel accomplished this by simply making the coupler pockets slightly larger and adding a longer shaft to its coupler. The GE motor found here is the one used on the Alcos, along with the trucks and single light bulb for the headlamp. The very first power truck of 1974 had a metal shaft running from axle to axle at the top of the power truck; this shaft changed to plastic in early 1975 and remained that way until the end of HO production (this holds true also for the first Alco power trucks). The motor carries a model number, with the month and year of manufacture stamped in black on its side, as did all the Alco diesels.

The same type of black plastic center casting is also present with small changes as is "LIONEL / MT. CLEMENS, MI. / 48043 / Molded in Canada". It is the only marking found on the Geep frame. Also present are the metal braces that run across the center of the hole, left to accept the trucks. With the front brace running completely across the hole, while the rear brace is cut out at its center allowing the power truck's drive shaft to pass through. This also will be found on the very early Alco frames. The extra metal weight was part of the shell and fastened to it. These Geeps also had the two rubber traction tires on the power truck.

Type V: Late 1974 Lionel GP-9

The changes made to the Alco frames apply here, with the metal weight being removed from the shell and a larger weight becoming part of the frame. These new weights extended from just behind the front truck body to the very end of the rear power truck. The shaft on the power truck changed to plastic. The light bulb was now fastened to a 1-inch-high plastic pin that pressed down into a hole in front of the metal frame. It was similar to the Alco mounting. Also changed was the front metal brace that passed through the hole left in the frame to accept the nonpowered truck. The brace was now cut out at its center split frame to accept the drive shaft for a power truck, but it would be 1975 before a double-drive unit was added to Lionel's line. The two rubber traction tires were still used and the motor was now a double shaft, with only one shaft being used.

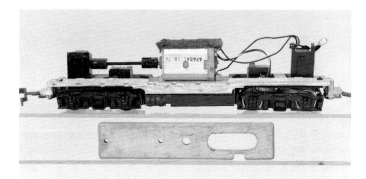

Type IV: Early 1974 Lionel GP-9

Type V: Late 1974 Lionel GP-9

Type VI: 1975 Lionel GP-9 (rear coupler installed upside down)

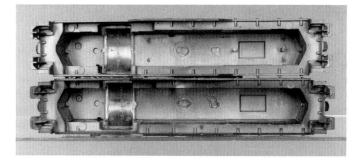

Comparison of shells used on Lionel-produced GP-9s. The top shell of 1974 has two cast-on pegs to hold the metal weight, while the bottom shell used from 1975 to 1977 does not have these pegs. Note the window material carrying a Lionel part number and the extra supports to accept handrail stanchions.

Type VI: 1975 Lionel GP-9

For 1975 little change was made to the frames themselves. The biggest change was the introduction of the second power truck, making the 1975 locomotives eight-wheel drive units. The traction tires were discontinued and the metal weight was a full inch smaller. It now ran from the rear of the front truck to just over the front edge of the rear truck. The motor used was the same as the Alco late 1974 motor, but now both shafts were being used.

Some of these Geeps, like the Grand Trunk, will be found with the motor stamped "1974" or "1975" but all will have the large weight of late 1974 and a single-powered truck. The weight helps to identify the production year, while in some cases the stamping on a motor can mislead a collector. In 1976–1977 the frames remained unchanged in the Geeps still being produced by Lionel for separate sale only.

Lionel-made GP-9 Shells

All of the Geeps produced by Lionel for the four years beginning with 1974 were made from the pre-1966 diework. All were equipped with wire handrails and sheet-metal stanchions. An assembly sheet was provided with each locomotive to assist the modeler in installing the handrail sets; they were the only part not fixed to the shell when purchased. Also present on the inside of these shells are reinforcement plastic studs used to accept the steel stanchions of the handrails. These studs, along with the two louvered areas just below the cab, will identify the shell as early 1974 Lionel production. When the 5511 Grand Trunk Geep was first shown in the 1975 catalogue, the louvers below the cab were eliminated for some unknown reason, but the shell does exist with the louvered area present. I believe the very early shells used on the 1974 UP, the gold Chessie, and the first Grand Trunk GP-9s were left over from 1960s production of HO, with the louvers subsequently removed from the original diework because of wear before they were used in the rest of the 1970s GP-9 production runs. Pictures depicting the Geeps for the last three years of Lionel HO still showed the louver area in *some* cases. This was simply a case of the old 1974 Geep photos being reused.

Two black plastic decorative horns are present, one on the short and one on the long hood. Clear window material is found in each cab area and carries the Lionel part number 50-5402-020; it was used on these locomotives for the full four years. Two clear double-lens headlights are also present, one at either end of the shell, with only the short hood end lighted. The very early Geeps of 1974 carry a metal weight fixed to the inner roof of their shells. All of the shells were made of light gray plastic, unlike the black plastic used in the pre-1966 Geeps. All of the shells were painted and lettering was Lionel's well-known stamping process.

Some of these locomotives — the Union Pacific for one — can be found with the road name stamped so heavily it can be read from inside the shell. Other Geeps, such as the 5700 Penn Central of 1977, will be found with repainted blue Grand Trunk shells.

All grille work, rivets, louvers, and grabirons are cast into the shell. The only real change made to the original diework for these new units were the louvered area under the cab and the steps, which now had open backs — unlike the closed pre-1966 locomotive steps.

Another small change is seen at the coupler area between the steps: the cutout area is wider than was the case on pre-1966 Geeps. This was done to accommodate the larger coupler pocket cast into the new frames of the 1970 line. In 1976 production was shifted to Hong Kong on *some* of these Geeps, while others were still produced by Lionel. All of the Geeps are very collectible today, with the Hong Kong items harder to locate. It also appears from 1976 on that the Lionel-made Geeps were only available as separate-sale items, with the Hong Kong GP-9s heading the sets, catalogued and available separately. Note: It is unclear how the very early 1974-type shell appeared on a locomotive introduced a full year after production started, as is the case of the 1975 5-5511 Grand Trunk Geep.

Listings of Lionel-made GP-9s

GM 50: See (5-5403) and (5-)5516

(5-)5402 UNION PACIFIC: First catalogued Geep produced by Lionel; catalogued in 1974-75 in set 5-1481; never shown as a separate item; available as such until 1976; shown in 1977 catalogue heading set 5-2782, although the Hong Kong–made 5-5714 actually was included in the set.

Shell finished in bright yellow; light gray roof, steps, and walkways; thin red stripe separating colors; road name on hood, UP slogan "We can / handle it." stamped below cab window, "5402" on lower side panels below cab all in semigloss red; found with both Type I and II frames. First of the three Geeps known to have the louvered area under its cab.

          30   **40**   **60**

(5-5403) GM 50 B & O CHESSIE (Gold): First catalogued 1974 in set 5-1480; returned in 1975 in same set; never shown as separate sale but road name was available as such from 1975 to end of 1976, when production switched to Hong Kong. Catalogue number 5-5403 only on carton; only GP-9 not to carry Lionel catalogue number in some form; catalogued in 1974 and 1976 with Chessie cat's head logo on its nose. Has only been found with the "50" stamping outlined in a box as described below.

Shell painted flat gold; flat dark blue stamped lettering; "Chessie System" incorporating cat's head logo appears on hood with large "B & O" below cab window and "GM 50" directly below it, with large "50" outlined in a box on the nose below headlights; can be found with Type I or II frame. The second Geep known to have the louvered area under its cab.   **30**   **40**   **65**

(5-)5511 GRAND TRUNK: Introduced in 1975 as one of first double-drive diesels, the unit does exist with the early shell of 1974 with louvered area; only shown in 1975-76 catalogue for separate sale, using 5-5511 but found two ways: with Type III frame and double drive of 1975 and Type II split frame with single drive of 1974, using both the 1974 and 1975 marked motors.

Note: Some collectors believe the unit was also available in uncatalogued sets in late 1975 while others believe it was available uncatalogued in 1976-77 and made up of surplus parts (some extra Grand Trunk shells *were* repainted for the black uncatalogued 5700 Penn Central Geep of 1977); having at least ten of each type of frame unit, I also believe the units were available in 1977 made up from parts (all of my units carry "5511" only on the cab with "5-5511 Grand Trunk GP-9" on the white carton only; all are mint and purchased at TCA or LCCA meets from several individuals; all but one are missing the louvered area beneath the cab).

Shell painted flat medium blue; short hood's nose glossy orange; white-stamped "5511" on cab side, "GT" on long hood side, 1/8" stripe along lower side panels at floor line.

(A) Type II frame.	**20**	**45**	**65**
(B) Type III frame.	**30**	**40**	**60**

(5-)5513 AMERICAN FLYER: Uncatalogued; introduced in special Sears set 5-6592 in 1975; available as separate item from Lionel dealers in 1976.

Shell painted red, white, and blue; center white panels have blue-stamped "AMERICAN FLYER" across long hood, flanked by three blue stars; centered directly below is "5513"; four white stars on blue lower side panel below stamped American flag on cab; decorative horns; window material; wire handrails; traction tires. Only available with the Type II split frame with one power truck. Difficult to find in good condition.   **40**   **50**   **65**

(5-)5514 SOUTHERN: Introduced 1975; catalogued again separately in 1976. Replaced in the sets of 1976-77 by the Hong Kong–made model. (See also 5-5711.)

Top: The first two Alcos introduced in 1974, 5-5400 Santa Fe and 5-5401 Great Northern; note the green roof, contrasted to the black one used on the Canadian GN unit, T-12002. Second: 5-5504 Freedom Train FA-1 and 5-5505 Rock Island — both new in 1975, with only the RI having the new eight-wheel drive train. Third shelf: Uncatalogued 5-5506 Sears Union Pacific, with its flat paint and nose decal, and the glossy-painted regular line Alco without decal but using the same number. Bottom: 5-5507 Amtrak and 5-5509 Southern Pacific. Some of these second-generation diesels have been found with the early shell with weight attached; these could be considered uncommon.

Top: Two known 5-5600 Santa Fe freight Alcos: Completely Lionel-made unit of 1976 and 1977 unit with same shell but a Hong Kong drive train. Bottom: The 5-5614 CN Alco and the uncatalogued 5-5613 GN. Both units are the same, including the numbers on the shells, as those sold in the Canadian market (see Chapter VI); the U.S. 5600-series numbers were used on the cartons only.

Top: First two GP-9s of 1974, with louvers: 5-5402 Union Pacific and 5-5403 gold Chessie. Second: 5-5511 Grand Trunk and uncatalogued 5-5513 Sears American Flyer Geep, both from 1975. Third: 5-5514 Southern and 5-5515 Frisco, also new in 1975; not all were eight-wheel drive although they were catalogued that way. Below: 5-5700 Penn Central, new in 1977; most collectors agree it was made up of extra inventory parts. All these models were equipped with metal handrail sets, but three are shown here without them.

	Gd	Exc	Mt

Shell painted dark green; white stripe above walkway around entire body; thin gold stripe separating colors; gold road name on long hood and "5514" below cab windows; decaled logo on nose. The 1975 locomotive has Type II split frame, single drive though introduced as double drive; the 1976 locomotive has Type III frame with double drive. One of the more difficult locomotives to locate.

Note: I have seen photographs of this unit with stamped logo. Verification requested.

(A) Decaled logo.	30	65	70
(B) Stamped logo.	35	60	75

(5-)5515 FRISCO: Introduced 1975; returned unchanged 1976, still available as separate-sale item only; there is speculation it was available in an uncatalogued set in 1975 (verification requested).

Shell painted bright glossy red; white band circling body and holding flat red road name stamped on long hood; glossy red "5515" stamped on cab's side panel; decorative horns; window material; wire handrails. Difficult to find and prized by HO collectors.   **35   60   75**

(5-)5516 GM 50 B & O CHESSIE (Gold): Available as separate-sale item from J.C. Penney 1975; information on 5-5403 applies, but Type III frame and double drive; new catalogue number on carton and outlined with thin boxlike line on side panels, front of cab, and below walkway; may be preproduction item. J. Otterbein Collection; value unknown.

NRS

(5-)5700 PENN CENTRAL: Uncatalogued; last Lionel-produced Geep (Hong Kong had become source of production); assumed made up from leftover parts and assigned Lionel number.

Shell painted semiglossy black; white-stamped lettering: very small "PENN CENTRAL" at center of long hood, preceded by large "PC" logo; "5700" on cab side; decorative horns; window material; wire handrails; available 1976 with Type III frame and double drive and in 1977 with both Type III and Type II split frame with single drive; will be found with repainted Grand Trunk shells. Scarce.

(A) Type II frame.	25	45	65
(B) Type III frame.	25	40	65

HONG KONG PRODUCTION

FA-1: The 5600 Santa Fe

First seen in the 1976 catalogue, this half-and-half locomotive can be found in the same 2680 carryover set of 1977 that was headed by the same locomotive of 100 percent Lionel manufacture in 1976. The model was also available for separate sale in 1977 (see page 19) and used the same 5-5600 catalogue number with no mention of the drive train change to Hong Kong manufacture.

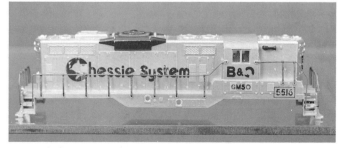

The gold Chessie GP-9, new in 1975 but never shown with the number in the catalogue. It was the first gold Chessie shell to carry a catalogue number and possibly was part of a preproduction run. The dynamic brake unit on the roof and the Lionel number are blue.

This unit uses the same shell as in the 1976 model, and all information given earlier in the section about Lionel-built Alco shells applies. The major difference in the two is the Hong Kong–made frame and drive train that was used in 1977, shown here. This frame, which I number **Type VII**, carries the Hong Kong and the Lionel name with the same lead or sheet-metal weights and three-pole pancake-type motor used on the foreign-made Geeps.

Just how many of these units were made up could not be determined, but once again it looks like Lionel was just using up shell inventory. Nevertheless, this half-and-half unit was sold as Lionel, although many collectors do not know it exists; it is not the easiest model to find.

The belief that the unit was also available in the Canadian line with the Hong Kong drive could not be validated to my satisfaction. There are *two* types of 5600 Santa Fe Alcos, found in sets and separately, using the same catalogue number of 5-5600. K. Armenti Collection; sets and separately: G. Horan and F. Coppola Collection. This type of Hong Kong frame was first produced for use in the warranty service exchange program of 1975. Caution should be used in purchasing models with this type of frame unless absolutely mint. The 5-5600 SF Confederation Flyer and the T-12001 CN and the T-12002 GN are the only units found in sealed sets with this type of frame as reported by some of my Canadian friends.

GP-9 Frames

Types VIII and IX

The frames and drive train used on the "new" Geep were poor performers, with less pulling power than the Lionel-manufactured Geeps, and it was not long before the HO operators realized that these were also cheap engines that did not live up to their expectations.

The new frames were now completely plastic and closely followed the construction of the frames used on the Hong Kong–made Alco units of that same time period. There were two types of frames and both carry the "Fundimensions Lionel Hong Kong" names molded into them. Four lugs cast in the side of the frame hold the shell firmly in place.

The frames and trucks were black unpainted plastic with all gears used in the front power truck also made of plastic. Two of the gears used had a metal shaft, while the remaining three were all plastic. The eight wheels and their axles were of polished metal, with only one fitted with a rubber traction tire.

The motor itself was a small three-pole pancake-type found on all the foreign-made locomotives of the time. The two NMRA-type (officially known as X2F) plastic horn hook couplers were held to the frame with a single brass screw, while two copper electrical pickup shoes were found on the rear truck. Some of the units were manufactured with a 2½-inch-long lead weight mounted at the center of the frame and held in place with a single Phillips-head screw that was seen under the outer frame (**Type VIII**). Others were made with the weight consisting of a series of 3-inch metal plates, held in place with two Phillips-head screws that could only be seen by removing the shell (**Type IX**). A single light bulb was mounted in a hole in the metal weight and was insulated with a tube-type insulation that the bulb slid down into.

There is a cut-out portion in the frame, similar to that found on the Lionel-made frame, but the reinforcement lugs which support the handrails and fit into the cutout are not present on the shells of these units. All rivet detail below the floor line is also missing, and the side frames of the trucks have less detail than those on the Lionel model. To service the trucks the modeler would have to apply pressure to the outer truck cover between the wheels so that the cover pops off, exposing the gears or electrical pickup. Both trucks are free-swiveling, with the rear truck fastened to the frame with a plastic pin that passes through it and the top of the truck housing (some of the models first produced were made with a *metal* pin, but these were few in number). The front truck, on the other hand, was held by the frame itself, which passed through a slit cut into the sides of the motor's plastic case.

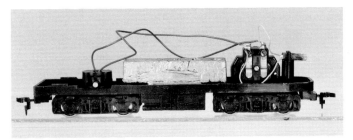

Type VII frame: Hong Kong–made drive; 1976 Alco with Lionel shell. The all-plastic drive was first used on the Kader-made Santa Fe Alco of 1976–1977. Note small pancake-type motor, large lead weight, and metal pin in rear truck. Bulb for headlight is completely hidden by sleeve of insulation at front of frame. There is more detail in the battery box area than in any other Kader-built locomotive.

Type VIII frame: Hong Kong–made GP-9 drive of 1976, with metal weight. Note that the detail found on Lionel models in the battery box area is missing, with only the air tanks shown.

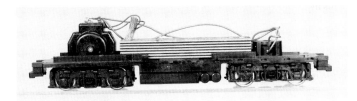

Type IX frame: Hong Kong–made GP-9 drive of 1977, with metal plate weight

GP-9 Shells

There were major differences of construction in these foreign-made shells, as opposed to the Lionel production. The entire shell was plastic, including the handrails that were now very thin and easily broken. In some cases the painting was excellent, while on others, such as the tricolored 5610 Chessie Geep, the decoration was poor. The paint on that model is thick and heavy and hides much of the rivet detail. The lettering in some cases is sharp and clear while in others it is thick and appears much too large.

There is speculation that Lionel decorated some of these shells, but there is no confirmation of this. The basic shells are known to exist in orange, gray, black, and tan plastic, with all shells then being painted.

The reinforcement lugs used for the handrails are not present on these shells as they were on the Lionel-made shell. Another difference lies in the four tabs molded into the inner roof: their purpose was to hold the long clear plastic tube used to light the cab and two headlights found at both ends of the shell. The shell also exists with the light shaft glued directly to the roof. Needless to say, this method of lighting leaves something to be desired. Unlike the Geeps made by Lionel, the Hong Kong model has plastic handrails already installed on its shell; the Lionel instruction and troubleshooting sheets were not included with these locomotives.

The clear window material found on these shells is a Lionel product and does carry the Lionel part number molded into it. I believe these Geeps were made and decorated solely in Hong Kong by Kader Industries, with the tooling for the window material sent to Hong Kong for manufacture.

Another major difference is the absence of the two louvered doors that were present under the cab of the early Lionel-made Geeps. Here the area is flat and free of any detail and in all but two cases holds the unit catalogue number.

Furthermore, some shells have the plastic handrail stanchions melted over at their ends after passing through the body while others are glued in place. It was not Lionel's custom to glue or melt anything in place in the earlier HO line, with the exception of the cab window material, which was often glued in place. All of these foreign-made Geeps are difficult to locate. The 5610 Chessie and 5710 Norfolk & Western are the only foreign-made Geeps to be catalogued showing a Lionel number on the cab. Once again we discover a challenge awaiting the HO collector.

Listings of Hong Kong–produced GP-9s

	Gd	Exc	Mt

GM 50: See (5-5612)

(5-)5610 C & O CHESSIE (Tricolored): First catalogued in 1976 in set 5-2681, it returned in 1977 as an uncatalogued separate-sale item and in uncatalogued set 5-2793.

Shell has very dark blue roof, lower side panels, and step area; wide yellow band encircling the entire shell; "C & O" on cab side; "Chessie System" incorporating Chessie cat's head logo stamped on long hood; Lionel "5610" below cab; all lettering dark glossy blue; heavy flat body paint. Two decorative horns, window material, plastic handrails with ends melted over; long clear two-piece shaft mounted on the four cast-on lugs in roof; Type IX frame. Uncommon and difficult to find.

	30	45	65

(5-)5611 ILLINOIS CENTRAL GULF: Uncatalogued Sears item; available 1976-77 separately and in 1977 in two-piece uncatalogued set, which included the Taiwan-manufactured 98602 IC caboose — one of the few cars to carry the Lionel name and built date on the side. The two-car set (catalogued as 49-9828, indicating an item made for Sears) had the two pieces packed in separate white Lionel boxes in a brown cardboard master carton with white and black label.

Basic orange plastic shell painted bright flat orange; top side panels and roof of long hood finished in a flat white; road name stamped across long hood in glossy black; Lionel "5611" on cab side; IC logo stamped on the orange nose; cab window material; clear light shaft glued directly to roof; no cast-on lugs; handrails glued in place with no sign of the melted area on most Geeps; Type VIII frame. Very difficult to locate.

	25	45	70

(5-5612) GM 50 B & O CHESSIE (Gold): Catalogued 1977 in set number 5-2683.

Shell finished in bright gold as were two earlier Lionel-made gold Chessies; "Chessie System" with cat's head logo stamped across long hood; large "B & O" on cab side; "GM 50" directly below; 50 years emblem appearing on its nose; all lettering glossy blue unlike Lionel's flat blue stamping; basic shell light tan with flat black paint on inner sides and roof behind cab, where light bulb slides between the two-piece light shaft (only locomotive to have this blackened area). Horns, cab windows, and plastic handrails; four cast-on lugs in shell roof; no louvered area below cab; Type VIII frame. This unit is mistaken for the early Lionel-made unit, and many collectors do not know it was included in the Hong Kong production runs.

	25	40	65

Two shells used by Kader of Hong Kong in 1976–1977 for Lionel production. Top: GP-9 shell made from Kader dies, when Lionel tooling finally wore out just before production was switched to Hong Kong in late 1975. Bottom: GP-30 shell of 1976, also Kader tooling. Note there are clear light shafts glued to the cast-on roof tabs on both of Kader-made GP-9 and GP-30 shells, with the Lionel part number seen on the GP-9 window material. Handrail reinforcement studs are melted flat after passing through the shell of the GP-9.

Comparison of Lionel-made GP-9 shells. The early 5402 has louvers under cab window, the later 5511 does not (although an earlier 1975 uncatalogued 5511 does exist with the louvered area). All Hong Kong–made Geeps come without this detail.

	Gd	Exc	Mt

(5-)5710 NORFOLK & WESTERN: Catalogued in 1977 only in set 5-2780; sold separately as late as 1979 as were most all other Geeps.

Black shell painted flat black; large "NW" centered on long hood; Lionel "5710" below cab windows; lettering all heavy white stamping; window material, horns, handrails, two light shafts present; handrail ends melted over inside of shell; Type VIII frame. 1977 catalogue shows 5710 N & W with metal handrails, like earlier 5514 Southern and 5402 UP had. C. Sommer comment.

Note: Also known to exist with Lionel number stamped in thin, washed-out white that does not match the hood's heavy stamping of "NW".

	25	40	60

(5-)5711 SOUTHERN: Available 1976 separately; catalogued 1977 in set 5-2781; although *catalogue* shows "5514" on the unit's cab, this number had changed to 5711 and the unit was now Hong Kong–produced.

Gray shell painted semigloss dark green; glossy thin gold stripe separating green body from white stripe; flat, washed-out Lionel "5711" on cab side and road name across long hood; poor-quality decal on nose;

The first of the Hong Kong–made Geeps. Top: 5-5610 Chessie and 5-5611 Illinois Central Gulf. Middle left: 5-5612 gold Chessie, like the ones above, new in 1976. Middle right: The first of the new road names for 1977, the 5-5710 Norfolk & Western. Bottom: 5-5711 Southern and 5-5714 UP, produced by Kader; note these and N & W above all have oversized plastic handrails.

	Gd	Exc	Mt

handrail ends melted over; light shafts glued to roof studs; horns and window material; Type IX frame.

Notes: This unit is often mistaken for the 1975 Lionel-built 5514 Southern locomotive (see page 21); I cannot accept speculation that this shell was decorated by Lionel although it is the best decorated of the foreign-made Geeps. Very difficult to locate. **25 45 60**

(5-)5714 UNION PACIFIC: Introduced 1977 in set 5-2782; catalogued showing Lionel catalogue number 5402 on its side; last of the Hong Kong Geeps offered, with no mention ever made of the production change; catalogue number 5-5714 never shown in the catalogue (as was the case with all foreign-made units).

Basic gray shell painted in flat latex-looking yellow and gray separated by thin red stripe; "We can / handle it." on cab side, Lionel "5714" directly below; road name across long hood; all lettering and striping in glossy red stamping; light shafts glued to roof tabs; Type VIII frame. One of the better-looking Geeps produced in Hong Kong, and difficult to find.

Note: Also exists with light shafts glued directly to the roof, with handrails also glued on. **25 45 60**

LIONEL-PRODUCED U-18-B

First shown in the 1976 catalogue, this locomotive really was new to the HO market. Lionel even thought about the modeler, offering one model in an unmarked, unpainted shell. Charlie Sommer points out that there was high demand for the U-18-Bs not only from Lionel HO collectors but from modelers requiring U-18-B shells for their layouts.

The ad introducing the new diesel made a point that Lionel produced the only model of the U-18 on the market at the time, with over seven hundred service stations ready to back up its new products. The new locomotive was dropped from the catalogue the very next year. So much for Lionel being a major factor in the HO train market, which was another claim Lionel used when this locomotive was introduced in *Model Railroader* in its December 1975 advertisement. As for service, few

parts were available and an exchange program for defective units was already in place for the service centers.

The model was available in 1976 and 1977 as a separate-sale item, in three road names, with all of these models and the unmarked one fairly hard to locate. This locomotive, one of their best-selling items, also has the distinction of being *the first and last really new piece of motive power offered by Lionel*. It was Lionel-manufactured and -decorated. One wonders what Lionel could have accomplished in the HO field had they introduced this type of new item to HOers in 1974, instead of starting out by marketing something everyone else already had available. This locomotive will rate high on the collector's list and will be as valuable as the Freedom Train sets, as few HO people knew it was even available in plastic.

Type X Frame

The frame used for the new locomotive was the same type used on the GP-9s of 1975 — a combination of metal and plastic, with no screws used for assembly. One change was the cast-metal weight, which was now ½ inch longer, and the single bulb used to light the cab area was held to the weight with black friction tape. The black plastic pin used to hold the bulb on the GP-9s and Alcos was eliminated.

The same GE motor of 1975 was used, the black plastic U clamps were still used to hold the weight to the frame, and the trucks were the same found on the GP-9s. All eight wheels were powered with the same manual tab-type couplers used on the GP-9s of 1975. The black belly tanks at the frame's center changed slightly with less rivet detail present. Still present were "Lionel Mt. Clemens, Mich.", "Molded in Canada", and the zip code number molded into it.

Lionel-made U-18-B Shells

The U-18-B shells were all manufactured from new Lionel tooling and were decorated by Lionel with sharp, clear lettering and eye-catching paint jobs. The basic shell is known to exist in white, light gray, and black, with the white shell found only on the unpainted 5520 Soo Line model. The shell itself differs from all other Lionel models in that it was cast in three separate pieces. All were glued together and all had cutouts or tabs cast into them for assembly purposes. See closeup of shells.

The lower casting was made up of the lower side panels and included the pilot, steps, and walkways. A cutout was cast into both sides at its center, along with one at each end to accept the assembly tabs cast into the other two parts. The second casting consisted of the long hood, and the third was the short front hood and the cab itself. All parts were glued at the floor line area using the cutouts and tabs on all three parts. All fit well, and it is difficult to tell that the shell is not a single casting.

All four models have black plastic decorative horns on the roof at the end of the long hood. Unpainted black plastic handrails and clear cab window material are present, along with number boards and headlight lens at both ends (with only the cab end of the unit lighted). Holes were cast into the shells to accept the handrails. Unlike the wire handrails used on the GP-9s, this model had handrails made entirely of black plastic. They were installed by the modeler, using the instruction sheet that was included (shown on pages 98–99).

No Lionel part numbers appear on these shells. A part number — 50-5520-043 for right, 50-5520-042 for left — did appear on each spur holding one side and one end railing. Good, clear louver and rivet detail are present on the roof, sides, and the ends of the shell.

Listings of Lionel-made U-18-Bs

	Gd	Exc	Mt

(5-)5520 SOO LINE: Available 1976-77 as a separate-sale item only; catalogued for first year only.

Basic white shell, with both ends and lower side panels below walkways finished in bright semigloss red; otherwise unpainted; "5520" in small black stamping on cab side and road name at center of long hood outlined with thin black line.
Note: Some collectors believe this shell exists with the white area painted but I have been unable to locate such a model and believe it was left unpainted to save production time and money. Extremely difficult to find in good condition.   **45   60   80**

Type X frame: Lionel eight-wheel drive for U-18-B of 1976 (couplers have been removed to show cast-on pockets)

Underside of U-18-B shell introduced in 1976. The hole seen just behind the cab roof accepts the set of five decorative horns on the roof. The three different-sized tabs on each side protrude into the shell's cavity and are part of the end platforms and side walkways casting, while the hood and cab were a separate casting glued to these tabs. A tab at each end of the shell can be seen: these were used in the same manner. This shell is the only one known made in this manner and glued together. The heat generated from running the model will open these glued joints and although the collector will pass this model by, the shell is not actually damaged.

The left column shows Hong Kong–produced GP-30s introduced in 1976 and the right Lionel U-18-Bs, also new in 1976. Left, top to bottom: Uncatalogued 5-5622 SF in passenger colors, 5-5623 BN, and controversial 5-5717 Conrail (this uncatalogued unit does not carry a Lionel number but may have been available in small quantities with a repainted Bachmann-decorated shell; verification requested). Right, top to bottom: 5-5520 Soo Line, 5-5521 CP Rail, and 5-5522 Rio Grande — these U-boats were all eight-wheel drive with plastic handrails. Undecorated gray U-boat also available is not shown.

	Gd	Exc	Mt

(5-)5521 CP RAIL: First catalogued in 1976 separately; available uncatalogued 1977.

Basic black or gray shell finished in semigloss red except for lower side panel and step at ends which were painted black; all lettering white block-type stamping except for black and white logo at end of long hood; road name on front of long hood; nose of locomotive holds white stripes; "5521" on cab side; handrails, horns, and window material; no part numbers found; Type V frame.

Note: Can be found in two shades of red because of basic shell color; considered rare in either shade.

(A) Light shell.	40	65	85
(B) Dark shell.	40	65	85

(5-)5522 RIO GRANDE: Available catalogued 1976 and uncatalogued 1977.

Basic black or gray shell painted semigloss black; thin orange strip runs length of lower side panels just below floor line; "5522" below cab window; road name spelled out at center of long hood and also on nose of the unit; all lettering stamped in bright orange; front wall and step area at both ends and short hood are orange, with end of long hood finished with orange striping; roof horns, handrails, and cab window material; no Lionel part numbers; Type V frame.

Notes: A striking model, favored by all collectors; considered the rarest of the painted U-18s. I have seen more than one of this particular model with front number boards holding white-stamped "5522" on a black background but I do not believe Lionel ever issued these models with anything but clear plastic number board inserts. Verification requested. Unit available in two different types of black finish. 1976 catalogue shows car numbered 5523 (incorrectly). C. Sommer comment.

(A) Glossy shell.	40	60	85
(B) Dull shell.	40	60	85

(5-5523) Unmarked Shell: It appears the unmarked shell was not stocked by many dealers and that not many were even produced. This version considered rare; I have only seen one. Not shown in the photograph, it has a gray shell — the only way it was known to have been made. The black horns and clear window material are present, but the handrails were not installed when purchased. **NRS**

HONG KONG–PRODUCED GP-30S

First introduced in 1976, this new type of power unit showed once again that someone at Lionel still had interest in trying to expand their HO line of equipment. But the locomotive turned out to be one of Lionel's last offering of HO power units.

Produced in Hong Kong by Kader Ltd., Lionel's GP-30 is the very same unit sold by Bachmann Bros. of Philadelphia, Pennsylvania, in the late 1970s — except that the series of metal plates used for weight in the Bachmann-sold unit was replaced by a cast-lead weight in 1976. The 1977 model used a sheet-metal weight. In most cases the decoration of the shell was also quite different, as shown in the photograph on page 55.

The Lionel model was first catalogued in set 5-2682 in 1976 in the BN road name and was available, unchanged except for the metal weight, the next year; it was also available these last two years as an uncatalogued item for separate sale. When first shown in the 1976 catalogue, the artwork used was of little help in identifying the unit. The shell carries no Lionel catalogue or part number of any kind. More confusion is caused by the picture of the GP-30 in the Conrail road name, which was shown on the front cover of the 1977 catalogue. The 5-5717 locomotive from all indications may have been available in late 1977 with the plentiful Burlington Northern shells used, repainted. A third road name, Union Pacific, has surfaced at meets, with Lionel frames and cartons, but there are no known UP GP-30s produced for Lionel in the 1970s line.

A fourth GP-30 was produced as an uncatalogued item using the 5-5622 catalogue number and the Santa Fe road name — in passenger colors. This locomotive was available in 1976 in an uncatalogued Sears freight set as well as being a separate-sale item, also uncatalogued, in 1976 and 1977. This unit, especially in the Santa Fe name, is most difficult to locate today.

All three of the Lionel GP-30s were decorated in a flat paint, with some having semigloss lettering and others having flat-finish lettering, while the Bachmann models of the 1970s have semigloss and high-gloss bodies with high-gloss lettering. All are lighted with a single bulb.

Type XI Frame

Frames used on the Lionel models were all made of unpainted black plastic in 1976 with a solid lead cast weight held to the frame with a single Phillips-head screw that could be seen from under the model: these I number **Type XI**. In 1977 the weight changed to a series of metal plates. NMRA horn hook couplers were used and were held to the frame by a single screw. The coupler pocket did not have a cover. Information cast into the frame reads "1976 Fundimensions Lionel, Hong Kong", along with the letter "C" in a circle. Two large tabs cast into the side of the frame pass through the shell at its center to hold the shell in place.

Poor detail is found on the truck side frames, but the detail found on the shell — such as rivets and louvers — is quite good. The roof of the cab held a cluster of three-piece decorative horns and bell, both of unpainted black plastic. Clear window materials in the cab, one headlight lens in the nose, and black unpainted handrails complete the detail.

This unit did not have good pulling power. The same small three-pole pancake-type motor powers the unit, which was equipped with one rubber traction tire.

Units other than the BN may be considered uncommon.

Listings of Hong Kong–made GP-30s

	Gd	Exc	Mt

181: See (5-5623)

(5-)5622 SANTA FE: Available from Sears, uncatalogued 1976-77.

White or red shell painted in passenger colors (flat silver long hood and sides; flat red cab, nose, pilots, and walkways); colors separated on roof and side with thin black and yellow lines; glossy red road name on long hood; Santa Fe logo on red nose; bright yellow-stamped Lionel "5622" on cab side; window material, number boards, headlight lens, and clear light shaft material; black unpainted handrails, bell, silver-painted decorative horns; Type VII frame.

(A) Stamped logo on nose (Sears).	30	50	75
(B) Decaled logo on nose.	30	50	75

(5-5623) 181 BURLINGTON NORTHERN: Catalogued 1976, introduced in set 5-2682 (appearing with new Taiwan-produced cars, the GT boxcar, 8601 BN caboose, the new 8621 coil car in the Pittsburgh & Lake Erie road name); this first GP-30 set returned in 1977; never shown as separate-sale item but available 1976-77 as such.

Black plastic shell painted flat green with roof and top row of side panels, floor line, and pilot at both ends finished in flat black; all lettering semigloss white block-type stamping; road name on cab side with large white "B" incorporating a green "N" on the long hood; "181" also appears at the end of the long hood; white stripes on nose of shell; unpainted handrails, decorative horns and bell on cab roof, clear window material, headlight lens, number boards; clear shaft glued directly to the inner roof of the shell to carry light to both ends of the shell; no Lionel numbers. The cab is a separate casting and will pop off to allow the modeler to service the motor (although with some degree of difficulty); new Type VII frame.

	30	40	50

Comments on the 5717 Conrail and the 5729 UP GP-30s

The front cover of the 1977 catalogue shows a unit with an unreadable number visible on the side of the cab. It also clearly show the Conrail logo stopping short of the first large side panel behind the cab. The road name is shown starting at the very end of the long hood — unlike my unit, pictured on page 27. No confirmation as to whether this road name was ever actually used by Lionel was available. I believe it was possible that a few of the Burlington Northern shells were repainted because of poor sales of that road name and reintroduced with the new road name in 1977. After all, it was done with the 5-5700 Penn Central shells that started out as Grand Trunk Geeps in 1975. In my research for this book I have gathered many Bachmann GP-30s, both old and new production. All have the same type of painting and lettering. I also have units that I know have been custom painted. None of these units show printing underneath the Conrail colors.

The unit pictured on page 27 is a repainted Burlington Northern shell; close examination reveals the lettering still present. Comparing it to my many Lionel GP-30s, one sees that the same flat paint was used, along with the same washed-out-looking white stamping of letters and numbers, but the Lionel 5717 number is not present. The same type of overspray also exists inside the shell, as found on most all shells painted for Lionel. Any good custom painter I have ever talked to always uses unfinished shells for their painting; if these are not available they will take the time to strip a decorated shell for their customers.

Lionel, on the other hand, was known in the past to have taken this type of shortcut in production. But if this is Lionel production, then why no Lionel catalogue number? The paint on the Conrail Geep shown is much lighter than that used on the 8701 Conrail boxcar, which was also new in 1977. The white lettering on the boxcar is very similar to the Geep lettering in its washed-out look. It may be that the Conrail Geep was a Hong Kong factory-repainted Burlington Northern shell, available in 1977, but I have my doubts. You be the judge.

Regarding the 5-5729 Union Pacific GP-30, some of the confusion about the Union Pacific road name could have come from ads run in *Model Railroader* in April of 1978, showing a Bachmann GP-30 for sale at $7.99 in the UP road name, with the Lionel name present. The locomotive is carried on sale lists by mail-order dealers even today. But the road name was not available as a Lionel item as far as can be determined. Verification requested on such a model.

HONG KONG–MADE GS-4

The new GS-4 introduced in 1975 was made in Hong Kong; both the locomotive and tender carry the Lionel Hong Kong name on their frames. It was first shown in the 1975 catalogue as the 5-6501, heading one of the two bicentennial sets. In 1976 a second road name was added to the GS-4s offered. This Southern Pacific-type locomotive was to be the only steam engine Lionel offered in the 1970s HO line.

The 5-6500 Southern Pacific was introduced for separate sale, with the 5-6501 returning separately and still heading the Freedom Train set, number 5- 2586. The set had five cars, in contrast to the smaller diesel set that held only four cars. Both road names were available again in 1977 in the same sets although they were shown only for separate sale. In 1977 the GS-4 returned in a third road, "The Western Pacific", catalogued in a six-car freight set (5-2783) and as a separate sale item (5-6502). Only available for a year or two, all of the GS-4s present a challenge to HO collectors, with the Western Pacific being the most difficult to find and the Freedom locomotive being the most sought after today. The changes made in the Kader Bachmann tooling of 1975 for this locomotive helps make the early Lionel GS-4 very collectible.

Type XII Frame

The engine was produced with a plastic and die-cast frame and boiler (**Type XII**). The boiler shell was cast in two separate sections with extremely good detail. The boiler shell was decorated with wire handrails and brass popoff valves. A dummy coupler was mounted on the pilot. Two ½-inch screws held the shell to the frame; one was located above the front truck and the second was hidden above the rear truck. The modeler had to use care in removing this rear screw, as covered in the instruction sheet packed with the locomotive. All piping and all ladders on the boiler are plastic. A single light bulb lights both of the headlight lenses at the front of the smokebox. The tender had no electric pickup. Values provided include locomotive and tender.

A large metal weight runs from the front of the smokebox to just behind the last drive wheel and serves more than one purpose. The weight also held the grain-of-wheat-type bulb to light the headlights. Of the eight drivers only the rear axle is powered and driven by a small three-pole metal-geared, enclosed-type motor mounted just above the rear axle and held in place by (and was part of) the metal weight. Although the catalogue stated that the drive train and worm gear used was a Lionel design, the motor was not the GE-type motor of 1974 but was the second specially made motor for these Lionel models. The other six metal-rimmed plastic-centered drivers are powered by the sheet-metal drive rods only. A stamped sheet-metal valve gear is also found. The front and rear trucks were plastic frames with metal wheel sets and excellent detail.

Note: Lionel's catalogue number will only be found on the carton of each unit.

482: See (5-6502)
4449: See (5-6501)
4454: See (5-6500)

(5-6500) 4454 SOUTHERN PACIFIC: First available 1976, shown only as separate-sale item but available in at least one uncatalogued set (5-2684), as was the uncatalogued matching caboose (see page 43).

Shell decorated with bright flat orange stripe running from end of the cab down the lower streamline side panel and across the pilot and back up the opposite side; reddish-colored flat stripe appears above the orange beginning at the cab and extending down the side to end above the first driver; remainder of shell finished in flat black, with the three colors separated by thin silver striping; "Daylight" slogan in silver stamping on orange side panel above first driver with silver "4454" stamped below

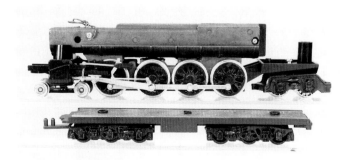

Type XII Hong Kong GS-4 drive and frame of 1975 used on all three GS-4 steam locomotives without change through 1977.

Type XI frame: Hong Kong drive of 1976 with lead weight used on first GP-30s, metal plates were used on 1977 frames.

Kader-made GS-4 steam locomotives — the only ones in the later Lionel HO line. Top to bottom: 5-6500 Southern Pacific, new in 1976, 5-6501 Freedom Train, new in 1975 in the special bicentennial set, and the 5-6502 Western Pacific, new in 1977 and the most difficult of the three to locate. The Southern Pacific marketed in the U.S. was also offered in Canada using the T-12030 Canadian number.

	Gd	Exc	Mt

cab windows; wire handrails on pilot and along boiler, with the smokebox and two nonworking marker lights painted silver. Most common of the three available road names.

The tender sides are painted with the same striping; black top giving very long streamlined look; wire handrails detail the top of the tender; six-wheel plastic trucks; outer floor carries the same Lionel Hong Kong markings as the locomotive frame. **60 75 90**

(5-6501) 4449 AMERICAN FREEDOM TRAIN: First shown in the 1975 catalogue, in artwork not depicting the locomotive accurately (see page 14); remained in the line until end of production in 1977; shown separately and in set 5-2586 in 1976 (as actually sold); the set carried the fifth car, a 105, which is quite rare today; the other four cars were all used with the diesel unit at the front.

The decoration of the locomotive is the only change from the Southern Pacific colors with the boiler painted flat dark blue, with pilot and lower streamline panels lighter blue with ¼" red stripe at the top; colors are separated and outlined with thin white striping; a third ⅜" stripe in flat white starts at the first driver and runs to rear of cab above the boiler walkway; all three colors continue across the twelve-wheel tender's side, with "AMERICAN FREEDOM TRAIN" stamped in dark blue across the large white area; three white stars appear in the red and blue striping at the end of shell just above floor line; "4449" stamped just below cab windows; Hong Kong and Lionel names on frame; all striping crosses the back of the cab and both ends of the tender; wire handrails, silver smokebox front, and double headlight. Most sought after of the three steam-type locomotives. **75 90 125**

Comment: The author has a 6501 in his collection with the skirt signed by the engineer and fireman responsible for getting the Freedom Train

across the United States; both men said they had signed many pictures and programs, but that was the first time anyone had ever asked that a model be autographed.

(5-6502) 482 WESTERN PACIFIC: Catalogued separately and in one six-car set, 5-2783, in 1977 only.

All detail found on the first two road names is here; the all-black, flat paint used makes it an eye-catching locomotive; silver smokebox front and thin white line running the length of the boiler and the tender side serves as contrast to complement fine detailing; this unit only one of the three without striping across the back of the cab and tender ends; double-outlined road name and logo stamped in white at center of tender side; "482" stamped in white just below cab windows. The most difficult of the steam units to find as it was available only one year. **70 90 100**

RAILSCOPE FA-1

It was in 1988 that one more innovation came to Lionel HO. Lionel was marketing a high-tech self-contained video camera in its models in O Gauge and somehow managed to make the unit small enough to fit into two HO FA-1 A units. Operating it was like sitting in the cab of your own train. The unit operated off two 9-volt alkaline-type batteries — one in the 3001 camera unit and one for the TV signal receiver disguised as a wood pile — and required no power from the track. A small Lionel TV was also available with the A units, but the customer's own television would work as well. An eight-page instruction and trouble-shooting booklet was included in the package.

Actually the new unit was not a part of the 1974–1977 line of HO marketed by General Mills, but a product of the new LTI (Lionel Trains

Incorporated). The shells of the A units were the same diework used in the 1974–1977 Alcos, and therefore it is included here as the first and last power unit made by Lionel Trains, Inc. in HO — at least at this point in time. There was however some modification to the tooling, with the drive train being of Kader manufacture using two of their pancake-type motors. Kader shipped these units directly to Mt. Clemens, along with the electrical component supplied by a subcontractor for assembly.

Lionel's 1989 full-page ad was designed to increase the unit's poor sales. It seemed the HO modeler was not sure it could actually work, and price topped $300. There was even a free battery-holder kit offered to push sales. Today the two A units can be purchased for under $125 (less the TV). HO operators also understood that drawbacks were that it is only black and white and that it ate up batteries. Current retail value for the AA unit is about $129. G. Bunza comment.

3001 RAILSCOPE CAMERA UNIT: Shell was made from same diework as FA-1 from 1974-77 HO line, except for softer plastic used; shell painted dark gloss blue on roof and top row of side panels, including the windshield; remainder of the shell was a light semigloss gray; white silk-screened "LIONEL LINES" and "3001" across middle side panels; "MADE BY / LIONEL" in last lower panel at rear; detail similar to FA-1 diework except thinner, dark frosted window material used in the cab; three oversized Phillips-head screws holding the cab to the all-plastic black frame were located on each side at front cab door, with one at the rear end of the cab.

The frame held two nonpowered plastic trucks with metal wheels; on/off switch operating the camera was mounted above the rear truck; camera unit operated through a hole cut below the nonworking headlight lens; fuel trank housed the 9-volt battery; "Lionel Trains Inc. Mt. Clemens, MI" and zip code number 48045 molded into the cover.

Collector value unknown

3003 RAILSCOPE POWER UNIT: Shell same as 3001 except for "3003" on side; frame still had fuel tank but it was cast into the frame

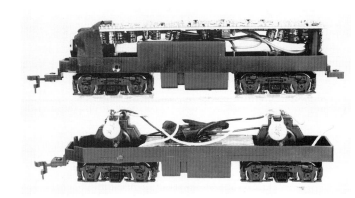

Special Hong Kong–made frames used on the RailScope units, with a Lionel die used for the shell. There are large holes to secure the Lionel-made shell on the video unit.

GP-9 custom painted by Bev-Bel: kit 906

Bev-Bel kit 902 and custom-painted locomotive by Tom's Engine Yard.

Custom-painted Alcos offered by Bev-Bel Corporation, never part of the Lionel HO line: kits 900 and 901

The two Hong Kong–built RailScope units with shells made from Lionel diework.

with a lead weight fastened with one Phillips-head screw; both four-wheel trucks were powered, each with its own pancake-type motor mounted on the truck; couplers on both units fastened with one brass screw to the cast-on coupler pockets that protruded through the shell (these are easily broken off); four plastic pins cast into the frame held the shell in place. Shells known to swell on the roofs from heat trapped inside the shells.   **Collector value unknown**

CUSTOM-PAINTED LIONEL POWER UNITS

While preparing this text I decided to include known custom-painted Lionel models after being offered the Conrail GP-9 shown on page 31 for $125 in 1989, at a meet in Allentown, Pennsylvania. It was presented by the would-be seller as one of the few that was made up because Lionel was thinking of adding new road names to its HO line of power units in late 1976.

The story made sense, but I had owned mockup models in my earlier Lionel HO collection, and this unit was decorated like none I had ever seen before. Being a builder of HO models for some time and having done some painting, I left the model on the seller's table. No box was seen at the time.

A half hour later I ran into a friend, Mike Nechapor, who is a custom painter of some stature. He assured me it was a custom-painted model, probably Bev-Bel, and that it should be labeled as such, with a kit number other than a Lionel number. Returning to the table I saw a white Lionel carton with the outline of a label that had been removed; no numbers were present. I immediately thought of the faked Lionel logo that had shown up on Athearn-made cars a year after the original publication of the Greenberg Guide to the earlier Lionel HO had been published. Here we go again, I thought: the seller knows who made this unit but isn't saying. I decided to buy the unit for $35. It was definitely Lionel manufacture but was never offered in Lionel's line of HO power units.

I have since found the other four units pictured on the opposite page — all custom painted, all Lionel production. Two of the Alcos shown were sold to me as they should have been, as Bev-Bel kits, with a white glued-on label stating "Made Exclusively for Bev-Bel Corp", along with their kit number. The kit number also identifies who painted the model for Bev-Bel. The tuscan Lehigh Valley Alco, also a Lionel model, was sold to me as a custom-painted unit by Tom's Engine Yard of Coplay, Pennsylvania. None were palmed off as a one-of-a-kind Lionel.

A letter and phone call to Irv Belkin, owner of the Bev-Bel Corp., assured me that his company did sell Lionel units that were redecorated and sold in their original boxes as Bev-Bel items only. They did no work for Lionel. Phone calls and letters went out also to the C & M Shops of Newfoundland, New Jersey, and Cudec, Inc. of Fairfield, New Jersey. Both Ray Thrayfell and Steve Young assured me they had done work for Bev-Bel, but not for Lionel. The same holds true for Tom's Engine Yard: he paints in small numbers for his own customers only and does not create rare models. Because of the federal EPA laws passed in late 1970, controlling the exhaust of paint fumes into the air, the companies mentioned no longer paint but are still in the business of silk-screening, hot stamping, and special lettering jobs for the hobbyist. All of the custom-painted models were in road names not available in the Lionel line of HO and were made for that reason. They were never meant to confuse the collector, but these models are all very collectible in their own right — but not as Lionel-offered models.

Once again, we in HO must keep a sharp eye open for the fast-buck guys who try to create a rare model by removing models from their cartons or removing their labels. From my experience with genuine Lionel mockups, I know that all had decaled numbers (usually oval-shaped 0s) and road names. The paint job always looked like it was done by hand, and they were never found in a stamped box. Most were marked nonproduction. The point is that there were no Lionel models offered in the 1970s that carry the custom-painted look. Remember, when you think you have found a rare model, do not be afraid to ask some questions before you buy.

CATALOGUE NUMBER	ROAD NAME	YEAR	MANUFACTURER	COLOR	NUMBER ON ITEM
BEV-BEL CORP.					
Alcos					
900	Penn. (solid stripe)	1975	Lionel	Brunswick green	5882
902	Lehigh and New England	1975	Lionel	Black/white	704
901	Western Maryland	1975	Lionel	Black	304
GPs					
904	Erie	1976	Lionel	Black/yellow	1263
906	Conrail	1976	Lionel	Blue/white	7478
TOM'S ENGINE YARD					
None	Lehigh Valley FA-1	1980	Lionel	Tuscan/black	542

CHAPTER III
Rolling Stock

This chapter covers first the freight cars, alphabetically by general category, and then the few passenger cars offered by Lionel in the United States. Within each type of car, items will be described in order of appearance, with Lionel-made items usually first. Not all details of dimensional data (such as capacity, and sometimes including inspection data) on the sides of cars are cited in the listings, but clear photographs of all cars described appear in this book. Frame markings are not described in each listing; please refer to the summary of marking styles in Chapter I. The introduction to each manufacturer's line, before the descriptive listings, reminds you of typical frame markings. There is a photograph of all freight loads at the end of this chapter. Chapter VI covers Canadian rolling stock.

Note: As with the locomotives, the freight cars are listed by Lionel catalogue number, with any portion not appearing on the side of the car in parentheses. A differing side-of-car number will follow the parentheses as needed. Because of their basic similarity, any four-digit car number prefixed by a numeral other than "5" will be listed in the sequence of 5-series numbers. Thus if you are trying to identify a specific car, look at the last four numbers and see if it is listed in the basic listing by catalogue number. Remember, side-of-car numbers that do not stem from the catalogue number are cited in sequence, but you will be referred to the listing under the catalogue number.

BOXCARS, REEFERS, AND STOCK CARS

See the four photographs on this and the following pages comparing details of the Lionel- and Kader-made models, as well as the illustrations on page 13 of Chapter I.

40-foot Lionel-made Boxcars

The boxcars Lionel produced in the 1970s were direct descendants of the 0874-type boxcars introduced in 1964–1966, just before Lionel dropped out of the HO market. These cars were by far the nicer looking of the boxcars in the 1970s line. Most are hard to find today since they were available only for a year or two.

All of the cars were of light construction but had excellent detail on the shell and frame. All steps, grabirons, and ladders were cast into the body, as were the roofwalks and number boards that appeared at both ends of the car. The doors were the operating type and moved freely on four claw foot-type glides. Two number boards are present, one small and one much larger, at the bottom of each door. Rivet detail is small but extremely clear and is present on the door, sides, roof, and ends of each car. All lettering, in Lionel's well-known stamping, is sharp and crisp in all cases. One black plastic brakewheel is also present.

The solid black plastic talgo-type truck has the NMRA-style couplers that have the manual uncoupling tab at one side, as introduced in the early HO line in the 1960s. Solid plastic wheel sets were used, and the truck was secured to the frame with one Phillips-head screw. The same three-piece frame, also from the 1960 line of HO, is also present

and has the sheet-metal weight between the inside floor and outside bracing. The Lionel name appears at the center of the frame and is quite small. Air valves and brake cylinders are also cast into the outside bracing. The part number 0864-376 is found on the inner roof of the shells of all Lionel-made boxcars, while the number 0866-208 appears

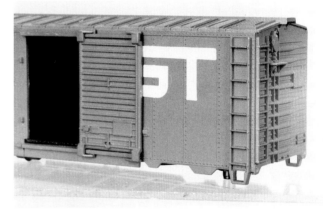

A Lionel-made 40-foot boxcar available in 1974–1976. Note the claw feet that the door rides on, with no door stops present, and the eight-rung ladder, cast-on roofwalk, and steps larger than those found on the Kader-made cars. Brakewheel is missing from model shown.

A Kader-made 40-foot boxcar shell introduced in 1976 and available until 1977 differed in many ways from the Lionel-made cars. Note the separate roofwalk, the seven-rung ladder, and the door that slides and is held in place by the door rails, the oversized door stops, and very small slanted steps.

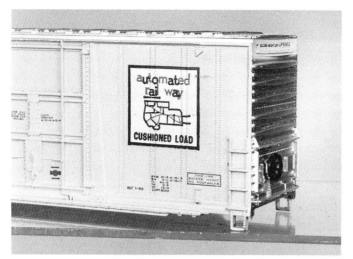

Closeup of the only shell used in the Kader-made car offered as Lionel in 1976–1977. Note the thin steps that were shown broken in the 1977 catalogue, the only year the car appeared in all four road names offered and the height of the car "notice" posted at the top of the car end. No roofwalks were used on this type of car because of its extra height.

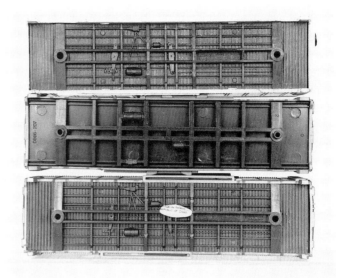

Three 40-foot boxcar underframes. Top: The Kader-made hi-cube with thin shell casting and the Lionel name molded in the frame. Bottom: Also a Kader standard 40-foot boxcar with same information but also bearing the oval gold sticker. Note the different width of main support and bolsters. Middle: Lionel model is shown, less its metal weight, to expose the part number. Note the change in the bolster to support the Lionel-type talgo truck.

Eight of the ten 40-foot boxcars manufactured by Lionel. Top: 5-8400 CP Rail and 5-8401 Grand Trunk, new for 1974. Second: 5-8510 BAR car and 5-8511 Spalding. Third: 5-8512 AMF and 5-8513 Milwaukee Road. Bottom: 5-8514 UP and 5-8515 WP boxcars. The last six were introduced in 1975, and all are sought after. Note the crisp clear decoration — not seen on the Taiwan boxcars added in 1976.

Top: The last two Lionel-made HO boxcars, the 5-8516 C & O and 5-8517 uncatalogued Sears car available in special sets in 1975. Then shown are the first and last of the 1976–1977 Taiwan-manufactured cars, starting with the 5-8613 UP and 5-8614 GT, followed by the 1977 production of the 5-8701 Conrail, 5-8702 Southern, 5-8703 Chessie, and the 5-8704 Railbox. The collector will find these cars, difficult to locate, not as nicely decorated as the Lionel models.

	Gd	Exc	Mt

on all outer frames. Floors carry the number 0866-207, and 0864-377 appears on all doors.

1976 saw the new production of the 8613 Union Pacific and 8614 Grand Trunk boxcars switched to Taiwan, which caused the catalogue number to change to the 8600 series. However, the catalogue still showed the Lionel-made cars with the Lionel numbers.

(5-8400) 88400 CP RAIL: First boxcar introduced in the 1970s line; only available in two sets in 1974; catalogue number only used on carton.

Gray or red shell painted flat red; large, heavy gloss, white lettering to the right of door shows road name with smaller "CP" and "88400" directly below; large black and white insignia to left of door; data present.

	8	**20**	**25**

(5-8401) 88401 GRAND TRUNK WESTERN: Catalogued in 1974-75 in one set, showing the wrong catalogue number; available 1975-77 separately, shown with correct number; catalogue number only on carton.

Black or gray shell, painted medium flat blue; large flat white "GT" on right side of door with "GRAND TRUNK / WESTERN" at opposite end; below is "GTW 88401" with data underneath; lettering underlined with white line.

	8	**20**	**25**

(5-8510) 88510 BANGOR AND AROOSTOCK: New in 1975; catalogued separately 1975-76; catalogue number only on carton.

White shell painted in flat red and blue; white-painted roof with matching roofwalk and doors; one half car side shows BAR logo in a light aqua and white; other half holds road name at top, spelled out in white; white-stamped "B A R / 88510" and data below. Most eye-catching of all the Lionel cars.

	10	**20**	**25**

(5-8511) 88511 SPALDING SPORTING GOODS: New in 1975; first of only two sports manufacturers' names Lionel used; catalogued separately 1975-76 (never available in a set); catalogue number only on carton.

Yellow shell painted in flat yellow; flat bright orange roof with matching doors; large "SPALDING / A Questor Company / SPORTING GOODS" and R in a circle at one end with "SSGX 88511" underlined; flat black-stamped data beneath; large basketball and "SPALDING / Official / TOP-FLITE / 100" stamped in black. A prize for the collector.

	10	**20**	**25**

(5-8512) 88512 AMF SPORTING GOODS: Catalogued separately 1975-76; catalogue number only on carton.

Gray shell painted bright silver with matching doors; flat black-painted roof; flat black-stamped letter; AMF name and "88512" underlined; data at one end and large black bowling ball and four falling bowling pins in red, white, and black on other end.

	10	**20**	**25**

Gd Exc Mt

(5-8513) 88513 MILWAUKEE ROAD: Catalogued separately 1975-76; some cartons carry "Made in Taiwan R.O.C." stamped on one side but car is Lionel production item.

Red shell painted flat red; silver roof; flat white-stamped lettering; road name logo on side at one end, other side spells out road name; "MILW / 88513" and data below road name. Plain looking; difficult to find.

10 25 30

(5-8514) 88514 UNION PACIFIC: New in 1975; replaced in 1976 by Taiwan-made car (see 5-8613 below) in the sets of 1976, although "88514" was still shown as the car number in the catalogue illustration; no prefix used on carton.

Brown or black shell painted flat rich brown; flat white block-type stamping; "We can / handle it. / the Union Pacific railroad people" on side at one end and UP shield in red, white, and blue, with "UP 88514" on the car side at other end, with data below. Sharp, clean-looking model.

10 25 30

(5-8515) 88515 WESTERN PACIFIC: Available separately only 1975-76; carton carries imported parts message but is a Lionel product.

White or gray shell painted bright flat orange; lettering in very small black stamping; "SHOCK PROTECTED SHIPMENT" high on one side with road name on the background of a silver feather, "88515" underlined, with data below; other end holds WP logo in white, red, and black, with "CUSHION UNDERFRAME" and data below. Lettering style gives a very crowded appearance. Rare.

20 25 35

(5-8516) 88516 CHESAPEAKE & OHIO: Uncatalogued; available 1975-76 in the American Flyer GP-9 special Sears set 56593 (most of the unpainted rolling stock is found in these early special Sears sets).

Unpainted medium blue plastic shell with matching doors; white-stamped lettering; to left of door, small road name with "C & O / 88516" below, both underlined, data at bottom; to right of door larger "C AND / O / FOR / PROGRESS", and data at bottom. Car body has slight shine to it except for areas of lettering where heat stamping dulled the surface. **Note:** Rare, even though some collectors say it was available separately as a Lionel item.

20 25 30

(5-8517) 88517 SEARS: Uncatalogued; available 1975-76 in Sears sets.

White or gray shell painted semigloss light green; to left of door large "Sears" outlined in a rectangle, with "R" in a circle outside box, data below; to right of door "SRCX 88517" with thin line above and below, "Sears, Roebuck and Co." below number; ⅛" stripe running length of shell, centered; flat white-stamped markings (one of few cars using script instead of block-type lettering).

15 20 25

(5-8580) 88580 SALADA: Promotional item not for sale to general public; plain brown carton without picture window or printing but with label affixed stating Lionel name and number 88580. There are two cars per carton. D. Simonini comment.

Solid red-painted body with matching doors; white-stamped "Salada" in white circle to right of door, data below; to left of door, "For Beyond Thirst, Salada Iced Tea", Lionel number 88580 below, with data; all other detail the same as found on other Lionel-made boxcars. Extremely rare promotional item of 1975 and early 1976. Don Simonini Collection.

NRS

40-foot Taiwan-made Boxcars

The 1976 catalogue still used pictures of the Lionel-made 8514 Union Pacific and the 8401 Grand Trunk, which were available separately. But in the sets, these two cars had actually been replaced by the new Taiwan-produced cars, with no mention of this fact by Lionel. The only hint of a change was a notation on the white carton "made in Taiwan R.O.C." and, of course, the number used on the carton and item changed to the 8600 series.

The carton still carried the prefix 5-, but like the Lionel-made cars, it is not present on the car side.

The two cars produced in 1976 were the brown 5-8613 Union Pacific and the blue 5-8614 Grand Trunk. In 1977 four new cars were added and the catalogue number changed to the 8700 series. These cars were the blue 8701 Conrail, the red 8702 Southern, the dark blue 8703 Chessie, and the dark yellow 8704 Railbox. They were to be the last boxcars offered by Lionel.

These cars were not made from Lionel tooling and were of a lighter construction. The trucks and couplers were of poorer quality and the decoration was also poor in most cases. Many colors of plastic were used to produce shells that were always painted. Most cars can be found in different shades of color depending on the basic shell color. The shells are lightweight, with separate roofwalks that *almost* hide the hole in the roof. One black plastic brakewheel is present, and there is good rivet detail on the car sides and ends. The sliding steel door holds two number boards and has rivet detail, but it does not operate well because it was merely pinched between the car side and the extra-thick door rails. The doors are often lost for this reason. All ladders, steps, and grabirons were cast into the shell. Most lettering was of the block type, applied by rubber stamping. The two 1976 cars carry the five-digit Lionel catalogue number, while the four cars offered in 1977 have only the last four Lionel catalogue numbers.

The frames of these cars are black plastic, with all valves and brake cylinders cast into them. The Lionel name and "Made in Taiwan" are cast into the main floor support. Sometimes an oval gold sticker is also present. Unlike the Lionel-made cars, these have no detail on the inner floor, which is completely covered with the metal weight and held to the car with the same plastic pin that secures the truck to the frame. The trucks are the talgo-type, black plastic with split axles and NMRA-type couplers. Some cars will be found with steel axles.

These cars were only available as a Lionel product for the two-year period 1976–1977 and so are difficult to locate today.

Gd Exc Mt

5-8613 UNION PACIFIC: Uncatalogued; available 1976 in sets and separately, and in sets in 1977.

White, brown, or gray shell painted light chocolate brown; to left of door, UP shield in red, white, and blue, smaller UP and "5-8613" below, data to right of door, "We can / handle it." and more data; all lettering in washed-out white stamping; gold sticker present on frame.

10 15 25

5(-)8614 GRAND TRUNK WESTERN: Uncatalogued; available 1976 in sets, and separately and in sets 1977.

White, blue, or gray shell painted flat blue; markings same as (5-8401), except for "58614".

10 15 25

(5-)8701 CONRAIL: Available only in 1977, separately and reportedly in one uncatalogued set (not verified).

White, tan, or blue shell painted flat light blue; to left of door bright white road name, "CR 8701" below, data at bottom; data also at the other end of car, showing two-step stamping method (accounting for different shades of lettering); to right of door very large Conrail logo; numbers and data in washed-out white. Bound to soon become collector's nightmare to locate.

10 15 20

(5-)8702 SOUTHERN: Available only 1977. One of the cars used by other HO suppliers.

Orange, red, or white shell painted flat red; washed-out white lettering, with bright green dot in the "O" of the road name to left of the door with small slogan "GIVES A GREEN LIGHT TO INNOVATIONS" below and larger "8702" and data below that; opposite end carries "SOUTHERN / SERVES / THE SOUTH" and data below. Four sizes of lettering gives crowded appearance.

(5)-8703 CHESSIE SYSTEM: Available only 1977.

White, blue, or gray shell painted very dark blue; all lettering washed-out yellow and much smaller than any other car; to left of door road name

	Gd	Exc	Mt

with small "C & O" and "8703" below, with data; to right of door Chessie cat's head logo, with data below.

Note: Made for other HO suppliers, less the Lionel number.

| | **10** | **15** | **25** |

(5-)8704 RAILBOX: Available only 1977.

Yellow shell painted bright yellow; deep black eye-catching lettering; to left, "railbox" incorporating large outline "r", with "RBOX / 8704", data below; to right of door, dark blue and red logo and "The nationwide boxcar pool" and data below; gold sticker on frame.

Note: There is speculation this car was decorated by Lionel because of the markings, the sharpest and clearest of all six Taiwan-made boxcars. Another one that will surely increase in value. **10 15 25**

Taiwan-made Hi-Cube Boxcars

These cars were 40-foot, smooth-sided, steel-type cars. Lionel's model of the hi-cube boxcar was first catalogued in 1976 and was part of the new Chessie GP-9 set 5-2681 as well as being available for separate sale. When it reappeared in 1977, using the same catalogue number, it was catalogued in three sets and separately with three new road names; the UP is the most common of the hi-cubes. The same type of car by the same manufacturer was also available from two other HO suppliers at the same time: here especially the car number and the Lionel name on the frame become very important to the Lionel HO collector.

All four cars were manufactured by Kader Industries in their Taiwan plant. The black plastic frame is stamped "Lionel" and "Made in Taiwan" but also carries the letters "R.O.C." for "Republic of China" — the first items to do so. The frames are weighted and have the talgo-type truck and NMRA-type couplers. The shells were one-piece castings in a variety of colors, all painted and carrying a white band at the top of the car end lettered "Excess height car" in black, followed by the Lionel catalogue number. The early 8612 UP car was the only model to carry the catalogue number on this white band. All body detail was cast in place, one brakewheel and no roofwalks were used. "Made in Taiwan" and "R.O.C." are found at one corner of the white carton as well as on the frame.

5(-)8612 UNION PACIFIC: Available 1976-77.

Blue, dark gray, light gray, yellow, or white shell painted bright yellow (shade varies); silver-painted roof and car ends, white band and letters at top of each end; blue-lettered door with large red, white, and blue UP shield to left, "UP / 58612" below with data, red Return Empty Car notice; to right of door "automated / railway" and "CUSHIONED LOAD" with a map, lettered in red and blue on white background outlined in blue, data below.

Notes: Of the four cars offered, this is the nicest looking but appears to have very crowded lettering because of the many notices; only one of the four to carry five-digit Lionel number. The number is repeated on the Excess Height notice. The car with the lighter sides is harder to find.

(A) Dark sides (blue or dark gray shell), 1976.	**8**	**10**	**15**
(B) Light sides (white, light gray, or yellow shell), 1977.			
	10	**15**	**20**

(5-)8710 THE ROCK: Available separately only 1977; 5-8710 found only on carton.

White or light blue shell painted flat powder blue; black- and white-stamped lettering; left side holds road name spelled out with "THE ROCK" above, "ROCK 8710" below with data; to right of door, large "R" and data; unpainted black frame. **10 15 20**

(5-)8711 ILLINOIS CENTRAL GULF: Available only 1977, separately; 5-8711 on carton only.

Orange or white shell painted flat bright orange, with flat black-painted door; left side carries road name in three lines, "ICG 8711", data, and "when empty / return to"; to right of door, large white-lettered "i" in a black circle

	Gd	Exc	Mt

(the logo looks almost pink on some of the orange shells). Difficult to find.

(A) Dark shell.	**7**	**9**	**12**
(B) Light shell.	**8**	**12**	**15**

(5-)8712 BURLINGTON NORTHERN: Available only 1977, separately.

Yellow or gray shell painted medium green; white-stamped lettering; left side holds road name in two lines of block-type letters, "BN / 8712" below, data at bottom; to right of door large "B" incorporating an "N".

Note: This car presents a much plainer appearance; also difficult to find.

(A) Light shell.	**6**	**10**	**15**
(B) Dark shell.	**8**	**12**	**15**

Austrian-produced 50-foot Mechanical Reefers

To locate all eleven of the reefers sold as Lionel is a special challenge. It is understandable that Lionel had these particular cars made by other manufacturers since there were no 50-foot refrigerator cars offered in the 1957–1966 HO line. New diework would have been especially costly.

The first 50-foot reefers introduced by Lionel in 1974 and available until 1977 included the names of Pacific Fruit Express, Railway Express Agency, Gold Medal Flour, Schaefer Beer, Heinz Foods, and the Frisco line. All were produced in Austria by Roco, and "AUSTRIA" and the diamond-shaped "ROCO" logo are visible on the frame but the Lionel name is not to be found.

All these cars were riveted steel-sided mechanical-type reefers, with lots of excellent rivet detail. They were made entirely of plastic, the only metal being the weight fastened to the inside of the car frame and the truck axles. All the cars had basic white or tan shells, painted, with most having stamped lettering; the Railway Express car was the only one to carry a decaled logo. Two of these cars do exist with silkscreened lettering, as cited in the descriptive listings following.

All cars had unpainted black brakewheels, trucks, frames, and separate roofwalks. The frames were held to the car with a slot at each end that snapped over a tab molded into the car's shell. Couplers were the NMRA-type on a talgo-type truck, which was held in place by a plastic pin that was part of the truck frame and passed through the floor. The frame has good rivet detail, brakes, reservoirs, and valves, all cast in place. These cars carry the five-digit Lionel catalogue number on their sides. All ladders and grabirons were cast into the shell, as were the seven tapered steps.

Each company behind the private name that Lionel used on the reefer cars was contacted during the preparation of this book; only General Mills, Inc. (Gold Medal Flour) stated there was an agreement with Lionel regarding use of their name in the decoration of the HO reefer line.

(5-8411) 78411 PACIFIC FRUIT EXPRESS: Available 1974-77 in sets, and separately in 1975 and 1976.

Orange-painted sides, black-painted roof and car ends; black-stamped lettering; Lionel "78411" on side; no Lionel name found on car; plastic talgo-type trucks. **8 10 15**

(5-8412) 78412 RAILWAY EXPRESS AGENCY: Available in sets 1974-77, and separately 1975-77.

Green body; gold lettering; red decaled logo; separate unpainted black brakewheel, roofwalk, and frame; NMRA-type couplers; steel axles on talgo-type truck; "78412" on side. Also found with silkscreened lettering. Only refrigerator car to use a decal in its decoration.

(A) Stamped lettering.	**10**	**15**	**20**
(B) Silkscreened lettering.	**15**	**20**	**25**

(5-8540) 78540 GOLD MEDAL FLOUR: Available 1975-77 but not catalogued the last year.

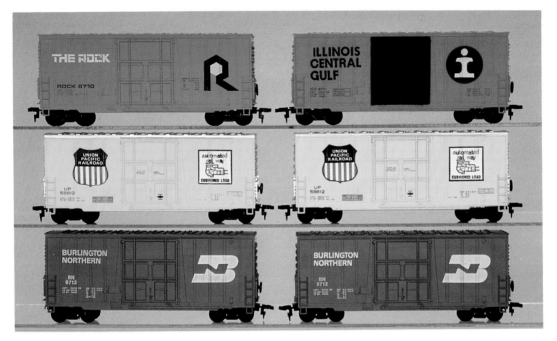

The four road names available in the new hi-cube boxcars made in Taiwan 1976–1977. The 5-8612 UP car on the second shelf, the first of the 1976 series, is shown in the light and dark painted shell, and the 5-8712 BN car of 1977 is also shown with light and dark shells. The 5-8710 Rock and 5-8711 Illinois Central of 1977 are only known to exist with the shade of paint shown here.

	Gd	Exc	Mt

White-painted sides; orange roof and ends; dark blue-stamped lettering; orange and blue logo with slogan "Eventually / Why / Not / Now?" and data to left; "W.C.F.X. 78540" to right of door, above, left, of circular orange and blue logo with "WASHBURN CROSBY / FLOUR" in outer circle, more data below; unpainted black brakewheel, roofwalk, and frame; NMRA-type couplers and talgo-type truck with metal weights. Gold Medal Flour is produced by General Mills Foods, Inc., the same company marketing Lionel trains at that time. **8   10   15**

(5-8541) 78541 SCHAEFER BEER: Catalogued 1975 and 1976 separately only though available uncatalogued in 1977.

White-painted sides; red roof and car ends; unpainted black roofwalk, brakewheel, and frame; red lettering with yellow and gold highlights; logo and beer glasses on side; "78541" on side; seven cast-on steps; NMRA-type couplers and talgo-type truck. **10   12   18**

(5-8542) 78542 HEINZ FOODS: Catalogued separately 1975-76; when first shown half the lettering was black — since car never made that way, the 1976 catalogue corrected the error.

Bright red-painted body; heavy white printing of Heinz logo to left with "NCRX 78542" below, slogan "PURE FOOD / PRODUCTS" and data to right; unpainted black brakewheel, separate roofwalk, and frame; seven cast-on steps; much rivet detail; NMRA-type couplers, talgo-type truck with weight. Fairly hard to find, a favorite of HO collectors; known to exist with the much thicker silkscreened lettering.

	Gd	Exc	Mt
(A) Stamped lettering.	8	12	18
(B) Silkscreened lettering.	10	15	20

(5-8543) 78543 FRISCO: Introduced 1975, shown erroneously with logo "Ship it on / the Frisco!" in black — in 1976 catalogued correctly with "it" appearing in white on black background.

Light tan-painted; "FRISCO" in black on white background, outlined in black, white-stamped data on right, slogan next to "SL SF / 78543" and more data; unpainted black brakewheel, roofwalk, and frame. Great-looking car and difficult to find. **10   15   20**

Taiwan Reefer Production

In 1977 four new names were added to the six Austrian-made models. They were Tropicana Orange Juice, Budweiser, Coors, and Schlitz. These four cars had welded steel sides, with rivet detail found only at the door area and at the end of the car side. The Lionel catalogue number changed to the 8700 series, designating the change to Taiwan manufacture — a fact not mentioned by Lionel.

All four cars had painted bodies with matching roofwalks and car ends; the same unpainted black brakewheel was present as was the weighted frame, of welded side construction. There was no rivet work to speak of except for the door and car ends and it was smaller and less clear. The trucks were still the talgo type with NMRA-type couplers, but they too were of poorer quality. A solid plastic pin was used to hold the truck to the frame, which carries "Made in Taiwan" and the Lionel name, which is slightly larger. Most but not all of the cars carry a gold-colored oval-shaped paper sticker ½-inch long, with "Made in Taiwan / Republic of China" in black stamping on it. All lettering was silk-screened and of good quality. The cars carry only the last four digits of the Lionel catalogue number although the prefix number "5" was still on the cartons. All four of these are difficult to find since they were available for only one year.

Also produced this year was the only known 40-foot reefer sold as Lionel in this time period. The car was also the only wood-sided-type reefer offered. It never appeared in any Lionel catalogue. Packaged in the white carton, with a white label glued to one end reading "Coors Reefer 5-8739"; the car itself carries the number 8740.

While researching this particular model I received a reply to a letter written to Coors Brewing Co. explaining that Coors policy is not to license any company to use the Coors name on products that may impact on the thinking of anyone under twenty-one years of age. This may explain the small number of these cars that seem to be available to today's collectors, many of whom do not even know the car exists.

(5-8739) 8740 COORS (Wood 40-Footer): Uncatalogued; available 1977 only, also in uncatalogued set 5-2793. C. Sommer comment.

Bright white-painted sides scribed vertically for wooden board effect; flat tuscan roof and car ends; all detail — closed steps (the only car in the line to have them), ladders, roofwalk, and ice hatches — cast into shell; "Coors® / GOLDEN" in black and gold to left of plug door; red, blue, and green logo highlighted with two thin black circles on right side, with "VENTILATOR" and "REFRIGERATOR" above; "A.D.C.X. 8740" (same number as Coors 50-footer) below; all lettering appears silk-screened; gold sticker present on frame.

All six of the Austrian-made reefers. Left to right, top to bottom: 5-8411 PFE and 5-8412 Railway Express of 1974, 5-8540 Gold Medal, 5-8541 Schaefer Beer, 5-8542 Heinz, and 5-8543 Frisco. The last four were catalogued new in 1975.

Top left is the only 40-foot wood reefer in the entire line, the 5-8739, new in 1977. It is followed by 50-footers, all new for 1977 and made by Kader in Taiwan: 5-8740 Coors, 5-8741 Budweiser, 5-8742 Tropicana, and 5-8743 Schlitz.

	Gd	Exc	Mt

Notes: This car could easily be mistaken for a Tyco reefer of the same era because of its shell style and closed steps. There is speculation the car was made for the Canadian market but never delivered to Parker Brothers and was sold in the same manner as the abundant 5-5613 Canadian National and 5-5614 Great Northern FA-1s. Extremely difficult to locate and rising in price quickly. Collections of J. Otterbein, K. Armenti, K. Fairchild, G. Horan, C. Sommer. **15   25   40**

	Gd	Exc	Mt

(5-)8740 COORS BEER (Steel-sided 50-Footer): New in 1977.

White-painted sides; tuscan-painted roof, roofwalk, and car ends; black and gold lettering; Coors name and logo very thickly applied; "A.D.C.X. 8740" on side; one brakewheel, NMRA-type couplers, talgo-type trucks; rivets shown only at door area and car end.

10   15   20

	Gd	Exc	Mt

(5-)8741 BUDWEISER (50-Footer): New in 1977.

Flat white-painted sides; bright flat reddish orange-painted roof, roof-walk, and car ends; red and black lettering; two logos in gold, red, and black; "STLR. C. CO. / 8741" with logo on right; all other detail same as 5-8740.   10   15   20

(5-)8742 TROPICANA ORANGE JUICE (50-Footer): 1977.

Flat white-painted sides; high-gloss dark green roof, roofwalk, and car ends; green-, black-, and orange-stamped block-type lettering; otherwise same detail as other reefers; tricolored logo to left of door, "TPIX / 8742" left of it near roof, data below.   10   15   20

(5-)8743 SCHLITZ BEER (50-Footer): New in 1977.

Flat white-painted sides; flat medium brown roof, roofwalk, and car ends; high-gloss medium brown lettering in script; blue, brown, and white logo outlined with yellow border to left of door with data below; "8743" to right of door below slogan, center of side on this car; details otherwise same as other three reefers.   10   15   20

Lionel-produced Stock Cars

Lionel made one 40-foot wooden-type stock car in the four years the later HO line was offered. It appeared in six road names. All were produced much like the boxcars, with a one-piece shell and all ladders, steps, the three number boards, and roofwalk cast into it. The sliding claw-foot door had open slats, as did the sides, and since they were very thin castings they were easily broken. All had stamped lettering, the same boxcar-type frame bearing the Lionel name, the same talgo-type trucks and couplers, and one brakewheel. All shell castings were close to the color they were later painted. All Lionel-made stock cars carry part numbers on their inner roofs. Four of the cars carry separate billboards, new in 1975, that were plastic and had four small plastic studs on their backs; the studs pressed through the open slats and held the boards firmly in place. These removable billboards covered two of the cast-on number boards found on the shells. The four billboard-type cars were all very colorful and are fairly hard to find with their signs intact. The three cars without the billboards are slightly easier to find.

(5-8402) 78402 THE KATY: Catalogued in sets 1974-76; available separately 1975-76; replaced 1977 by only known Taiwan-made stock car, also a Katy, 5-8770, covered at the end of the listings below.

Shell painted flat red; bright yellow-stamped lettering; Katy name and "SERVES THE / SOUTHWEST" to right of door; two smaller number boards at other end hold "M-K-T" and "78402"; no data. One of the more common stock cars.   8   10   12

(5-8570) 78570 D & RGW (DENVER RIO GRANDE): Catalogued 1975-76 separately only; catalogue number only found on carton.

Shell painted flat black with matching door; white-stamped "D & RGW / 78570" below to right of door; two smaller number boards to left of door covered by the new large billboards introduced this year (light tan with steer's head in yellow, brown, white, black, and blue).

Notes: *Some* of the large billboards have pins on their backs melted at the end to help hold them to the car; no printing is found on the original number boards if the add-on boards are removed. The car is shown in 1975 catalogue in dark brown but is only known to exist in the flat black color.   10   15   25

(5-8571) 78571 RATH: Catalogued for separate sale only 1975-76; catalogue number only on carton.

Shell painted flat yellow; large number board to right of door has crisp black-stamped "R.P.R.X. / 78571"; red, white, and blue removable billboard to left of door has Indian head logo and flat black Rath name. Difficult to find complete.   12   15   25

	Gd	Exc	Mt

(5-8572) 78572 NORTHERN PACIFIC: Catalogued (as reddish in color) 1975 and in 1976 only known to exist in brown and silver.

Medium brown-painted sides; roof and ends bright silver (only stock car not painted solid color); large separate "PIG PALACE" billboard; white-stamped road name and "78572" on cast number board at opposite end. One of nicest looking cars in line; difficult to find with billboard intact.   15   20   25

(5-8573) 78573 D & RGW (DENVER) RIO GRANDE: Un-catalogued; available in Sears sets 1975-76, and separately in white Lionel carton 1976.

Glossy blue unpainted shell; large cast-on board has name and "the ACTION road"; two smaller boards carry white-stamped "D & RGW" and "78573". Extremely difficult to find. Verification is requested on this car with a painted blue shell.   15   20   25

(5-8574) 78574 SOUTHERN: Uncatalogued; available separately 1975-76 and in uncatalogued Sears set 5-6590; catalogue number on carton only.

Unpainted medium green shell; yellow lettering; logo on largest cast-on board to right of door; smaller boards hold name and Lionel "78574".

On the left, the Lionel stock car offered 1975–1976, and to the right, the Kader-made car of 1977. Note the much thicker steps, larger number board, and cast-on roofwalk on the Lionel model. The Kader shell used a thinner brakewheel, with no end number board present, and it carries data not found on the Lionel model.

Underframes of the 40-foot stock cars. Top is the Lionel model with the truck removed to show the metal weight and number on the bolster. On the bottom, the Kader-built car of 1977, with simulated wooden frame. Note the truck and coupler difference and thinner casting of the Kader car, with the Lionel name and "MADE IN TAIWAN" on the frame.

Gd Exc Mt

Many collectors do not realize this car exists; most difficult to locate. The car can be partially seen in the photograph of the boiler house kit on page 11 of the 1977 catalogue.   15   20   25

(5-8575) 78575 NYC (NEW YORK CENTRAL) POULTRY: Catalogued 1975-76. The last of the billboard-type stock cars offered.

Light emerald green-painted shell; bright yellow removable billboard with large tan chicken to left of door; cast-on number board at opposite end holds "NYC / 78575". Difficult to find with number board intact.

10   15   20

Taiwan-produced Stock Car

(5-)8770 THE KATY: Available as Lionel only 1977; produced in Taiwan for Lionel in two known variations.

Shell of each version painted flat red, latexlike finish; doors cast in black plastic are painted red on outside only; four thin straight steps, ladders, and three number boards cast into shell; separate roofwalk held to roof with four plastic pins passing through roof and melted over at the ends; one brakewheel; largest number board to right of door has name and "SERVES THE / SOUTHWEST" below; two smaller boards hold "MISSOURI-KANSAS-TEXAS" and "M-K-T / 8770"; data present; black plastic frame is weighted, with all detail below floor cast in place; talgo-type truck, NMRA-type couplers; frame carries "Republic of China", spelled out instead of "R.O.C.".

Notes: Poorly painted car and very small lettering; easily confused with same car — less the Lionel number — made for other HO suppliers at the time. Again, the Lionel number and name on the frame are important clues for the collector.

(A) Thin steps, as described above.   10   15   20
(B) Thicker, sturdier steps, mismatched painted door and roofwalk. C. Sommer comment.   NRS

CABOOSES, CRANES, AND WORK CABOOSES

Lionel Caboose Production, 1974–1975

The first cabooses introduced in the 1974 line of sets — there were no separate-sale items — were 100 percent Lionel manufacture. The tooling used for these models of the 36-foot steel type with off-center cupola was the original diework used on the 1960s Lionel-made cabooses. Very little change was made to the dies. The car was still a three-piece casting, consisting of floor, car shell, and cupola. The smokejack and ladders were separate castings of unpainted black plastic. The shell itself still has the fine rivet detail cast into its steel-type sides and ends. The ladders are fastened to the shell with four small plastic tabs that protrude from the roof ends (the original roof had holes to accept the wire ladders).

The cupola still pops off when the middle is pressed. The most noticeable change to the shell was made at the floor line: the four small tabs that hung down past the frame at the frame-support points and truck-bolster ends were still present, but they were now cast into a 1/16-inch overhang around the entire shell and hid the frame sides completely. The tabs under each door do the same job as on the original caboose — securing the shell to the frame. The slot cut into the shell's side for this purpose on the original caboose is absent from these new models.

The new frames differ in a few areas. The flat, smooth look of the original outside frame is now made to resemble wood planking on the undercarriage of the car. Steps, toolboxes, and coupler pockets are all cast in place as were the originals, but the coupler pockets are now much wider. Two plastic pins, cast into the coupler cover, were pressed up into

the body to hold the coupler in place. No printing of any type appears on the new frame, and there are no part numbers present. The only part number found on these new cars is located on the inner roof of the cupola; it reads "50-3406-010", which is present on all the Lionel-made cabooses. The talgo-type trucks are still used, but the attached coupler pockets are not. Body-mounted finger tab couplers are present. Trucks made entirely of black plastic are held to the frame with one Phillips-head-type screw. A metal weight is also fastened to the inside of the frame — this was the only metal used in the car. The ladders, brakewheel and stand, and the handrails are in a separate one-piece casting of black unpainted plastic with the bottom support pushing into the top of the frame and details each car end. All lettering was done in the Lionel heat-stamping method. No illuminated cars were ever produced.

The cars were available in 1974 and 1975 and were sold as separate items in the second year, though never catalogued that way. Some of the cars are known to exist with both painted and unpainted shells, but no changes in the catalogue number were made. All of the cars carry a full five-digit Lionel number on their sides but not always the catalogue number used on the carton. The production of cabooses switched to Taiwan manufacturing in 1976 with no reason ever given by Lionel. Most collectors agree the move was because of the power units now being made in Taiwan.

Gd Exc Mt

(5-8405) 98405 ATSF (SANTA FE): Catalogued 1974 in sets only, the car was available separately until early 1975; replaced in 1976 by Taiwan-made 5-8603; catalogue number appears only on carton.

Bright red-painted shell (exists with unpainted shell in sets of early 1975); unpainted black frame; yellow-stamped lettering; large SF logo below cupola; "ATSF / 98405" at center of side; smokejack, one-piece ladders, brakewheel, handrails.
(A) Painted shell.   5   8   12
(B) Unpainted shell.   8   12   15

(5-8406) 98406 UNION PACIFIC: Catalogued 1974 in sets only; available separately 1975-76; polished-looking unpainted version in uncatalogued Sears sets of 1975-76; both cars found separately with "UP / 98406" on sides; both replaced in 1977 by Taiwan-made 5-8724 UP caboose.

Flat yellow-painted shell; glossy red-stamped lettering; large UP road name in two lines, small "U.P. / 98406"; smokejack, ladders, and trucks same as other Lionel-made cabooses.
Note: Your author owns two painted shells with decaled UP shields but does not accept them as factory.
(A) Painted shell.   8   10   15
(B) Unpainted shell.   10   15   20

(5-8418) 98418 CHESSIE SYSTEM: Introduced 1974 with gold GP-9 Chessie set, number 5-1480; Lionel's first catalogued set (although shown last in the catalogue); sold separately 1975; replaced by Taiwan-made 5-8600 in 1976; Lionel catalogue number 5-8418 only on carton.

Follows description in section introduction but was first to carry a two-tone paint scheme: body and walls of cupola painted flat yellow with both roofs semigloss silver; "Chessie System" incorporating large cat's head logo stamped across seven lower center side panels, very small "C & O" below roof line, very small Lionel "98418" below that; all lettering in very dark blue stamping. Not as hard to locate as Taiwan car of 1976-77.   10   15   20

(5-8419) X98419 GREAT NORTHERN: Catalogued in sets 1974-75; available 1975-76 separately; this road name never produced in Taiwan; no Lionel name found on car.

Body and cupola sides painted bright red, main and cupola roofs flat black; yellow-stamped lettering; road name above windows; "X98419" below in lower side panels; logo stamped in black, white, and yellow

Seven Lionel-made stock cars, left to right, top to bottom: 5-8402 Katy of 1974, followed by six from 1975, 5-8570 D & RGW, 5-8571 Rath, 5-8572 NP, 5-8573 D & RGW, 5-8574 Southern, 5-8575 NYC. The last car, bottom right, is the 5-8770 Katy new in 1977 and made in Taiwan. Note the thin straight steps. Note also that the D & RGW name and Katy were used twice and that there are large separate boards holding the company logo on four of the Lionel-made cars.

Left, the Lionel-produced caboose of 1974–1975, and on the right the Kader Taiwan-made car of 1976–1977. Many different details can easily be seen, although both cars have a one-piece hand-rail, brakewheel, and ladder casting. Note the Kader-made car carries the Lionel name and "BLT. 1-76" on its side, one of the very few models to do so.

Comparison of the caboose frames with the Lionel-made car at top, with no markings of any type present. Body-mounted couplers are used although talgo-type truck is present. The Kader-made car on the bottom appeared in the U.S. and Canadian lines and shows the Lionel name with "Made in Taiwan" hidden under the truck. There are steel axles and an extra-long coupler shaft, with body-mounted coupler pockets removed.

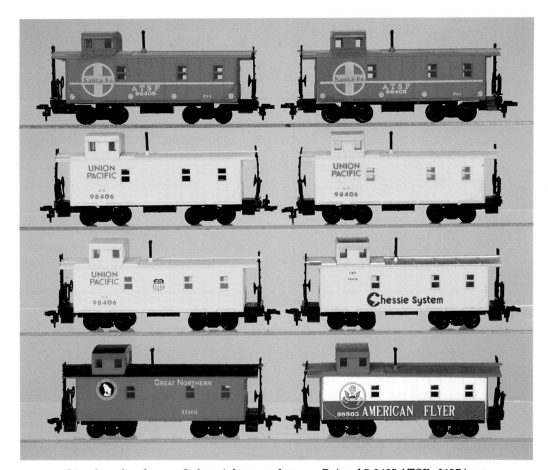

Lionel-made cabooses. Left to right, top to bottom: Painted 5-8405 ATSF of 1974, un-painted 1975 car, painted 5-8406 UP car of 1974, unpainted car of 1975, second early painted 1974 car with UP shield in decal (no such car was part of the Lionel line), painted 5-8418 Chessie of 1974, 5-8419 GN of 1974, and 5-8503 Sears American Flyer of 1975. Note cast-on roofwalks on all cabooses.

Nine known cabooses produced 1976–1977 by Kader in Taiwan; at least nine other power unit names were available in the line without matching cabooses. Top: 5-8600 Chessie, 5-8601 BN, 5-8602 ICG (all available 1976). Middle: Bright red 5-8603 ATSF of 1976, dark red 5-8603 packaged in some 1977 sets, 5-8604 SP (the last car added in 1976). Bottom: 5-8720 NW, 5-8721 Southern, 5-8724 UP — all introduced in 1977. Note separate roofwalks on all cars.

	Gd	Exc	Mt

below cupola at roof line; car has dull areas on both sides, similar to 1975-76 C & O boxcar; smokejack, ladders, brakewheels.

	Gd	Exc	Mt
(A) Painted shell.	10	15	20
(B) Unpainted shell. G. Bunza Collection.	8	12	15

(5-8503) 98503 AMERICAN FLYER: Uncatalogued; produced for Sears special sets in 1975; available separately 1976 and as part of two-piece set that included the matching GP-9; these two uncatalogued items carry the number 94-9832 on the corrugated box and the individual Lionel number on the separate white cartons packed inside.

The unpainted red shell has top side panels painted flat white, bottom medium blue; large white-stamped road name on blue; stamped presidential seal below cupola and extending into blue and white side panels, "98503" below; smokejack, ladders, and brakewheel. One of the more common cabooses having been available through Sears and as a Lionel item and two-piece set. **8 10 15**

Taiwan Caboose Production, 1976–1977

In 1976 most caboose production switched over to Taiwan, with many changes made to the 36-foot steel-type cars with off-center cupola. First of all, the rivet detail on the shell was much larger than on the Lionel shells. The smokejack was also thicker, with the roofwalk being a two-piece separate casting instead of Lionel's cast-on roofwalks. The cupola also had changed. It was higher, and the roof was above the top of the smokejack, instead of the opposite. There were also over-sized grabirons at all four corners of the cupola roof, unlike Lionel's smooth roof. The cupola windows were also larger on these new cars. The ladders ran up over the roof of these cars and then curved back down to fit into holes in the roofwalk and held in place. The ladders, brakewheel, and handrails were of one casting but much thinner than Lionel's.

All under-floor detail was cast into the frame, along with "Made in Taiwan" and "Lionel". Some of these cars also carry an oval-shaped gold paper sticker printed with "Made in Taiwan" and "Republic of China"; some of the stickers had "R.O.C.". Other cars had no stickers at all. In any case, the stickers were not necessary as "Lionel / Made in Taiwan" was molded into the frame itself.

The talgo-type truck, with metal axles and extra-long coupler shafts, are used, along with a flat metal weight fastened to the inside of the frame. The four tabs in the shell's side, at the floor line, hide the end of the truck bolsters and floor supports. Lionel chose to extend the shell's side down to help hide these tabs and cover the side of the frame. The frame was held to the shell by a small tab cast into both ends of the shell; it was simply pressed into the slot in the frame. The trucks were fastened by a small plastic pin, while the coupler was held in place by a snap-on coupler cover that promptly fell apart if the car was dropped or fell. Then the truck had to be removed to repair the coupler. The 1977 run of cars also exist with plastic axles on their trucks.

All of the Taiwan-made cars had painted shells, and all are becoming increasingly more difficult to locate, being available for just the last two years Lionel was involved with HO. Once again, the number on the car side and the Lionel name on the frame become most important to the collector.

None of the cars were ever shown in the catalogue for separate sale, but they were all available that way. There were nine other road names offered as power units that did not have matching cabooses.

There is speculation that the car was made in the Western Pacific and Penn Central road names and then simply used in the Bachmann line of HO when Lionel dropped out. Shells would have carried the 8700-series numbers if produced for Lionel.

5(-)8600 CHESSIE SYSTEM: First Taiwan-made caboose, introduced 1976 in set 5-2683, along with the new 5-5612 golden Chessie GP-9 of that year, also produced in Hong Kong; no mention of the

manufacturing changes was ever made in the catalogue; available 1976-77 separately but never catalogued that way.

Shell painted flat yellow; main and cupola roof finished bright silver; very dark blue-stamped lettering; road name incorporating cat's head logo in lower side panels, very small "C & O / 58600" below cupola; "Made in Taiwan" cast into frame and gold sticker present.

Notes: There is speculation that Lionel decorated some of these Taiwan-manufactured cars; having no confirmation, I do not believe Lionel ever decorated foreign-made cabooses. Of the fifteen 5-8600s I own, half have the gold paper sticker, half do not. Difficult car to find; often confused with Lionel 5-8418 of 1974-75. **8 10 15**

(5-8601) 98601 BURLINGTON NORTHERN: Catalogued in sets 1976-77; also available separately the same two years.

Shell painted flat medium green; roof and entire cupola painted flat black; washed-out white stamping; large "BN" at cupola end, road name below; far end of side carries "98601"; frame carries Lionel name (also without Lionel name) and "Made in Taiwan" and gold sticker.

Note: Very common at least in eastern U.S.; many of the cars found in the later white Lionel cartons without any printing — these unmarked cartons were most often used in sets only. **5 6 8**

(5-8602) 98602 ILLINOIS CENTRAL GULF: Never catalogued but offered in special two-piece set, including the GP-9 in Illinois Central livery and sold as set 49-9828, 1976. Set packed in plain brown carton bearing Lionel name and address on the side, white label on top announcing contents, and the two items were in individual white Lionel cartons inside. Caboose was available separately in 1977 with Lionel "5-8602" on carton.

Shell painted flat orange; main and cupola roofs finished bright silver; black semigloss stamped lettering; logo directly under cupola; road name spread across nine of the fourteen lower side panels in bold stamping, along with Lionel "98602" at one end, Lionel name, and "Blt. 1-76" smaller at other end. First of only two cars to carry the Lionel name and built date on its side. One of most difficult cabooses to find — many collectors do not know the car exists. **15 20 25**

5(-)8603 SANTA FE: Catalogued 1976 in set 5-2680, in a bright red finish; available separately 1976-77 but not catalogued that way.

Shell of 1976 car painted bright red, including roofwalk and cupola (car in some 1977 sets much darker red with unpainted black roofwalk); yellow-stamped Santa Fe logo, road name, 1/16" stripe on side; white-stamped "ATSF" in lower center side panels, "58603" below; four miniature logos at floor line, small "CE-3" at one end; frame has gold sticker.

Note: Difficult to locate, especially the darker car, which I believe was never meant to be shipped from Taiwan as a Lionel product but was made for Bachmann or AHM by Kader. Verficiation of this darker car requested.

	Gd	Exc	Mt
(A) Bright red, 1976.	8	10	15
(B) Dark red, 1977.	10	15	25

(5-8604) 98604 SOUTHERN PACIFIC: Available separately 1976-77 and in uncatalogued Southern Pacific GS-4 set in 1976; also available in at least two known Canadian catalogued sets.

Shell painted flat light brown; roof and entire cupola finished in bright silver; lower side panels and toolbox area painted flat light orange; road name appears in nine of the lower panels; only the second car to carry the Lionel name and built date at one end of the side, "98604" at other; silver-stamped lettering with silver stripe above and below; frame has gold sticker. Striking model. **10 15 25**

(5-)8720 NW (NORFOLK & WESTERN): Introduced in set 5-2780 in 1977; available separately 1977 but never catalogued that way; catalogue number appears on carton.

Shell painted black; large white-stamped "NW" below cupola and small Lionel "8720" below it; frame has gold sticker. Same frame and

	Gd	Exc	Mt

shell used in 1976; because of sparse lettering, it has a plain, drab look; extremely difficult to find. **10 15 20**

(5-)8721 SOUTHERN: Introduced 1977 in set 5-2781; available separately later in 1977; catalogue number only on carton.

Shell including roofwalk painted flat red; white-stamped logo, "SOUTHERN / X8721", appearing directly below cupola, similar to NW caboose; some cars carry gold sticker. **8 10 15**

(5-)8724 UNION PACIFIC: Introduced in set 5-2782 in 1977; available separately later that year.

Shell including roofwalk painted flat yellow; road name above windows at center of shell, Lionel "8724" below in very small red stamping. Same ladders, smokejack, brakewheels, and trucks used on all three 1977 cars. A challenge for the collector. **8 10 15**

Austrian-produced Crane Car

The only crane car in the Lionel HO line was introduced in the very first catalogued set number 5-1480 in 1974 and was available all four years the line was sold. This car was again available in that set in 1975, and for the last two years it was in set number 5-2683. It was always accompanied by C & O work caboose 5-8404 in the sets made by Lionel. The number 5-3401 and the C & O markings were used in all four sets and appeared in decal form, applied by the modeler. The crane car was available from 1975 until the end of 1977 as a separate-sale item, though it was never catalogued that way.

An Austrian Roco-made item, the crane was manually operated and would swivel 360 degrees, while the boom itself would crank up and down with the two small thumb screws provided with the car (see the photograph on the next page). The thin black line used to raise and lower the boom, which was attached to two small spools in the cab, is usually broken or missing, and it is a real job to restring the unit.

Except for the metal axles and one boom hook, the car was completely plastic, unpainted, and equipped with six-wheel trucks and horn hook couplers. "Made in Austria" is cast into the outer frame, but the Lionel name is not present anywhere on the model. The cab boom and platform had good, clear detail, with "Bucyrus Erie" on the boom.

In 1975 and 1976, the crane was available with 50-foot work caboose 5-8421, with decal markings on the crane changed to Union Pacific and number 5-3400. These two cars came in a special set, number 5-8422, which is extremely difficult to find complete. In late 1975 through 1977 the same crane was also available with a 40-foot uncatalogued work caboose (5-8403), in some sets and separately. The Union Pacific road name was still used, in decal form, along with "33400" on the crane. It is difficult to find the crane with the decals in good shape. The UP road name is the hardest to locate. The crane was also available in the Canadian line along with the 50-foot work caboose, catalogue number T-08422, with the same U.S. decals included in this uncatalogued set. See the instruction sheets reproduced on page 106.

(5-3400) 33400 (decaled) UNION PACIFIC CRANE: 1975.
For description, see text above. **10 15 20**

(5-3401) 33401 C & O CRANE: 1974.
For description, see text above. **10 15 20**

Lionel-produced Work Caboose

First introduced in the new 1974 sets, this caboose was available all four years the line was offered. It appeared in only two road names — Union Pacific and Chesapeake & Ohio, with the former the most difficult to find — as Lionel production, with the original mold of the 1960s used. The car was a 40-foot car that had four main castings: the main floor and car sides were one casting, while the cab and frame were separating ones, and the toolbox and fencing made up the fourth casting, which was always unpainted. All parts snapped into prepunched holes in the floor of the car, with

no glue used. Plastic trucks had finger tab couplers, and a blackened metal weight is hidden between the floor and underframe of the car. The Lionel name is on the main beam of the frame, along with the brake housing and valves, which are cast into it. The only two screws used hold the truck frame and metal weight to the main floor of the car.

The 40-foot caboose does exist with both painted and unpainted bodies and cabs. All four of the castings have better-than-average detail, and all are marked in Lionel's stamping method. The cab end carries an unpainted, one-piece black plastic casting that holds the ladder, brakewheel, and handrails; a black smokejack is mounted on the cab's roof. A Lionel part number, 0819-206, can be found on all Lionel-produced work caboose cabs, on the inner roof.

In 1975 a new caboose in the Union Pacific road name was introduced in a special two-car set, number 5-8422, which included the Roco crane car of 1974 and a new 50-foot work caboose. This caboose once again showed Lionel trying to market "new" items in HO.

The body of the car was only slightly changed. The cast-on stake pockets on the side of the car were all the same size, unlike the 40-foot Lionel-made cars with the center pocket being much larger than the other ten. This new car was made exactly like the 40-foot cars, with the same four castings used on the smaller car. Of course the car body and toolboxes were longer. The same trucks, couplers, and handrails are present. A small change was seen on the toolbox and fence casting: the wooden board effect on this new car ran vertically, unlike the 40-foot horizontal wooden board look of the smaller car. The main frame has rivet detail, and the valves and brake housing are cast in place. The Lionel name is cast into the frame, along with "Mt. Clemens, MI." and zip code number 48043. The part number 0819-206 is also present on the cab's inner roof. All lettering is done in bright red stamping. This car was shown for the last time in 1976. It is the rarest of the three Lionel-made work cabooses and is unknown to many HO collectors.

All three cars used the 8400-series numbers. Why the Union Pacific road name was chosen for a second type of work caboose is not known.

The two-car 5-8422 UP set came packed in the dark blue window-type carton and carried "5-8422" on one end. The crane itself was packed inside a white individual carton with cardboard liner, while the caboose was held only by the liner; both items could be seen in the window of the master carton.

	Gd	Exc	Mt

(5-8403) 98403 UNION PACIFIC (40-Footer): Uncatalogued, the car was available the last three years of production both in sets and separately.

Body and cab found in bright yellow in both painted and unpainted versions; both marked in bright red silk screening on three cast-on number boards; largest board between windows has road name, two smaller ones carry data and "98403"; toolbox and handrails, but no smokejack; unpainted black plastic toolbox and fencing.
(A) Painted. **15 20 30**
(B) Unpainted. **15 25 35**

(5-8404) 98404 CHESAPEAKE & OHIO: Catalogued 1974-77.

Very dark blue-painted body and cab; bright yellow silkscreened lettering on boards as with UP car; large board holds "C AND O / FOR / PROGRESS" and "98404" appears on small board closest to fence end of the car; unpainted black plastic smokejack, toolbox, and handrails. Car also exists in an unpainted version.
(A) Painted shell. **10 15 20**
(B) Unpainted shell. **15 20 25**

(5-8421) 98421 UNION PACIFIC (50-Footer): Available in special two-car set 5-8422 in 1975-77; available uncatalogued in Canada as number T-08422. Catalogue never stated the car was a new 50-foot car.

Unpainted yellow cab; red-stamped lettering on three number boards; road name appears on largest board, two smaller ones holding data and "98421"; smokejack, handrails; toolboxes and fence unpainted gray. Extremely difficult to find complete. **20 25 35**

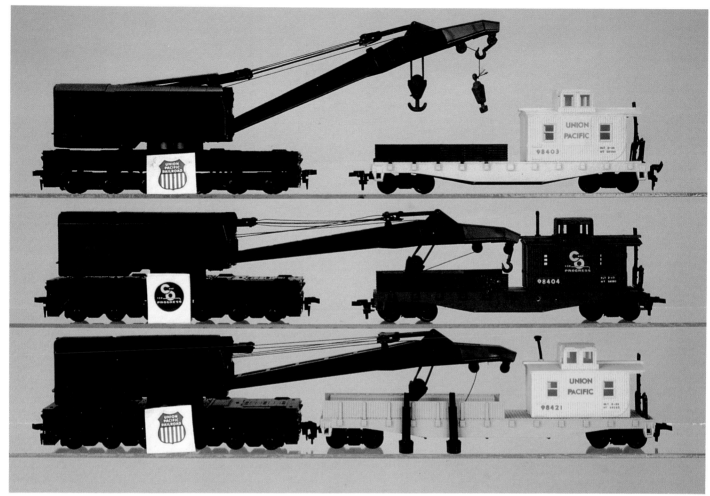

Roco-made crane cars with their counterparts, the Lionel-made work cabooses. The crane was lettered by a decal that the buyer would apply. Top to bottom: 5-3400 UP crane of 1975 with 40-foot 5-8403 caboose, 5-3401 C & O crane of 1974 with 5-8404 C & O caboose, 5-3400 crane again with the 5-8421 50-foot work caboose (only available in two-car set 5-8422, new in 1975); the catalogue made no mention of the new 50-foot car.

FLATCARS

Once again we find that Lionel decided at the very beginning, in their haste to get into the HO market, not to use their diework but have 40-foot flatcars made in Austria by Roco; in 1975 a flat made from Lionel tooling did appear: it was first available in the uncatalogued Sears sets of 1975–1976. All three of the Austrian-built flatcars were available for the full four-year period (in sets in 1974, and separately 1975–1977). All carry the Roco logo and "AUSTRIA" on the frames.

One new 50-foot and two 48-foot heavy-duty flatcars were added in 1977. These new cars were all manufactured for Lionel in Taiwan by Kader Industries and were not items new to the HO market. Neither the Lionel-made 40-foot car of 1975 nor the three cars added to the line in 1977 were ever shown in the U.S. catalogue. All four of these cars were available as separate Lionel items. To add to the confusion, some of the cars, such as the 8760 and 8761 UP cars, carry a four-digit Lionel number while others, such as the 28413 UP and 28414 SF 40-foot cars of Roco production, have the five-digit number. Still others, such as the GN log car numbered 5-8762, carry numbers not used by Lionel. Two cars, the black Austrian and white Lionel 40-foot flatcars, are not marked at all.

All of the cartons for the Taiwan-made cars carry notation of the country of origin on their sides or backs. The Kader-made flatcar frames are marked in various ways, as shown in the chart on page 12, Chapter I.

Lionel-made Flatcar

The flatcar introduced in 1975 had Lionel pre-1966 diework and simply used the unpunched body designed for the new work caboose of that year. The shell carries the Lionel part number 50-8520-012, which is plainly seen on the underside of the car, along with the punch marks needed for the work caboose. The car differs from the Austrian-made cars available in that the steps and grabirons are larger, and the stake pockets have horizontal bracing whereas the Austrian cars had smaller steps with smooth-sided stake pockets. No doubt Lionel's own flatcar line had the potential for growth, but there were three Austrian-made flats available at the same time, and it must have been cheaper for Lionel to have the cars made elsewhere.

(5-8520) UNMARKED WHITE FLATCAR: First used in Sears sets of 1975-76, holding a load of stakes and tan plastic crates; second version using the same catalogue number on its carton had no load in 1976 and was available separately and uncatalogued in 1977, when the car had stakes only and was available uncatalogued. This car has the distinction of being the only Lionel-made flatcar during the entire four-year period, available separately. All three version used the same catalogue number.

Unpainted white shell has no markings of any kind; only the Lionel name on the frame identifies it; frame presses into shell and is held with two Phillips-head screws that also secured the trucks with metal axles.

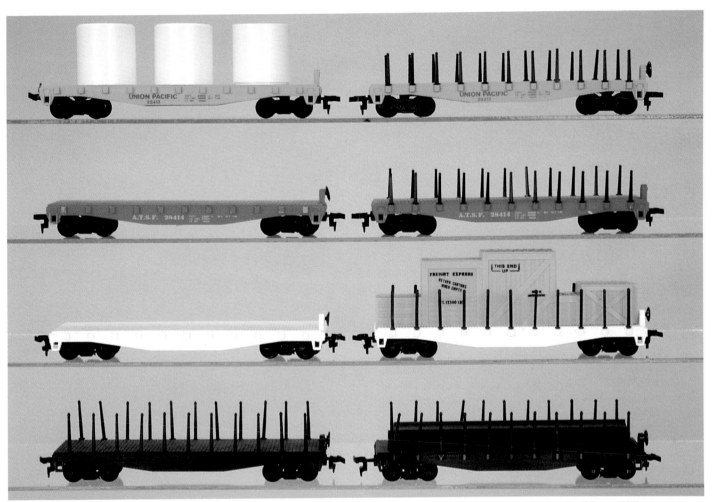

Two variations of the Austrian-made 40-foot flatcars available as Lionel. Top: 5-8413 UP with pipe load in a 1977 set, with the same car available separately in 1974–1976 with and without stakes. Second: 5-8414 SF of 1976–1977 without stakes, and from 1974–1975 with stakes. Third: Lionel-made 5-8520 flatcar of 1976–1977, unmarked with no load, and in Sears sets of 1975–1976 with stakes and crates; the car was also available in 1976–1977 separately without a load. Bottom: Unmarked 5-8415 of 1974–1977 in two variations — with stakes in 1977 and with I-beams and stakes in 1974–1976. Catalogue numbers on the cartons remained as listed, no matter what the flatcar held. The crates do not carry the Lionel name, as they did in the pre-1966 line.

Top: 5-8760 50-foot UP flatcar with stakes, of 1976, and 5-8761 48-foot fish-belly flatcar of 1977. Bottom: To the right of the only tank car offered, the 5-8416, the 5-8762 GN fish-belly car of 1977. All cars are Kader-made models from Taiwan.

Comparison of the four types of flatcars offered as Lionel. Left to right: Lionel model of 1975–1977; Austrian Roco car, available 1974–1977; Hong Kong Kader 50- and 48-foot heavy-duty flatcar models. Note the fragile protruding steps on the last car.

	Gd	Exc	Mt

A metal weight is held between the shell and frame with the same two screws; one standing brakewheel; the load of tan plastic crates also from pre-1966 diework are lettered in black stamping and read "FREIGHT EXPRESS" in block style; notations of Return Empty, Made in U.S., and weight. No Lionel name found on the pre-1966 crates.

Note: The crates are usually found glued in place, which always damages the car floor; the crates were not glued by Lionel but held with a rubber band that promptly broke. When in sets, in an original white carton, no catalogue number was found.

	Gd	Exc	Mt
(A) With crates and stakes, Sears, 1975-76.	10	15	20
(B) Without load, 1976.	4	6	8
(C) With stakes only, 1977.	8	10	15

Austrian-made 40-foot Flatcars

All three of the cars offered were made of two plastic castings, with metal axles and the weight hidden between the shell and frame of the car. The car, including the frame, had lots of good rivet detail, with the vertical brake support, steps, and stake pockets all cast in place. Like the Lionel-made car, there were eleven stake pockets per side, but they were all the same size while the center pocket on the Lionel-produced car is much larger and stands away from the car side. The steps of these cars also differ in that the Lionel car has tapered steps with smooth sides, while the Austrian-made model uses the same type of step but has extra support on both sides. The grabirons on the Austrian cars are arch-shaped, while Lionel's model uses a straight grabiron, which is also larger and extends out past the step. There are talgo-type trucks, held in place with the same split-type pin used on the other Austrian-made cars, underframe detail, and NMRA-type couplers. The diamond-shaped ROCO logo and "AUSTRIA" are cast into the frame.

(5-8413) 28413 UNION PACIFIC: Catalogued in sets 1974-76 with twenty-two black stakes; available 1977 in sets with stakes and in one set, 5- 2783, with stakes and tan-colored crates; available as separate-sale item 1975-77 without the crates but not catalogued that way; catalogue number on carton; can be found without stakes as separate sales item, using same catalogue number 5-8413.

Shell painted flat yellow; semigloss red-stamped lettering at center of car with data, road name, and "28413"; one black plastic brakewheel; crate load same as used in 1960s HO, has sharp, clear black stamping but no Lionel name.

	Gd	Exc	Mt
(A) With stakes.	6	8	12
(B) Without stakes.	6	8	10
(C) With stakes and crates in sets, 1977.	8	10	15

Comparison of flatcar underframes. Top to bottom: Lionel 40-footer of 1975; Roco 40-footer, available all four years; Kader 50-footer, new in 1976; 1976–1977 48-foot fish-belly heavy-duty flatcar, also by Kader; this last car was also available in the Canadian line. Note the differing trucks, wheel sets, and couplers.

	Gd	Exc	Mt

(5-8414) 28414 SANTA FE: Catalogued in sets 1974-75; returned to catalogue 1977; available 1974-77 in sets and separately, with and without stakes.

Shell painted semigloss red; sharp yellow-stamped lettering found between third and ninth coupler pocket on side, giving crowded appearance; same black stake used on UP car; "28414" on side.

Note: I believe the omission of stakes was simply factory error.

	Gd	Exc	Mt
(A) With stakes.	8	10	12
(B) Without stakes.	6	8	10

(5-8415) UNMARKED BLACK FLATCAR: Catalogued 1974-77 in sets, with stakes and three brownish plastic simulated girders as load; available 1976-77 separately with and without stakes and in same carton with same catalogue number, but never catalogued that way.

Entire car unpainted black plastic, with no lettering. Unappealing.

	Gd	Exc	Mt
(A) With load (stakes and I-beams), 1974-77.	6	8	12
(B) With stakes only, 1976-77.	6	8	10
(C) Without load, 1976-77.	5	6	8

Taiwan-made 48- and 50-foot Flatcars

In 1977 three new flatcars were introduced into the Lionel HO line — none of them were ever shown in a U.S. catalogue. All three were manufactured for Lionel in Taiwan and represented the idea of increasing the size of the line but not the quality. Noting the Lionel number and name is again extremely important, as all three cars were available through other HO suppliers.

The first car, the 8760 UP, was a standard 51-foot flatcar (the actual car was indeed 51 feet in length, but collectors refer to it as a 40-footer). The model consisted of two separate castings — the frame and side with all under-floor detail cast in place, and the outer floor of the car showing the wooden board effect and with six tabs cast into the underside. The tabs were pushed into slots in the car frame to hold the two halves together; the metal weight was hidden between them. Good rivet detail was present, as it was on the second car, introduced in 1977, which was modeled after the steel floor-type car.

The 48-foot, 200-ton flatcar, available in two road names (8761 UP and 8762 GN), was equipped with four trucks and was also made of two castings — the floor was cast flat and glued to the frame. The frame casting was very thick and had a low side wall at its center, giving it the name "fish belly." No valve or brake housing is found under the floor. Four extra-heavy steps are cast into each corner, and there is a lot of rivet detail under the car. The four trucks are fastened with plastic pins to a swivel bar that in turn is held to the frame with the same type of plastic pin. Castings at both ends of the car hold the two vertical brakewheels, and four ½ by ¾-inch metal weights are hidden at each corner of the frame. The cars carried three logs of poor-quality plastic that were held with three copper wires twisted to resemble chain.

	Gd	Exc	Mt

42764: See (T-20221) at end of flatcar listings.

(5-)8760 UNION PACIFIC: Available 1977; full catalogue number only on carton.

Entire car painted flat yellow; red-stamped lettering includes road name and "SERVES ALL THE WEST"; data and Lionel "8760"; one black plastic vertical brakewheel; plastic talgo-type trucks held with solid plastic pin; NMRA-type couplers; four flat straight steps cast into body; twenty-eight stakes, about ½" higher than those on 40-foot Taiwan-made cars; "Made in Taiwan R.O.C." on the frames of some cars, and some with "MADE IN TAIWAN / LIONEL"; gold sticker present. Difficult to find, especially with stakes complete and unbroken.

	8	10	12

(5-)8761 UNION PACIFIC (Heavy-Duty 48-Footer): Available 1977; catalogue number on carton only.

Entire car painted in thick flat yellow; red-stamped lettering with road name and "8761" at center, data at both ends of car side; two vertical brakewheels; four four-wheeled black plastic trucks attached to a swivel bar fastened to the frame with a single plastic pin; grabirons on all four corners of the floor; three dark brown plastic logs as load are ½" diameter, have ⅛" hole in one end, and are held to the car with three pieces of copper wire twisted to resemble chain that passes through three of the thirteen pinholes present on each side of the floor.

	10	12	15

(5-8762/T-20221) 42764 GREAT NORTHERN: Made for Canadian market, catalogued as T-20221; can be found in white cartons used in the United States; uncatalogued in the United States.

Entire car painted light blue; washed-out white-stamped lettering; "42764" on side — not a Lionel number; Lionel name and "Made in Taiwan" on frame; information under 5-8761 UP car applies here, with the exception of light brown ⅜"-diameter logs used here (no holes appear in either end of these smaller logs). Available in both Canada and the U.S.; one would think this is easily found, but it is not and prices are steadily rising.

	10	15	20

GONDOLAS, HOPPERS, AND A TANK CAR

Austrian-produced 40-foot Steel Gondolas

In the early Lionel HO of the 1950s and 1960s, Lionel sold only one gondola car of its own. In 1957, there was a Rivarossi-made gondola with two road names, and the Athearn production of 1958–1959 included one 50-foot gondola in one road name, but two colors. (See Volume I for details on this aspect of early HO manufacture.) Then came the

Lionel production of one type of car, with one road name in five colors, with four types of loads available.

In the 1970s none of the Lionel HO gondolas were of Lionel manufacture, and no Lionel diework was ever used. The earliest cars were made in Austria and were the best quality offered. They were available catalogued until 1976 when production moved to Taiwan. One shell type was Austrian-produced, with four colors and road names available in the four years Lionel offered the line.

The 40-foot Austrian-made cars were of a two-piece casting with painted plastic body with lots of good, clear rivet detail on sides, ends, and inside the car, with six side braces also present. Ladders, grabirons, and tapered steps were all cast into the shell, and cast-on tabs pass through the separate black plastic frame to secure it to the car shell. There are talgo-type trucks with steel axles and NMRA-type couplers, and the brake housing and valves are cast into the frame as on other Austrian-made models. Further evidence of quality is the metal weight that was hidden between the shell and frame. "AUSTRIA" and the Roco logo are molded into the frame.

None of these cars were ever catalogued separately, but they were available until 1976. All of them are difficult to find.

	Gd	Exc	Mt

(5-8407) 18407 RIO GRANDE: Catalogued in sets 1974-75, with load of three white plastic culvert pipes, but also available separately, uncatalogued, without a load, in 1976; available again separately 1975-76, uncatalogued, with a simulated gray sand load. The car was replaced in 1977 by Taiwan-made car 5-8730; catalogue number on carton only.

Entire car painted flat bright orange; crisp black-stamped lettering; data on first panel; large "Rio / Grande" and "the ACTION road" below on third and fourth panels; "D & RGW / 18407" and data on right panels.

	Gd	Exc	Mt
(A) With pipe load, 1974-75.	6	10	12
(B) Without load, 1976.	3	5	7
(C) With sand load, 1976-77.	4	6	8

(5-8408) 18408 B & O CHESSIE SYSTEM: Catalogued in sets 1974-75; available separately 1975 though not catalogued that way and never carried a load; road name returned 1977 as Taiwan manufacture, catalogued as 5-8731; catalogue number only on carton.

Shell painted semigloss dark blue; faded yellow-stamped lettering; "B & O / 18408" beneath on second panel, data on third; Chessie cat's head logo centered.

	6	10	15

(5-8409) 18409 NORFOLK & WESTERN: Uncatalogued; available separately 1975 without a load; returned in 1976 with sand load; available in uncatalogued set 5-1493 and in Sears set 5-6590; catalogue number only on carton.

Entire car painted rich dark brown; flat white-stamped lettering; all but one panel lettered, giving crowded although sharp and clean appearance; data before and after "N & W / 18409", thin white line above and below stamping, road name, and large "N & W" toward right end with more data. Most difficult to locate; many HO collectors unaware of this car.

	Gd	Exc	Mt
(A) Without load, 1975.	8	10	12
(B) With sand load, 1976.	10	12	15

(5-8410) 18410 SOUTHERN PACIFIC: Catalogued only in sets 1974-75, never shown carrying a load; available separately although not catalogued as such 1975; catalogue number only on carton.

Shell painted semigloss red; white-stamped lettering on all but two end panels; road name, data, and logo spread across side; very wide "SP / 18410" on second panels.

	10	15	20

Taiwan-produced 40-foot Steel Gondolas

In 1977 the manufacture of the 40-foot gondolas relocated to Taiwan. The Southern Pacific and the Norfolk and Western road names

The first four road names used on HO gondolas. Top and second, left: 5-8407 Rio Grande, available with sand in 1975, with pipe in 1975 sets, and without a load in 1974–1975. Second, right: 5-8410 Southern, which never carried a load. Third: 5-8408 Chessie with sand in 1975 and without load, 1974–1975. Bottom: 5-8409 N & W with sand in 1975 and without a load in 1974. As with the flatcars, the catalogue number on the carton did not change with a change in load situation, although the carton liner did.

Last two gondolas offered: 5-8731 Chessie and 5-8730 D & RGW, both available with and without loads and both Kader-made from Taiwan.

The covered gondolas of 1976, made in Taiwan and also available in the Canadian line: 5-8620 B & LE and 5-8621 P & LE.

were dropped, and only two of the road names — the Rio Grande and the B & O Chessie — were reintroduced.

Why did this change take place, since the newer cars were of clearly poorer quality, with a one-piece shell? One can only speculate that the reasons were economical. Both of the cars of 1977 were one-piece casting, which include the frame of the car and all detail cast in place, and the detail was much smaller and less clear than was the case with the Austrian models. A large mold plug is located at the center of the frame along with the Lionel name, "Made in Taiwan", and the gold sticker. The talgo-type truck is used and held with a single plastic pin pressed into the shell floor. Split axles, NMRA-type couplers, one brakewheel, and a metal weight are to be found. The weight inside the car is painted to match the shell and holds the rivet detail, so one must look closely to see that it is not part of the shell.

Both cars were painted and had fairly sharp and clear stamped lettering. Both were decorated very much like the car of Austrian manufacture. And both cars have thicker shell castings and tapered steps, with the ladders found on the car ends having only three rungs (unlike the four-rung ladder found on the Austrian-made cars).

Neither car was ever catalogued as a separate-sale item, but each was available that way. The cars came with the three culvert pipes as load in sets; the Rio Grande was available without a load in the Burlington set 5-2682. When sold separately, both can be found with a simulated sand load, or with no load at all. No catalogue number change was ever made to indicate differences. The Lionel number 5-8730 or 5-8731 appears on the carton, loaded or not. In reality we have three variations of the 8730 car, and the cartons for them will confuse the collector. Some carry the notation "Made in Taiwan R.O.C.". While others carry "imported parts labeled to show country of origin", some collectors (I am not one of them) think that these Taiwan-made shells were shipped here to be decorated by Lionel. Liners for these cartons also differ in their shapes.

	Gd	Exc	Mt

(5-)8730 RIO GRANDE: 1977; catalogue number on carton only.

Car painted orange; semigloss black-stamped lettering on five of eight side panels; "D & RGW / 8730", road name, "the ACTION road" with other data on side; floor covered with one flat glued-on metal weight but center pin to hold it is not present.

Note: If found with simulated sand load, the load is of unpainted gray plastic and has eight studs cast into its bottom to hold the load to the car.

	Gd	Exc	Mt
(A) With sand load.	6	10	12
(B) With three culvert pipes.	8	12	15
(C) Without load.	5	7	10

(5-)8731 B & O CHESSIE: 1977; available in set 5-2783 with culvert pipes or separately with and without sand load; catalogue number same on carton, with or without load.

Entire body and metal weight painted flat very dark blue; washed-out-yellow lettering on four of five side panels; "B & O / 8731", data, Chessie cat's head logo, "Chessie / System".

	Gd	Exc	Mt
(A) With sand load.	6	10	12
(B) With three culvert pipes.	8	12	15
(C) Without load.	5	7	10

The four road names used on hopper cars. Top to bottom, left to right: 5-8417 Kader car of 1974, Lionel-made 5-8555 BN (unpainted car of 1976 and painted car of 1975), 5-8556 Rio Grande (painted car of 1975 and unpainted 1976 car), and two Taiwan-produced cars of 1977: 5-8755 CP Rail and 5-8756 uncatalogued BM.

Taiwan-produced 57-foot Covered Coil Car

These cars were specially built gondolas and were fairly close to the prototype car, which had hinged covers to protect the loads — usually large rolls of wire or aluminum or steel — from rain and snow. The covers would swing down on both sides of the car when pressed at both ends. Seven plastic rolls molded in one casting were used as a load in the car. Lionel's mistake here, as in other cases, was that the car was not new to the HO market. AHM and Bachmann Bros. of Philadelphia also sold this model, in some cases in the exact same colors and road names. Watch for the Lionel name, along with "Taiwan ROC", on the frame! This is the only car known to carry a white paper sticker.

These cars were first catalogued in 1976 and again in 1977 in sets only; they were available separately the same two years but not catalogued as such.

The cars are all plastic, with a metal weight fastened to the inside floor being the only metal present. The four square cast-on steps broke off easily, as did the covers. These covers were cast in two pieces with the latching part being added to the car much like a roofwalk was to a boxcar. All cars carry two standing brakewheels, with a third one attached to its cover. Four-wheel talgo-type trucks attached with a solid plastic pin and couplers with an extra-long shaft to clear the car body were all made of unpainted black plastic.

Closeup of the coil car (or covered gondola) first seen in the 1976 catalogue in two road names and never shown separately. Note the heavy step and end walkway that provides access to the control wheel for the cover of the car.

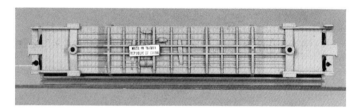

Underside of the Kader-made coil car, new in 1976, with trucks removed for this photograph. The car was cast in three pieces, including two doors. Note white paper sticker present even though the same information is cast into the right side of car floor; this is the only car known to use a white sticker.

	Gd	Exc	Mt

31002: See (5-8620)

42279: See (5-8621)

(5-8620) 31002 BESSEMER & LAKE ERIE: Catalogued in 1976 in set 5-2681.

Body painted a flat deep orange; covers painted thick silver color, with dark blue-stamped "B & L.E." and "31002"; white block-type lettering; black, white, and orange B & LE logo.

Note: The only known coil cars to carry a Lionel catalogue number on sides are the Canadian line cars (see Chapter VI). This car difficult to find with Lionel name.   **10   15   20**

(5-8621) 42279 PITTSBURGH & LAKE ERIE: Catalogued in set 5-2682 in 1976-77.

Entire car painted flat aqua green; white-stamped "P & LE / 42279" on body and cover; red and black New York Systems logo, data; very light tan unpainted seven-coil load resembling wood boards nailed in place; four steps and underframe detail cast into shell; three brakewheels and talgo-type trucks.

Notes: The car as a model is very common at meets, but the Lionel-stamped car is not. The same coil car was shown in the 1977 catalogue in the GP-30 Burlington Northern set, 5-2682, in a light blue with P & LE markings; the car is not known to exist in this color and stamped with the Lionel name. Verification requested.   **10   15   20**

Lionel-produced Hopper Cars

The two Lionel-manufactured hoppers were uncatalogued but were available in 1975–1976 as separate items, in two road names, with painted and unpainted shells used. Reworked diework from the 1960s was used. The black plastic frame was a carryover from the early HO line, with the tab at each corner that snaps into the open end of the shell. The frame is stamped "Lionel Mt. Clemens MI", with zip code number 48043. Both cars were the 42-foot open-quad, offset type. The plastic shells had straight flat sides and held very small rivet detail — less of it than on the Taiwan-made cars. There was one plastic brakewheel and NMRA-type finger tab couplers on talgo-type trucks with a one-piece axle; the truck is held to the frame with a solid plastic pin. The metal weight is fastened to the inside of the car floor on two plastic pegs that are melted over and hidden from view by the simulated coal load.

The loads differ from the Taiwan car in that the Lionel part number 50-8555-015 is molded into them, and there are no tabs to hold them to the shell; the load simply pressed down into the shell. See loads pictured on page 55.

	Gd	Exc	Mt

(5-8555) 78555 BURLINGTON NORTHERN: Uncatalogued; available separately 1975-76 only.

Unpainted medium green shell; crisp white-stamped lettering; large "BN" in right end panel; road name with "BN / 78555" and data on left end; center panel holds very small "BLT. 1-72" only, giving car a bare appearance; "Mt. Clemens, MI" and zip code number on frame. Both versions of the Lionel BN car are difficult to find.

	Gd	Exc	Mt
(A) Painted shell, 1975.	10	15	20
(B) Unpainted shell, 1976.	8	12	15

(5-8556) 78556 (DENVER) RIO GRANDE: Uncatalogued; available separately 1975-76.

Unpainted light orange shell; heavy black lettering; road name and "the ACTION road" in center panels; to left, data; to right "D & RGW / 78556 / BLT. 3-66".

Note: The 1975 car was a darker orange-painted shell; the 1976 model was unpainted. Both variations are hard to find.

	Gd	Exc	Mt
(A) Darker orange-painted shell, 1975.	10	15	25
(B) Unpainted lighter orange shell, 1976.	10	15	20

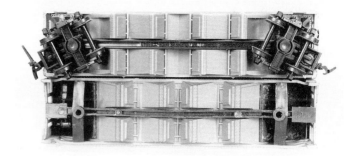

The only two types of hoppers offered as Lionel HO. Left: Lionel car, with much heavier casting, available in two road names from 1975 to 1977. Right: Kader-made car available 1974–1977 in three road names; it is much thinner. Note the differences in ladder steps and brakewheels.

Undersides of hoppers. On the top, Lionel-made car, with thicker body casting; below, the Kader model with the truck removed to expose the black metal weights. Both have talgo-type trucks, with the Kader car holding much more rivet detail.

Taiwan-produced Hoppers

The very first *hopper* Lionel offered in the 1970s HO line was of Taiwanese manufacture — in most cases the Lionel-made model came first. Two other road names were introduced in 1977. In 1974 the catalogue offered sets that included the 5-8417 Burlington Northern, which carried the 1974 series catalogue number on its tapered sides, with Lionel and Taiwan on the frame (the two Taiwan-made hoppers introduced in 1977 carry this same information, because the same diework was used for the frame). The frame for each car was black plastic with NMRA-type coupler and split axle talgo-type trucks that are held to the frame with one solid plastic pin pressed up into the frame; the frame fastened to the shell with a small stud at each end of the frame just above the coupler (the stud pressed into a hole cast into the bottom of the shell). A metal weight at each end of the shell was also held in place by the frame. Rivet detail is found on the car sides and ends and again on the four sets of unloading doors. Double-rung steps are found at each corner of the shell, with one black plastic brakewheel also present.

All three cars carry a simulated coal load, which differs from the Lionel load; most of the Taiwan-produced loads are black-painted gray plastic and do not carry a part number of any kind. Seven round mold marks are present inside, as are the four cast-on tabs used to hold the loads firmly in the body.

All of these cars can be considered rather rare, with the un-catalogued Boston & Maine car topping the list.

	Gd	Exc	Mt

(5-8417) 78417 BURLINGTON NORTHERN: Available 1974 in sets only; sold separately 1975-76, but not catalogued that way.

Medium green-painted body; white-stamped lettering; block-type road name and "BN / 78417" below, with data below that at one end; large "BN" at opposite end. Uncommon. **5 10 20**

(5-)8755 CP RAIL: Catalogued in all three new sets of 1977; available separately 1977, uncatalogued.

Shell painted flat red; washed-out white lettering that has been done with very thin stamping but has sharp edges and therefore quite readable; large road name over two side panels, with Lionel "8755" to right and data below. Uncommon. **5 10 20**

(5-)8756 BM (BOSTON & MAINE): Uncatalogued; available as separate item in 1977, and in uncatalogued set 5-2793.

Shell painted with same type of flat paint as on the CP Rail car, but in a bright powder blue; flat white-stamped "BM / 8756" between lines, BM logo, in a much heavier stamping, in black and white to right; data in center. Rare. **12 20 30**

Taiwan-produced 42-foot Tank Car

As was the case with the early HO line of the 1950s and 1960s, the tank car was the orphan of the car line. Only one type of tank car was used and this time with only one road name. The car was available for the full four years, allowing plenty of time to add new road names, but Lionel chose for some reason to use only the one car and road name.

The tank was a two-piece casting attached to the frame with a single plastic pin at its center. The frame was lightweight, with very thin cast-on steps that broke off easily. The frame had good rivet detail and the valves and brake housing were cast in place. On the frame are the Lionel name and "Made in Taiwan, Republic of China". A plastic pin held the talgo-type truck to the frame. There were NMRA-type couplers and a metal weight hidden inside the tank body. In 1976 one change was made when the truck's early steel axle was changed to a black plastic split axle type; there was no corresponding change in catalogue number. Both early and late trucks were of poor quality, detail-wise. The car can be found in Lionel sets of 1976–1977 without the Lionel name on its frame.

	Gd	Exc	Mt

(5-8416) 48416 DOW THREE-DOME TANK: Catalogued in sets 1974; also available separately 1975-77 but not catalogued that way.

Car painted flat black; rather small bright yellow lettering; Dow Chemical Company logo at right end; Lionel "48416"; wire handrails and stamped-metal ladders; one standing brakewheel is glued to the frame. The later cars of 1976-77 carry the gold oval sticker.

8 10 15

LIONEL-PRODUCED PASSENGER CARS

In 1975 the first passenger cars were offered by Lionel in the later HO line; these cars were introduced in the Freedom sets of 1975 but were illustrated in artwork. In 1976 they appeared in photographs as actually sold. All were produced in Mt. Clemens, Michigan.

Two separate castings were used for the cars, as had been done in the 1960s. On all cars, the outer body casting consisted of the floor, sides, and ends. The casting held rivet detail, window openings, steps, and undercarriage detail — all cast in place. There were three different versions of the inner casting, with window material changing on three of these castings.

In the 101, 105, and 110 display cars, the second casting consisted of the roof and clear window material that fit inside the outer body casting of each car. In the 101/105/110 display-type cars the casting has two raised windows on each side that line up with the opening in the outer body casting, the windows being about 1 inch square. This type of car

The only passenger cars offered in the 1970 line and first available in 1975. Top to bottom: 41 showcase car, 101 display car, 105 display car (only with the GS-4 set), 110 display car, and the 205 observation car. All are extremely light-weight castings and are easily broken.

also has a cardboard liner that holds the four printed pictures (made of paper and appearing like postage stamps) shown in the window areas. The cardboard liner fills the entire top casting but is not seen from the outside of the car.

In the number 41 showcase-type car, a second type of casting is used, there is no cardboard liner, and the entire inside of the car can be seen; this car has three windows, approximately 2¼ inches long and ¾ inch high, per side. The windows displays three models: a gold Liberty bell, an early black automobile, and a gray moonrover. All are unpainted colored plastic and are attached to the floor on plastic pegs cast into the floor.

In the 205 observation-type car, the third type of window casting is found. It has frosted window material that blocks the inside of the car from view. The outer shell of this car holds an observation deck and brass-colored railing; this car was also available with unpainted black railing.

Four-wheel talgo-type trucks were used on all cars, with finger tab couplers. None of the cars are lighted and all are extremely lightweight. The body of each car is white with a red stripe and has dark blue lower side panel and undercarriage and silver-painted roof. Numbers were

stamped in blue. All cars carry "AMERICAN FREEDOM TRAIN" on their sides, in blue.

A total of 22,500 of these cars were produced in 1975. According to Dan Johns, it was the first and last run, as the sets were not good sellers; all cars sold after 1975 came from existing stock. My research shows production runs of 5000 pieces for each of four car, with a shorter run of 2500 for the 105 display car, only available in the steam set. The total number of cars produced would have allowed just 2500 of each for the two Freedom sets offered. The short run of the 105 display car and its availability only in late 1975 and 1976 explain its rareness for the HO collector today.

	Gd	Exc	Mt
41 SHOW CAR	20	30	40
101 DISPLAY CAR	20	30	40
105 DISPLAY CAR	35	50	75
110 DISPLAY CAR	20	30	40
205 OBSERVATION CAR	20	30	40

Comparison of Bachmann-sold items of the late 1970s, on the left, with Lionel models of the earlier 1970s on the right. Note that the colors and in some cases the numbers are the same on each shell. The Lionel name molded into the frame of the models on the right is a very important identifier. All of the models shown were produced by Kader Industries, with only a few using a Lionel catalogue number on the model itself, as shown.

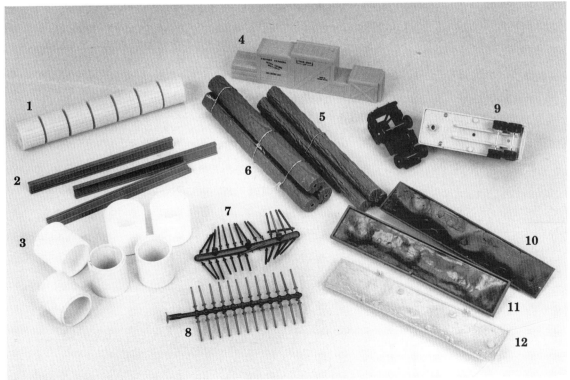

Freight car loads:

(1) coils for covered gondola

(2) I-beams for 40-foot flat-cars

(3) white culvert pipes for flatcars and gondolas (note the smaller gray pipes are Tyco products, never used on Lionel cars)

(4) crates for Lionel flatcars (no Lionel name present on MPC-era crates)

(5) small logs for 48-foot GN car

(6) large logs for 50-foot UP car

(7) stakes for 40-foot Roco-made flatcars

(8) stakes for 50-foot Kader-made flatcars

(9) metal tractor trailer available in 1977 sets

(10) Taiwan coal load

(11) Lionel coal load (number present)

(12) Taiwan sand load

CHAPTER IV
Accessories and Building Kits

LIONEL ACCESSORIES

When the Lionel HO line of 1974 was introduced, the only accessories available were a bumper, and a gray unpainted signal and trestle bridge, along with some telephone poles and road signs in sets of twelve. These items were available all four years, but only in sets, with no individual catalogue numbers ever issued. The trestle bridge and signal bridge were made for Lionel by the Airfix Corporation of England. A black girder bridge and a gray arch bridge with trestle set were shown in 1975 and ran until the end of the line as separate-sale items. The arch bridge was also available in some of the sets for the four-year period.

The only track or switches catalogued were shown in the Canadian catalogue as separate-sale items and were made in Hong Kong. The track in the U.S. sets were mostly Atlas products and were never shown separately. The Canadian track assortment consisted of a manual and a remote switch, left or right, 9-inch straight track, and 18-inch-radius curved track, a 30-degree and a 90-degree crossing, and an unlighted and a lighted bumper.

In 1975, for the first time, a line of accessories was offered for separate sale with individual catalogue numbers. All of the accessories were packed in the early red, white, and blue boxes. All of these models were plastic except for the metal ladder found on the tower unit and the base of the girder bridge; the lighted beacon tower besides the metal ladder also had a metal rod that held the light housing to its base and provided the second of the electric leads needed to light the unit.

One item requires special comment. It is the gantry crane, catalogued in 1975 as Lionel item 5-4502. It was dropped from the catalogue the very next year — I choose with good reason not to believe this model was ever actually offered in the Lionel HO line, since I have been unable to locate either a model or a collector who has seen one.

If it had been made, it would be safe to assume the same Lionel superstructure used on the 5-4501 beacon would have been used here, with the number on the red base changing to 5-4502. The Roco-made crane of 1974 would have been installed on the base, since it was the only crane offered in the line. But Roco only shipped the model as a crane mounted on a flatcar. In order for Lionel to use the crane cab for another purpose, three steps would have been required. First, the flatcar body would have to be removed — destroying the car in doing so, I might add. Second, the four legs cast into the crane floor, which held it to the car body, would also have to be removed. Third, a 1/16-inch hole would have to be drilled in the crane floor to accept the metal pole that holds the crane cab level on the tower. It is difficult to believe Lionel would have gone to so much trouble to expand the line by one model.

The gray and orange crane base shown in this chapter is a very close copy of the original Lionel crane, which was sold in kit form (3805) by the International Hobby Corporation of Philadelphia (it was manufactured by Mehanotehnka of Yugoslavia). The tower unit of the black crane shown is an original Lionel tower from the 1960s Lionel HO line, with a Roco-made crane mounted on it by an HO operator in the Philadelphia area. Conflicting information was received during the

The gantry crane, shown in the 1975 catalogue as 5-4502 but never made. The crane at the left is the AHM model kit 3805 and the one on the right was made up but is not a Lionel product except for its tower, which is original 1960s issue (note that the crane is not sitting level).

The detail photograph below shows the trouble Lionel would have had to go to in order to create such a crane using the Roco-made crane car and its own tower. One can see the damage caused by trying to make the four clips fit into the Lionel-made base. An original pedestal is shown at left, with the MPC issue next to it. The crane simply would not sit on the Lionel-made pedestal shown and is the reason it looks crooked on its tower. These illustrations are included to head off any models that may show up as "one of a kind." The crane was not put into production as Lionel.

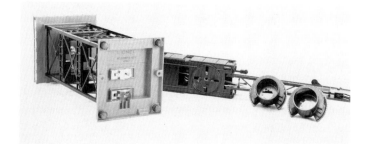

research for this book: former Lionel and Roco employees did not agree on whether the crane — other than the known crane car variation — was ever produced. Verification of such a tower model is requested.

	Gd	Exc	Mt

(5-4501) ROTARY BEACON: 1975; produced from the 1960s dies.

Unit had a black superstructure and light housing, red base and platform. There is one red and one green lens with a metal and plastic housing; the metal ladder and metal pole doubled as the electrical pickup to light the unit; "Lionel" and "Mt. Clemens, Mich. 48043" on base; four black rubber pads included. Difficult to find unbroken.

	15	20	25

(5-4502) GANTRY CRANE: See text above; not manufactured.

(5-4530) TRESTLE SET: 1974-77.

Forty-six piers in twelve different heights up to 3″ (there were four of each lettered A through K and two 3″ L sections, constructing two complete grades 0″ to 3″), forty-four risers, twenty-four clips, two wedges, and an arch bridge; "Lionel" and identifying letters (A-L) cast into each pier; set shown as gray, with piers also in dark brown, clips in black (only bridge was gray); one-piece instruction sheet included; packed in plastic bags.

	7	10	15

(5-4531) GIRDER BRIDGE: Catalogued 1975-77.

Black plastic sides and metal base from 1960s diework; no lettering on sides; Lionel name stamped on metal floor. Very common and not very desirable.

	5	8	10

Airfix-Lionel

The Airfix models included the two bridge kits first available in set number 1480 of 1975. The signal bridge kit was made in both gray and black unpainted plastic, with the bridge only available in gray. Only the signal bridge is known to carry the Airfix name on its base. The phone poles, road signs, and I-beams used on the flatcars were also Airfix products; this was never mentioned by Lionel. The models listed below are extremely hard to find unbroken and were not available separately.

UNNUMBERED SIGNAL BRIDGE:

(A) Gray.	4	8	12
(B) Black.	4	8	12
UNNUMBERED TRESTLE BRIDGE: Gray.	6	10	15

POLA-MADE LIONEL BUILDING KITS

(5-4551) PICKLE FACTORY: Appearing in back of 1975 catalogue, first catalogued building offered by Lionel in HO; available until end of 1977.

Light tan walls done in clapboard style; two light brown wooden boardlike vats; dark gray roofs resembling corrugated steel and flat metal panels; black smokestacks; dark brown roof supports, ladders, handrails, and walkways; Lionel and Pola names on light tan structure frame; clear window material, window template, and instructions included for cutting each window glaze; finished model is 12″ long, 5½ high, and 4½″ deep. The model did require gluing and is difficult to find built and in good shape.

	15	20	30

(5-4552) WATER TOWER AND SANDING STATION: Catalogued 1975-77 as Lionel-stamped item; holds Pola and Lionel names on the inner roof the water tower rests on. Packed in the red, white, and blue carton used on all 1974 locomotives and rolling stock.

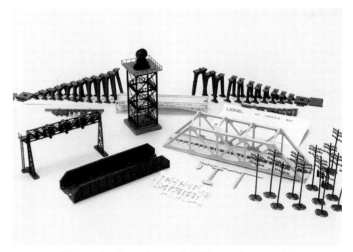

Shown back to front: 5-4530 trestle set with arch bridge, 5-4501 lighted beacon, uncatalogued signal bridge, and 5-4531 girder bridge in front of it, uncatalogued trestle bridge on right with uncatalogued set of road signs and set of telephone poles. The signal bridge, trestle bridge, road signs, and telephone poles were part of some of the sets offered 1975–1977 and were not assigned catalogue numbers.

	Gd	Exc	Mt

Dark red brick walls; gray roofs; lighter gray water tank and sanding station housing; dark brown ladders, walkways, and tool shed walls; light tan base, sand house walls, and simulated sand pile; clear window material and instruction sheet included; finished model stood nearly 10″ long, 5″ high, and 4″ deep.

	10	15	20

(5-4553) ENGINE HOUSE: Catalogued 1975; available as Lionel model until 1977; names found on dark gray frame.

Deep yellowish walls with wood panel effect; dark brown doors, window frames, and vents, all with excellent wood detail; dark gray shingled roof; clear window material and instruction sheet included; finished model 12″ long, 4″ high, and 5″ wide. The doors of the model moved on a pin cast into the doors top and bottom. Difficult to find with doors unbroken.

	10	15	20

(5-4554) PASSENGER STATION: Catalogued 1975-77; this kit found in Lionel packaging, without Lionel name on frame.

Red simulated brick walls, bluish gray slate roof panels; tan chimneys; white windows, doors, dormers, and trim; 16½″ long, 5½″ high, and 5″ deep. The kit required many hours of careful work for assembly, but it was worth the time to acquire this beautiful structure. Almost impossible to find built up and in good condition. C. Sommer reports the kit has been reissued in recent years, at a price of $50-70.

	25	35	50

(5-4555) STOCK YARD: Introduced 1976.

Light green clapboard-style walls and light gray simulated cedar roof on main building; dark brown water tower and supporting wood bracing; light gray windmill; white windows, doors, and railings; light tan fencing and corral gates; clear window material; three horses and figure pushing wheelbarrow, along with bag of potatoes, a barrel, and case of bottles make a complete kit almost impossible to find; finished kit 11″ long, 6″ wide, and 6½″ high. Shown with three kits never sold as Lionel: a new coaling tower, an ice station, and a grain elevator.

	10	15	25

(5-4556) BOILER HOUSE: Second new kit offered in 1976; second to be found in Lionel packaging without Lionel name on kit.

Four of the Pola-made Lionel building kits, new in 1975. From top, left to right: 5-4551 pickle factory, 5-4552 water tower, 5-4553 engine house, and 5-4557 rooming house. Note the small building in front of the rooming house is not shown or mentioned in the catalogue or instruction sheets. Pola produced these scale buildings for other distributors. There are no Lionel-sold variations known.

	Gd	Exc	Mt

Gray stonelike base; bluish gray roofs and overhangs; light tan vertical clapboard main walls; dark brown windows, doors, fence, and outside wood supports; dark red brick chimney, 7½"; silver wheelbarrow, barrels, tools, and boxes; finished kit 7½" high, 7" long, and 4½" deep. Another kit difficult to find complete.   **10   15   20**

(5-4557) ROOMING HOUSE: As above, 1976-77; neither Lionel nor Pola name appears on kit.

Tan main house walls; dark brown shed attached, including supports for off-white porch; white windows and doors; light gray roofs; clear window material; three figures, a bike, man with handtruck holding large bag; finished model 6½" high, 6" long, and 4½" wide. Difficult to find complete. When available in 1977, a small tan shed-type building was included; this extra was not mentioned in kit description nor in instruction sheet.   **10   15   25**

TRACTOR-TRAILERS

Available in 1977 in sets introduced new that year and un-catalogued near the end of 1977 as separate-sale items, these were packed in the same white cartons used for rolling stock. As shown in the photograph on page 59, the models were entirely metal except for the fourteen black plastic wheels; six sets of double wheels were present,

with each set cast in one apiece and detailed with tread marks, and two front tires were single-casting and completely smooth. All were mounted on wire axles. The tractor was a smooth casting while the trailer had ribs on its roof and sides. No back doors are present on the trailer. All the tractor-trailers were full painted, in the road name of the set they were offered in. The effective detailing includes doors, lights, grille, and bumper — usually missing from the sets. No catalogue numbers were ever assigned to these models.

	Gd	Exc	Mt

NORFOLK & WESTERN: 1977. Part of set 5-2780.

Black tractor with gray trailer; black paper sticker on trailer side, white NW stamping; bumper, radiator area, and air vents painted flat silver.

4   6   8

SOUTHERN: 1977. Part of set 5-2781.

Green tractor with gray trailer holding same paper sticker, green with yellow "SOUTHERN" on tractor and trailer; silver grille and bumper.

4   6   8

UNION PACIFIC: 1977. Part of set 5-2782.

Yellow tractor with silver-painted grille and bumper; gray trailer with yellow paper sticker holding red "UNION PACIFIC" stamping.

4   6   8

These Pola scale buildings were new in 1976. At top, 5-4554 passenger station, with 5-4556 boiler house on the left and 5-4555 stockyard (note horses!) below. The three metal trucks shown were introduced in three new sets of 1977 with names matching the power units in each set.

CHAPTER V
U.S. Catalogued and Uncatalogued Sets

In the following lists, a letter appears in parentheses after each item to designate the source of manufacture:

- (A) Austria
- (H) Hong Kong
- (L) Lionel
- (T) Taiwan

Note that color photographs of sets appear in this chapter; each illustrates the consists — for closer looks at individual cars, consult the appropriate chapters. The loads carried are shown on page 55. Scenic accessories and tractor-trailers are covered in Chapter IV. Illustrations of track, motive components, etc. are provided in Chapter VIII.

Note: Although the catalogue shows and states that "rerailer track" was included, these track sections were not available in the sets of 1974. What did come with the early 1974 sets was a snap-in plastic rerailer piece, about 2 inches long, that was pushed into the straight section of track. Cast into it was "1731 Bachmann". It was replaced in some of the sets beginning in 1975. A rerailer section of track marked with the Atlas name was available in some sets until 1977. All track and switches used in U.S.-marketed Lionel sets were of Atlas manufacture.

CATALOGUED SETS

	Gd	Exc	Mt

5-1480 THE CHESSIE: 1974-75.
5-5403 Gold Chessie GP-9 (L)
5-8415 Black unmarked flat with three I-beams and twelve stakes (A)
5-8407 Orange D & RGW gondola with three white plastic pipes (H)
5-8402 Red M-K-T stock car (L)
5-8411 Orange PFE 50' reefer (A)
5-3401 Black crane car, C & O decal (A)
5-8404 Blue C & O work caboose (L)
5-8417 Green BN hopper (T)
5-8416 Black Dow tank (T)
5-8418 Yellow and silver Chessie caboose (L)

The set also contains a kit for a signal and girder bridge plus twelve telephone poles and twelve road signs, an unlighted bumper snap-in rerailer, a manual switch, 4550 transformer, and twelve sections 18"-radius curved track and twelve sections 9"-long straight track.

	65	80	125

5-1481 THE UNION PACIFIC: 1974-75.
5-5402 Gray- and yellow-painted UP GP-9 (L)
5-8400 Red CP Rail boxcar (L)
5-8407 Orange D & RGW gondola, no load (A)
5-8402 Red M-K-T stock car (L)

	Gd	Exc	Mt

5-8415 Black unmarked flatcar with stakes and I-beams (A)
5-8412 Green Railway Express reefer (A)
5-8414 Red SF flatcar with stakes (A)
5-8406 Yellow-painted UP caboose (L)

Included thirteen sections track, snap-in rerailer, 4550 transformer, and booklet.

	50	75	100

5-1482 THE GREAT NORTHERN: 1974-75.
5-5401 Green and orange GN FA-1 (L)
5-8413 Yellow UP flatcar with stakes (A)
5-8401 Blue GT boxcar (L)
5-8415 Black unmarked flatcar with I-beams and stakes (A)
5-8402 Red M-K-T stock car (L)
5-8410 Red SP gondola, no load (A)
5-8419 Red and black GN caboose (L)

Included thirteen sections track, snap-in rerailer, instruction booklet, and 4550 transformer.

	50	75	100

5-1483 THE SANTA FE: 1974-75.
5-5400 Red and silver SF passenger Alco (L)
5-8415 Black unmarked flatcar with three I-beams and twelve stakes (A)
5-8400 Red CP Rail boxcar (L)
5-8408 Blue Chessie gondola, no load (A)
5-8405 Red unpainted SF caboose, yellow letters (L)

Included thirteen sections track, snap-in rerailer, instruction booklet, and 4550 transformer.

	50	75	100

5-2586 AMERICAN FREEDOM TRAIN, STEAM, 7-UNIT: 1975-76.
5-6501 Red, white, and blue GS-4 (H)
41 Display car (L)
101 Display car (L)
105 Showcase car (L); available only with set; extremely difficult to find set with 105 car
110 Display car (L)
205 Observation car (L)

Included thirteen sections track, rerailer track, instruction booklet, and 4550 transformer.

	200	325	400

5-2587 AMERICAN FREEDOM TRAIN, DIESEL, 5-UNIT: 1975-76.
5-5504 Red, white, and blue Alco diesel (L)
41 Display car (L)
101 Display car (L)
110 Display car (L)
205 Observation car (L)

Included same track components as steam unit set.

	125	225	300

	Gd	Exc	Mt

5-2680 THE SANTA FE: 1976-77.
5-5600 Blue and silver SF Alco freight (L); set also found with the 5600 Alco using a marked Hong Kong–made drive, in 1977 packaging.
5-8613 Brown UP boxcar (T)
5-8413 Yellow UP flatcar with stakes (A)
5-8603 Red-painted SF caboose, yellow trim, white numbers (T)

   Included twelve sections track, rerailer track section, and 4550 transformer. First set to hold track and transformer manufactured in Hong Kong. **50 65 90**

5-2681 THE CHESSIE: 1976-77.
5-5610 Tricolored Chessie GP-9 (H); extremely difficult to find
5-8612 Yellow and silver UP hi-cube boxcar (T)
5-8620 Silver and orange Bessemer & Lake Erie coil car (T)
5-8730 Orange D & RGW gondola, no load (T)
5-8600 Silver- and yellow-painted caboose (T)

   Included twelve sections curved track, snap-in rerailer, 4550 transformer, and instruction booklet. **75 90 125**

5-2682 THE BURLINGTON NORTHERN: 1976-77.
5-5623 Green and black BN GP-30 (H)
5-8614 Blue GT boxcar (T)
5-8621 Green P & LE coil car (T)
5-8417 Green and black BN hopper, with coal (T)
5-8730 Orange D & RGW, no load (T)
5-8416 Black Dow tank car (T)
5-8601 Green BN caboose (T)

   Included twelve telephone poles, twelve road signs, trestle set with arch bridge, eighteen sections curved track, eight sections straight track, rerailer track section, 4550 transformer, and instruction booklet. **80 100 125**

5-2683 CHESSIE GOLDEN ARROW: 1976-77.
   Almost the same as set 5-1480 catalogued in 1974, but has pair of manual switches to make the figure eight. The Geep was of Hong Kong manufacture while the stock and gondola cars were Taiwan-made. **85 100 120**

5-2780 NORFOLK & WESTERN EMPIRE: 1977.
5-5710 Black N & W GP-9 (H)
5-8755 Red CP Rail hopper with coal load (T)
5-8730 Orange D & RGW gondola with three culvert pipes shown, but with sand load in car (T)
5-8612 Yellow and silver UP hi-cube boxcar (T)
5-8720 Black-painted N & W caboose (T)

   Included die-cast tractor trailer in same road name (T), snap-in rerailer, twelve sections curved track, 4550 transformer, railroad map, booklet of railroad history, iron-on decal for a T-shirt, twelve telephone poles, and twelve road signs. **85 100 125**

5-2781 THE SOUTHERN EMPIRE: 1977.
5-5711 Green Southern GP-9 (H); catalogue shows 5514 Lionel-made Geep heading this set, but it came with the 5711.

   Same cars and extras as set 5-2780, but road name changes on caboose and trailer truck to match the locomotive. **85 105 125**

5-2782 THE UNION PACIFIC EMPIRE: 1977.
5-5714 Yellow-painted UP GP-9 (H)

   Same cars and extras as the first two sets new this year (above). The die-cast truck's road name changed to the UP, with the painted caboose shell holding number 8724 (T). This set also showed the Lionel-made Geep as its power unit.

Note: All three of the above sets can be found in the original box with the DRG & W gondola carrying a sand load that is not shown in the catalogue; three white culvert pipes also included in the set. **85 100 125**

5-2783 THE GREAT WESTERN FREIGHT: 1977.
5-6502 Black Western Pacific GS-4 (H)
5-8412 Green Railway Express reefer (A)
5-8416 Black Dow tank car (T)
5-8770 Red M-K-T stock car (T)
5-8760 Yellow UP flatcar with stakes and tan crates (A)
5-8731 Blue B & O gondola with three culvert pipes (T)
5-8725 Dark red WP caboose (T)

   Included signal and girder bridge kits, twelve telephone poles, twelve road signs, rerailer track, sixteen sections curved track, two sections straight track, and power pack. It was a made-up type of set, with the UP flatcar carrying crates and the Chessie gondola shown with three culvert pipes. Track, transformer, and instruction book included. **90 125 150**

UNCATALOGUED SETS

   Very little is known as fact about what was actually available as uncatalogued Lionel HO sets in the 1970s. We do know that there were special Sears, J.C. Penney, and many private dealer sets. We know that the uncatalogued sets that have been verified have very few pieces of rolling stock that were not regular line cars. But the power units found in these sets, on the other hand, were for the most part special decorated units made strictly for Sears or Penney. None were offered in the regular Lionel line until the middle of 1977, when Lionel was dumping its inventory. Without doubt there are more special dealer sets to be discovered and listed than those included in this edition.

   Advertising packets provided to the dealers by Lionel included photos, banners, tear sheets, and special pricing. No catalogue numbers were shown on the material, which allowed the dealer to make up and advertise many types of sets from existing inventory. The cartons used on these sets varied greatly; they and the accompanying paper are covered in Chapter VII. It appears that the slogan "Sears American Flyer by Lionel" was used on all set cartons sold by Sears; it appeared as part of the decoration or on the special glued-on Sears label. Further information on this appears in Chapter VII, on paper and packaging.

Note: Information on any set not listed is requested.

5-1493 Special Dealer Set: 1974-75.
5-5402 Yellow and gray UP GP-9 (L)
5-8402 Red M-K-T stock car (L)
5-8400 Red CP Rail boxcar (L)
5-8416 Black Dow tank car (T)
5-8415 Black unmarked flatcar with stakes and I-beams (A)
5-8409 Dark brown N & W 40' gondola, no load (A)
5-8414 Red SF flatcar with stakes and crates (A)
5-8412 Green Railway Express reefer (A)
5-8417 Green BN hopper with coal load (T)
5-3400 Black UP crane (A)
5-8403 Yellow- and black-painted UP 40' work caboose, black/dark blue tool boxes (L)

   Included girder bridge kit, signal bridge kit, twelve telephone poles, twelve road signs, two switches, two bumpers, instruction and warranty packet. C. Sommer Collection **NRS**

5-2684 Special Dealer CONTINENTAL EXPRESS SET: 1976.
5-6500 Daylight colors SP GS-4 (H)
5-8402 Red M-K-T stock car (L)

5-8412 Green Railway Express 50' reefer (A)
5-8408 Dark blue B & O 40' gondola with three culvert pipes (A)
5-8760 Yellow UP 50' flatcar with stakes and crates (T)
5-8416 Black Dow tank car (T)
5-8604 Daylight colors SP caboose (T)

Included girder bridge kit, signal bridge kit, telephone poles, signs, track, transformer, and instruction booklet. K. Armenti, C. Sommer Collections.

5-2685 Special Dealer Set: 1976; available again 1977 with catalogue number changing to **5-2692.**
5-5622 Red and silver Santa Fe passenger GP-30 (H)
5-8612 Yellow and silver UP hi-cube boxcar (T)
5-8413 Yellow UP 40' flatcar with three white culvert pipes (A)
5-8405 Red-painted SF caboose (L)

Included track, transformer, instruction booklet. Available in plain brown carton with glued-on label. K. Fairchild Collection.

5-2790 Special Dealer CHESSIE FREIGHT SET: 1977.
5-5612 Gold Chessie GP-9 (H)
5-862! Green 42279 Pittsburgh & Lake Erie coil car (T)
5-8711 Orange Illinois Central hi-cube boxcar (T)
5-8731 Blue B & O Chessie gondola, no load (T)
5-8600 Yellow and silver Chessie caboose (T)

Included twelve sections curved track, rerailer, and power pack. Packed in plain brown carton; white label on end bears "5-2790". Not one item in the set is Lionel production.

5-2791 Special Dealer/Dealer catalogue number 49-95064 BUR-LINGTON NORTHERN FREIGHT SET
5-5623 Green and black BN GP-30 (H)
5-8770 Red M-K-T stock car (L)
5-8614 Blue GT boxcar (L)
5-8613 Brown UP boxcar (T)
5-8730 Orange D & RGW gondola with sand load (T)
5-8415 Black unmarked flatcar wtih stakes and beams (shown) (A)
5-8601 Green BN caboose (T)

Included girder bridge kit, signal bridge kit, twelve telephone poles, twelve road signs, twelve sections curved track, three sections straight track, power pack, history booklet, iron-on. C. Sommer comment.

5-2792 Special Dealer BURLINGTON NORTHERN FREIGHT SET: 1977.
5-5623 Green and black BN GP-30 (H)
5-8702 Red Southern boxcar (T)
5-8704 Yellow Railbox boxcar (T)
5-8770 Red M-K-T stock car (L)
5-8730 Orange D & RGW gondola, no load (T)
5-8601 Green BN caboose (T)

Included girder bridge, signal bridge, rerailer, telephone poles, road signs, track, and power pack. Packaged in plain brown carton with white label.

5-2793 Special Dealer CHESSIE FREIGHT SET: 1977.
5-5610 Tricolor Chessie GP-9
5-8620 Orange and silver B & LE coil car (T)
5-8416 Black Dow tank car (T)
5-8740 White and brown Coors 40' reefer (T)
5-8761 Yellow UP flatcar with logs (T)
5-8770 Red M-K-T stock car (L)
5-8756 Light blue B & M hopper with coal (T)
5-8730 Orange D & RGW gondola with sand load (T)
5-8600 Yellow Chessie caboose (T)

Included sixteen sections curved track, two sections straight track, rerailer, girder bridge kit, two switches, twelve telephone poles, twelve

road signs, 4550 transformer, iron-on, map, history booklet, instruction booklet. C. Sommer comment.

5-2794 Special Dealer SOUTHERN PACIFIC FREIGHT SET: 1977.
5-6500 Daylight colors SP GS-4 (H)
5-8770 Red M-K-T stock car (T)
5-8416 Black Dow tank car (T)
5-8742 White and green Tropicana reefer (T)
5-8760 Yellow UP flatcar with crates and stakes (T)
5-8731 Blue Chessie gondola with sand load (T)
5-8604 Orange and brown SP caboose (T)

Included eighteen sections track, two remote switches, girder bridge, signal bridge, road signs, telephone poles, and power pack. Packaged in plain brown carton, white styrofoam liner; white label on end has "5-2794".

5-2798 Special Dealer BURLINGTON NORTHERN SET: 1977.
5-5623 Green and black BN GP-30 (H)
5-8613 Brown UP boxcar (T)
5-8761 Yellow UP 48' flatcar with logs (T)
5-8756 Blue B & M hopper with coal (T)
5-8416 Black Dow tank car (T)
5-8601 Green BN caboose (T)

Included Track and transformer

5-6590/Sears catalogue number 49-9546 AMERICAN FLYER SET OF 1975.
5-5513 Red, white, and blue American Flyer GP-9 (L)
5-8517 Light turquoise green Sears 40' boxcar (L)
5-8516 Dark blue C & O 40' boxcar (L)
5-8409 Dark brown N & W gondola, no load (A)
5-8415 Unpainted black unmarked 40' flatcar (A)
5-8503 Red, white, and blue American Flyer caboose (L)

Included track and transformer.

Note: The set is available in the red, white, and blue picture-window carton with styrofoam base; the green insert pictured the 5-6595 Union Pacific Alco set of 1976. G. Bunza Collection.

5-6592/Sears catalogue number 49-9547 AMERICAN FLYER SET OF 1976.
5-5513 Red, white, and blue American Flyer GP-9 (L)
5-8517 Light turquoise green Sears 40' boxcar (L)
5-8516 Dark blue C & O 40' (L)
5-8573 Dark blue D & RGW 40' stock car (L)
5-8410 Red SP 40' gondola (A)
5-8520 Unpainted white unmarked 40' flatcar with stakes and crates (L)
5-8503 Red, white, and blue American Flyer caboose (L)

Included track and transformer. Also available in the red, white, and blue two-piece box with styrofoam liner and green insert on the lid depicting the American Flyer GP-9 set listed above. K. Armenti, G. Horan, J. Otterbein Collections.

5-6590/Sears catalogue number 49-9549 UNION PACIFIC SET OF 1975.
5-5506 Yellow UP FA-1 with decal on nose, dull paint (L)
5-8574 Dark green SP 40' stock car (L)
5-8409 Dark brown N & W 40' gondola (A)
5-8517 Light turquoise green Sears 40' boxcar (L)
5-8415 Black unmarked 40' flatcar with stakes and I beams (A)
5-8406 Yellow-painted UP caboose (L)

Included track, transformer, and instruction booklet. G. Horan, F. Coppola, K. Armenti Collections.

Note: The set also exists with a lemon yellow cupola on the caboose that does not match the body. Part of the C. Sommer Collection.

The top two curves show the first two 1974 sets, headed by the Alco FA-1. Top curve: 5-1482 Great Northern, with its rare red Southern Pacific gondola; this is only the second known set the car came in. Second curve down: The five-piece Santa Fe 5-1483. Third row down: 5-2681 five-unit Chessie set of 1976. Front: The 5-2680 four-unit Santa Fe set of 1976. With the exception of the Alco shells, not one item in either of these last two 1976 sets was of Lionel manufacture.

The first two sets of 1974, headed by a GP-9. Top two curves: 5-1480 gold Chessie set, that also held bridges, telephone poles, and road signs never assigned a catalogue number. Only the locomotive, stock car, and two cabooses were of Lionel manufacture. The gondola pictured has load of sand in place of the three culvert pipes that were included in the set. Front two curves: 5-1481 UP set with locomotive, 40-foot boxcar, stock car, and caboose of Lionel manufacture, four remaining cars were Roco manufacture.

5-6595/Sears catalogue number 79-9551 UNION PACIFIC SET OF 1976.

Consists of same components as 5-6595 UP set of 1976. Verification requested. Both sets available in plain brown cartons with styrofoam liners and white label showing Alco set enclosed. "HO American Flyer" appears on white glued-on Sears label.

The sets catalogued in 1977 included die-cast metal trailer trucks as well as telephone poles, road signs, iron-ons, and paper items.

LIONEL HO SETS

Prices include delivery in USA.
Offer expires 11/30/78 or while stocks last.

THE CHESSIE FREIGHT $22.95

SET INCLUDES:
GP-9 CHESSIE "GOLD" DIESEL
CABLE CAR
HI-CUBE BOX CAR
GONDOLA
CHESSIE CABOOSE
12 SECTIONS OF TRACK
SNAP-IN RERAILER
POWER PACK

THE BURLINGTON FREIGHT SET $26.95

SET INCLUDES:
BN GP-30 DIESEL
TWO BOX CARS
CATTLE CAR
GONDOLA
BN CABOOSE
15 SECTIONS OF TRACK

SNAP-IN RERAILER
TELEPHONE POLES
GIRDER BRIDGE
SIGNAL BRIDGE
ROAD SIGN SET
POWER PACK

CONTINENTAL EXPRESS SET $49.95

SET INCLUDES:
SOUTHERN PACIFIC 4-8-4 GS-4
SP CABOOSE
CATTLE CAR
TANK CAR
REEFER
FLAT CAR with load
GONDOLA with load
18 SECTIONS OF TRACK

2 SWITCHES
GIRDER BRIDGE
SIGNAL BRIDGE
ROAD SIGN SET
POWER PACK

Here is how one dealer, Hi-Country Brass of Denver, advertised some uncatalogued sets.

The two bicentennial sets. Top two curves: Five-car GS-4 steam set 5-2586, with the rare 105 display car, second behind the locomotive. Bottom two rows: Smaller four-car diesel set 5-2587. The 1976 catalogue mistakenly referred to both sets as diesel powered sets.

Two sets of 1977. Top two curves: 5-2783 Great Western, headed by the GS-4 in a new road name. Note the culvert pipe in the Chessie gondola and the crates on the 8760 50-foot UP flatcar. Lower two rows: 5-2682 catalogued set; the catalogue clearly shows the Lionel 8401 GT boxcar that had been replaced by the 8614 Taiwan-made car shown. Not one piece in either set was a Lionel-made product except for the crates used on the flatcar.

Three new sets catalogued in 1977 hold the same three freight cars shown at top, along with the metal trailer trucks shown in the accessories chapter (IV); the road name used on the locomotive and caboose was the only difference in the three sets, from top to bottom: 5-2782, 5-2780, and 5-2781. Extra components were also shown in the catalogue, such as maps, T-shirt iron-ons, booklets, telephone poles, and road signs as shown on page 63.

Three uncatalogued sets from 1976–1977. Top curve: 2798 set of 1976, thought to have been a Sears set (with no labels on the brown carton, it could not be verified). Two middle rows: Dealer special set 2794, headed by the GS-4, issued in 1977. Front row: 2792 uncatalogued set of 1977, advertised by dealers in Model Railroader magazine. Not one piece in any of the three sets is a Lionel-made item.

Top curve: Uncatalogued 6592 American Flyer Sears set of 1975. Note the rare Southern Pacific gondola in red. Second curve from top: Uncatalogued Sears set 6595, headed by the UP Alco also issued in 1975. Third curve from top: Dealer special from the Ken Fairchild Collection, which was packaged in a plain brown flat carton 10 inches by 28 inches, with white glued-on label marked "1976. Number 2685". Front curve: Uncatalogued 2790 set of 1977, headed by gold Chessie.

CHAPTER VI
Canadian Market HO

The HO items sold in Canada and distributed by Parker Brothers of Concord, Ontario, present a challenge, the likes of which I have never witnessed elsewhere. In the preparation of this book, these items took more time to sort out than all the items manufactured outside the United States put together. I am still not sure all the Canadian models are covered in this edition, and verification is requested on some that are. One problem is that there is only one known catalogue issued for these models, which were available from 1975 to 1977. The catalogue issued in 1975 was also used in 1976. There is no evidence of a catalogue being issued in 1977, although special dealers' price lists were issued in this last year for Lionel HO. Furthermore, there were items sold in Canada that were available at the same time in the United States, with absolutely no difference in the model's number or decoration. The number on the carton was the only real change. The same U.S.–offered building kits were also sold, using the same U.S. carton and its number.

The models made expressly for Canadian customers carried Canadian road names and a catalogue number with a prefix "T", followed by five digits (the number appeared on the carton and and model itself), from 1975 to 1977. *Some* of the items sold in the States were simply packed in the striped Canadian carton, and thus only the carton had the "T" number; the number on the car itself was the same as that used in the United States. The same goes for decoration and road names. The T-20210 cable car and the T-20221 48-foot flatcar are two examples. Another is the 51-foot reefer sold in the United States. None were catalogued in Canada. There *was* a model of a 51-foot plug-door boxcar in the Canadian line, but this model was not offered in the U.S.

Among the Canadian locomotives only the FA-1 Alco in the Great Northern road name (catalogue number T-12002) and the Canadian National (T-12001) were manufactured by Lionel and can be found in the white U.S. cartons stamped "5614 G.N." and "5613 C.N."; both models still carry the Canadian "T" on their sides. They were definitely sold in this manner — this is not a case of someone switching cartons or models.

The inventory list at the back of this volume includes all known items sold in Canada, including the United States items that were merely repacked in Canadian cartons and stamped with the Canadian catalogue number. The catalogued items made for the Canadian market are:

- One GS-4 locomotive in one road name
- One GP-9 in three road names
- One GP-30 in one road name
- One Alco FA-1 in three road names
- One boxcar in five road names
- One stock car in two road names
- One gondola in two road names
- One three-dome tank car in one road name
- One hi-cube boxcar in two road names
- Two 51-foot boxcars in eleven road names
- Two 51-foot flatcars in two road names
- One cable car in two road names
- One crane car in one road name
- Two work cabooses in two road names
- One steel caboose in five road names
- Seven scale building kits
- Five catalogued sets
- Two uncatalogued sets

We know now that Kader Ltd. of Hong Kong was directly involved in the Canadian-marketed line of Lionel HO and special Parker Brothers models, shipping both decorated and undecorated models directly to Parker Brothers in Ontario, Canada. Parker then decorated some of these blank shells themselves in special road names only available in Canada and packaged them in their own red and orange cartons. The models were available in sets and separately from 1975 through 1977, with most shown in the one catalogue used in 1975–1976. Parker also did its own advertising, had their own catalogue and price sheets, and sold the line pretty much as they saw fit with little interference from Lionel U.S.A.

Speculation has it that Parker continued trade with Kader after Lionel left the HO market in 1977, but this could not be confirmed to your author's satisfaction, because Parker also left the train scene some years ago. During this time period it seems components were also shipped directly from Kader and included trucks, car frames, doors, etc. for use on the Canadian-sold models as Parker saw fit. Parker simply made up their own models from the parts. This would explain the Taiwan or Hong Kong name being found on a Kader-made frame with a shell from yet another manufacturer. An example would be the 5-8739 Coors 40-foot reefer thought to have been made exclusively for the Parker line of models but only found in the white U.S.–style carton. This particular car never appeared in either the U.S. or Canadian catalogues. This one-of-a-kind car has a Kader frame with a "Tyco-type" shell with closed steps. Parker was also known to have had dealings with other smaller companies based in Canada who also supplied components and decorated some of the shells used on the special rolling stock. Repainted shells were also part of the line and included the T-20210 brown Canadian National coil car. The car can be found with the original orange shell refinished in the dark brown CN color.

Eighty-five percent of the Canadian models offered were of foreign manufacture, with only a few of the power units offered made from Lionel tooling. There is no doubt that Kader Ltd. was the chief supplier. A smaller number of models came from Bachmann Brothers of Philadelphia, which as we know is another member of the Kader family. In a few cases the Bachmann- and Lionel-sold models of the time can be distinguished only by the name present on the car frame. The information used to identify the motors and frames of the models sold on the U.S. market can also be used to identify the Canadian items. One change seen is that the shells of the Kader-made Geeps are made of many colors of plastic that were eventually painted — unlike the shells found in the U.S. models, which are usually the color of the paint later used.

The catalogue issued in Canada shows the seven building kits sold in the United States (which used the same U.S. catalogue numbers), along with a full page showing the track assortment offered. All track and DC power packs offered in the Canadian line were all manufactured by Tindax, a subsidiary of Kader Ltd. No accessories are shown.

All the diesel units offered in the Parker Bros. Canadian Lionel line of the 1970s. All four Geeps were of Hong Kong manufacture, while the three Alcos were Lionel-made. Note that the first two Alocs in right column were the exact same units sold in the United States, using the 5600-series catalogue number in their white cartons in 1976–1977. Not shown: the GS-4 in the Southern Pacific and Freedom Train colors, the same models as the U.S. production being also available in Canada, separately and in sets 1975–1976 and using the very same U.S. number on the cab side. The Freedom locomotive was also available as a static model with a plastic case and wooden base.

| | Gd | Exc | Mt |

Most Canadian-sold models were very limited in number and many of them were available only in sets. These pose the ultimate challenge for the collector today. It appears that the special Parker-decorated shells are much harder to find than the Kader-decorated models.

Following first is coverage of locomotives available in Canada and secondly rolling stock; Canadian sets are listed at the end of this chapter. Note that the frame types referred to in the following listings are described and illustrated in Chapter II. Chapter VII describes the catalogues, paper, and packaging for the Canadian items as well as those marketed in the United States. Knowing how both Canadian and United States packaging and numbering were used is important in identification of authentic Lionel HO. There are some cars that are the same models used in both U.S. and Canadian markets; for these, the values suggested below would be a bit higher if the Canadian boxes are included.

POWER UNITS

Canadian-marketed FA-1s

T-12001 CANADIAN NATIONAL: Available 1975-77 in three-car set T-10050 and separately; Lionel product but no Lionel name on shell;

can be found in U.S. cartons with catalogue number 5-5613 on carton only.

Light gray shell finished in flat or semigloss black with three diagonal white stripes on lower side panels; flat orange nose covers sides to behind cab door; large white "CN" appears on nose; white catalogue number "T-12001" in lower side panel at rear; Lionel part number "50-5400-20" on clear cab window material; headlight lens and decorative horns; Type II late 1974 frame with four-wheel drive. Found also with Type VII Hong Kong frame.

(A) Flat finish.	25	40	60
(B) Glossy finish.	25	40	60

T-12002 GREAT NORTHERN: 1976-77; uncatalogued; can be found in U.S. cartons with Lionel catalogue number 5-5614 on carton only.

Gray Lionel-made shell finished in flat black, with flat orange lower and middle side panels and nose; 1/4" black band with two thin yellow stripes around shell separates orange panels; decaled logo below headlight; yellow-stamped road name and "T-12002" on black band; Type II or Type VII frame and motor; headlight and decorative horns. (Also found with Type VII Hong Kong drive; NRS.) **25 35 50**

UNNUMBERED CONFEDERATION FLYER: Catalogued 1975-76 in set T-10067, along with ten 50' steel plug-door boxcars and a caboose, but no catalogue number found on unit.

Canadian market 40-foot boxcars. Top: T-20120 BC boxcar of 1975 and T-20121 UP car of 1976, same as the U.S. model, including the car number on its shell (the T-number was used only on the carton). There are no separate roofwalks. The last three shelves hold the five road names used on the 40-foot Taiwan-made boxcars of 1975–1976: T-20100 DWC, T-20101 ON, T-20102 GT, T-20103 UP, and two variatons of the T-20105 CP Rail car. Note the lighter paint and smaller steps on the car on the bottom shelf, right. The T-20103 UP car is also a repacked US model, with the T-number only found on its Canadian carton. Two stock cars are pictured on page 72.

	Gd	Exc	Mt

Gray Lionel shell finished in glossy white with two ¼" reddish orange stripes across roof and windshield area, one stopping at floor line, other continuing along lower side panels to rear; bright blue block-lettered "THE CONFEDERATION FLYER" below "CANADA", in white letters outlined in red, on rear top side panels; outline of maple leaf symbol on top front panel; blue-stamped set name also on nose; clear window material and decorative horns; frame and motor Hong Kong–made — as used on 5-5600 SF Alco in the U.S. Model extremely difficult to find and the set is almost impossible to locate complete.

	40	75	100

Canadian-marketed Hong Kong–made GP-9s

These units were all of Hong Kong manufacture; the frames can be identified using the information on GP-9s sold in the United States, on pages 25–26.

T-12010 ONTARIO NORTHLAND: Catalogued 1975-77, heading five-car set T-10052; also available separately.

Gray or dark blue plastic shell with body painted bright yellow and roof, lower side panels, and cab sides finished in flat medium blue; cab roof painted light blue; white-stamped logo and "Rail / Services" on cab sides; very dark glossy blue road name, "T-12010", and three Z or lightning-shaped stripes on long hood; black plastic handrails, decorative horns, clear window material, and clear plastic shaft lighted both ends. Extremely difficult to find in good condition, as most of the Canadian items seem to be — perhaps because many Canadians are operators.

	50	75	100

T-12012 GRAND TRUNK: Catalogued separately 1975-77; available in two uncatalogued Simpson's department store sets.

Painted same as U.S. model: solid blue body with reddish orange ends; white-stamped markings and stripe at floor line and large "GT" at center of hood; "T-12012" on cab side; handrails, decorative horns, clear window material, and clear light shaft. Difficult to find. No matching caboose.

	30	50	75

T-12013 CANADIAN NATIONAL: Catalogued separately and in six- unit freight set with no number used on set box; available 1975-76.

Shell painted flat black with flat orange hood ends; thin white stripe along side at floor line; flat white-stamped "CN" at center of long hood and "T-12013" on cab side; handrails, horns, clear window material, and light shaft; black or dark blue unpainted plastic frame. One of hardest Canadian items to find.

	40	65	90

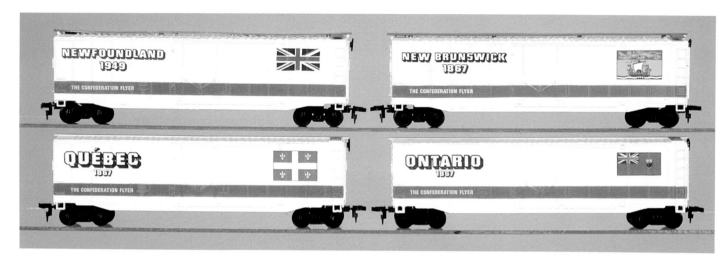

Four of the 50-foot boxcars used in the special Parker Confederation Flyer sets of 1975. No individual catalogue numbers are used. The Hong Kong cars are on the top, with separate roofwalks, and the Taiwan cars on the bottom shelf have cast-on roofwalks. All are extremely rare. The 50-foot BC boxcar is shown on page 72.

Top: The same two-car UP set used in the U.S. line, with its carton number bearing the Canadian T-08422 number. Models are marked as they were in the U.S. production. The bottom three shelves show cabooses with road names that match all the power units offered: T-20170 CP Rail, T-20171 CN, T-20172 ON, T-20176 SP, and the 1976 Hong Kong Confederation caboose that carried no numbers but had the Bachmann name on its frame.

	Gd	Exc	Mt

GP-30s

T-12020 CP RAIL: Catalogued 1975-76 in set T-10054 and separately in 1976.

Reddish orange shell in both painted and unpainted versions, with inside of unpainted version blackened so bulb did not light up cab sides; white stripes across nose and front wall; black stripes on white background on end of hood and wrapping around to end under second roof fan; white-stamped road name in center of hood; "T-12020" stamped on cab side; handrails, decorative horns, clear window material, light shaft, and plastic bell on cab roof; black steps at both ends of unit.

	Gd	Exc	Mt
(A) Painted.	50	70	100
(B) Unpainted.	40	60	90

GS-4

(T-12030) DAYLIGHT FLYER: The only catalogued steam unit shown in Canadian HO, in small four-car set; exactly the same as U.S. unit; catalogue number stamped on carton only; available as separate item and in uncatalogued Simpsons set.

See page 30 for descriptive details.

	Gd	Exc	Mt
(A) As catalogued item.	60	75	90
(B) Uncatalogued, same as U.S., static model with case and wood base.	50	60	75

ROLLING STOCK

Almost all of the rolling stock offered in the Canadian market was manufactured in Taiwan, with some of the 50' cars coming from Hong Kong; still other models were assembled and decorated in Canada. There are a few pieces of rolling stock that do not carry a Lionel catalogue number except on the carton. Most have the Lionel name on their frames and the word "Hong Kong" or "Taiwan" is also present (see also page 12). All of the rolling stock made for the Canadian market can be considered uncommon, with the boxcars heading the list. Many items were never shown in the catalogue, while many were available for only one year. These models now present a considerable challenge to the collector — just think, we could have bought them in 1976 for $2.25 each.

Boxcars and Stock Cars

40-foot Boxcars

The boxcars from Taiwan were made of shells in white, gray, black, and blue plastic; these cars will show up in different shades of body color. Almost all were painted with rubber-stamped lettering, with a few known to have the heavy silkscreen-type lettering. The boxcars have black plastic brakewheels and painted roofwalks that were separate castings added to the cars. One bad feature of the boxcars are the doors: the rails to hold them are thin and only serve to hold the door against the car side. The rail has a tendency to buckle and the door would slide off the car, resulting in the cars being found today without one or both doors.

The frame is of black unpainted plastic and all floor bracing, brake cylinders, and valves are cast on. Talgo-type trucks are used with metal axles and NMRA-type couplers. The Lionel name and "Made in Taiwan" are cast into the frame, and a blackened metal weight is fastened to the inside of the frame and held in place with the same plastic pin that holds the trucks with its top melted flat.

5-8613: See (T-20103)

	Gd	Exc	Mt

T-20100 DULUTH WINNIPEG & PACIFIC: Available 1975-76 separately and in one catalogued set.

White shell finished in a flat medium brown with sliding door painted flat turquoise green; white-stamped block-lettered road name, dimensional data, and "D.W.C. T- 20100" on left side of car; all lettering underscored with white lines, giving crowded appearance; lettering on right side of car has only small white dimensional data stamping. One of the most sought-after boxcars of the Canadian line.

	25	40	60

T-20101 ONTARIO NORTHLAND: Available 1975-76 separately or in sets but one of most difficult to locate.

White, blue, or gray plastic shell painted in flat blue, darker than that used on Grand Trunk car of same period; flat bright yellow ends and some lettering; road name to left and logo on right side of door, with white-stamped "ONT. / T-20101" and data, separated by three thin vertical yellow lines, below. Very handsome model due to sharp, clear printing.

	25	40	60

T-20102 GRAND TRUNK: Catalogued 1975-76 separately and in sets.

Black, gray, or pinkish brown shell painted completely blue; white-stamped lettering with washed-out appearance; road name, "GTW T-20102", and data all appear to left of door, large "GT" to right; thin white lines separate the lettering. More readily available but apt to become scarcer.

	15	20	30

(T-20103) 5-8613 UNION PACIFIC: Uncatalogued; available 1976-77 separately; Canadian "T-20103" on carton only, with U.S. "5- 8613" on car side. It is the only car in the entire line to carry the Lionel hyphenated prefix on its shell.

Description same as U.S. model (see page 36).

	10	15	25

T-20105 CP RAIL: Available separately and in sets 1975-76.

White, gray, or tan shell painted flat reddish orange; washed-out white-stamped lettering (this is only boxcar to carry its lettering on the same end of the car), with logo in black and white at opposite end of the car; "CP T-20105" below road name is followed by data so small they cannot be read. Most common of the boxcars.

	15	20	25

Hi-Cube Boxcars

5-8612: See (T-20121)

T-20120 BRITISH COLUMBIA RAILWAY: Catalogued in sets and separately 1975-76.

Shell painted flat dark green with doors lighter green; washed-out white-stamped "BCOL T-20120" and data to left of door, with opposite end carrying road name and logo in white and orange and more data and orange and black number board; all detail cast into shell, including straight steps at each corner; no roofwalks; frame, trucks, and weight are same as found on the 40' boxcars.

	15	25	35

(T-20121) 58612 UNION PACIFIC: Uncatalogued; same as made for U.S. market; Canadian "T-20121" on carton only, while car carries U.S. "58612".

See page 37 for detailed listing of U.S. car.

	5	8	10

50-foot Plug-door Boxcar

The models of this steel-sided boxcar has excellent rivet detail, with steps, ladders, door, door rails, and number boards all cast into the shell. The shell comes basically in blue, white, gray, or tan, but the shade of the car's paint was not affected by the difference. These boxcars were made in Taiwan and Hong Kong (separate roofwalks were present on the Hong Kong cars, while the Taiwan cars had cast-on roofwalks); regardless of origin, the car has a single brakewheel.

The top three shelves show, in the left column, two of the 50-foot cars offered in Canada: T-20201 BC boxcar and, T-20200 PC flatcar with containers, and 48-foot fish-belly T-20221GN flat with logs (same car available in U.S.); no Lionel number appears on these last two cars. The right column shows the three covered gondolas, beginning with the repainted T-22010 CN, T-20211 B & LE, and the T-20212 P & LE cars; the last two were also available on the U.S. market with no Lionel numbers on the car shells. The bottom shelf holds the only two ordinary gondolas offered: T-20125 CN and T-20126 D & RGW. Both were available with and without a load of sand. The number T-20126 is not on the car shell and once again the car is the very same model as the U.S. version.

Top: T-20130 CP Rail of 1975 and T-20131 BN of 1976. Middle: T-20140 CN and T-20141 Katy, also the same car as on the U.S. Market. Bottom: The only tank offered in Canada, T-20150 — one of the most difficult of Canadian models to find; note the blue background with white CGTX markings.

There are two types of unpainted black plastic frames with black plastic trucks used (shown on page 13), but both frames had a metal weight fixed to the inside. The early Taiwan frame had four cross braces and two truck bolsters, while the later Hong Kong frame had eight cross braces with two truck bolsters. The later frame has a smooth main floor with lots of rivet detail and has brake housing and cylinders cast on; the early frame held no rivet detail and has the wooden-board look, as did all the other Roco and Taiwan-made cars. The early frame carries "Made in Taiwan" with no Lionel name, while the later frame has the Lionel name and "Hong Kong" on the middle outside panel. Both types of frames may be found on any of the boxcars described below.

The trucks on the Taiwan-made cars have a plastic pin securing the trucks, while the trucks on the Hong Kong cars snap into a hole in the frame. The Taiwan cars have metal axles, with the Hong Kong cars having plastic ones with split or solid axles.

Listed below, after T-20201 British Columbia, is a group of ten cars that were only available in the Confederation Flyer set. The shells used in this set can be found with either the roofwalk cast into the Taiwan shell, or with the separate roofwalks (of the Hong Kong cars). The latter are rare. No separate catalogue number was used for these cars; the only number on each of these cars is the year that province joined the Confederation. No numbers are found on the individual cartons.

One other strange feature of the cars in the Confederation set, with the later Hong Kong frames, is the area where the Lionel name should be, on the main floor support; there is an oval-shaped melted area present, as if the name or another brand name was removed by a hot metal stamp being applied to the surface. The melted area is present on all the cars in all four of the sets in your author's collection.

	Gd	Exc	Mt

T-20201 BRITISH COLUMBIA: Catalogued 1975-76; available in two catalogued sets and separately.

Shell painted flat dark green with matching roofwalk; nonoperating door finished in flat lighter green; white-stamped road name, number board, and logo (in orange and white), all to right of door; data in three panels to left of door, along with "T-20201"; one brakewheel. It has been found with the early or late frame but only with separate roofwalk on a Taiwan-made shell.

(A) Early frame.	10	25	30
(B) Late frame.	15	20	25

UNNUMBERED CONFEDERATION FLYER SET BOXCARS: Available 1975-76. The cars listed below were only available in the set, which is almost impossible to find today; indeed, all of the individual cars are also rare now. As stated previously, these cars had no separate catalogue numbers; the only number appearing on the car was the year the province it represents joined the Canadian Confederation. All cars are painted exactly the same, with only the emblem and year changing.

Glossy white-finished shell with ¼" reddish orange stripe on side above floor line; separate roofwalk is orange; multicolored provincial emblem to right of door, name of province and date to left of door with white-stamped "THE CONFEDERATION FLYER" below on orange stripe; all cars can be found with early or late frames, with separate or cast-on roofwalk.

The ten cars are Alberta, 1905; British Columbia, 1871; Manitoba, 1870; New Brunswick, 1867; Newfoundland, 1949; Nova Scotia, 1867; Ontario, 1867; Prince Edward Island, 1873; Québec, 1867; and Saskatchewan, 1905.. The later Hong Kong cars are more difficult to find.

(A) Taiwan.	15	20	25
(B) Hong Kong.	15	25	35

40-foot Stock Cars

Although the 5-8574 Southern and the 5-8570 Rio Grande stock cars appear on the rear cover of the 1976 Canadian catalogue, they are not known to have been part of the Canadian line. The pictures are simply the same shots used in the U.S. advertising kits issued by Lionel in 1976, which were provided to Parker Brothers for their distribution. We would appreciate hearing of any collector having these two cars carrying a Canadian "T-" number on their sides. Below are listed the two observed Canadian-sold stock cars.

	Gd	Exc	Mt

8770: See (T-20141)

T-20140 CANADIAN NATIONAL CATTLE CAR: Catalogued 1975; available 1976 in sets and separately; although the car was made by the same Taiwan manufacturer as the 5-8770 Katy (see page 41 and below), the car differs from the car sold in the U.S. Lionel line.

Shell finished in dark brown with ½" white stripe around shell at floor line; the three small number boards hold the only lettering — two at left carry "CN T-20140" and all data; board at right holds a large "CN" — all in neat flat white stamping; steps cast into corners are thinner than those found on The Katy car; can be found with and without "Lionel" on frame; talgo-type trucks, separate roofwalk, metal weight, brakewheel same as on U.S. model.

	15	20	30

(T-20141) 8770 CANADIAN "The Katy" CATTLE CAR: Uncatalogued but available in 1977; exactly same as car described with U.S.-sold items (see page 41); "T-20141" on carton only.

Cabooses, Cranes, and Work Cabooses

Two types of cabooses were offered in Canadian HO. The first was the standard 36-foot steel body also offered in the U.S. line, and all information in Chapter III (pages 41–46) identifying this type of car applies here, except of course for the decoration and road names used. One basic difference was that the unpainted ladder and handrail castings used on the Canadian cars were always of the same unpainted color plastic as the frames, which detracted from the car's appearance. The same castings offered on the U.S. cars were always black plastic, matching the frames, which added to the cars' appearance.

The second type of car offered was totally new to the Canadian HO line and was never offered by Lionel U.S.A. This car was part of the Confederation Flyer set available in 1975–1976 and was never offered separately. The car was steel-sided, of welded construction; rivet detail was present on the unpainted black frame, however, and talgo-type trucks were used with extra-long coupler shafts and steel axles. The frame was stamped with the Bachmann Hong Kong name only, as it was made for the Bachmann HO line of cabooses in the late 1970s. The car was purchased through the Kader Corporation by Parker Brothers and shipped directly to Canada, as were the 50-foot plug-door boxcars also used in this Confederation Flyer set. Parker Brothers, in decorating the caboose, failed to remove the Bachmann name from its frame as was done on the boxcars. Both types of cabooses offered in the Canadian line can be considered rare and very collectible.

5-8604: See (T-20173)

T-(-)20170 CANADIAN PACIFIC: Catalogued 1975-76 in sets and separately.

White or gray shell painted flat orange-red, which did not match the GP-30 it came with in the T-10054 set of 1976; the car came with an unpainted yellow plastic frame, ladder, and handrail unit; faded white-stamped lettering, with "T20170" below cupola; sharply lettered safety warning, built date, and car weight; two brakewheels, smokejack, and roofwalk all unpainted black plastic; talgo trucks have split plastic axles.

	10	15	20

T-20171 CANADIAN NATIONAL: Catalogued separately and in set T-10050 in 1976.

Shell painted flat burnt orange that clashes with glossy white unpainted plastic handrail, ladder, and underframe; the main and the cupola roofs painted black; faded white-stamped lettering: "CNR" at cupola end,

	Gd	Exc	Mt

partially covering green maple leaf, with "SERVES / ALL / CANADA" in a box below; "T-20171" and road name in lower side panels at opposite end; no built date or data; black smokejack, brakewheels, and roofwalk; trucks same as CP caboose, but with steel axles; "Lionel" and "Made in Taiwan" appear on frame.   **10   15   20**

T-20172 ONTARIO NORTHLAND: Catalogued in sets (it was the tail car in set T-10052) and available separately 1975-76.

Shell decoration follows that of locomotive, with flat bright yellow-painted body, flat dark blue roof and separate roofwalk, and semigloss light powder blue cupola; three semigloss dark blue Z stripes below cupola; dark blue road name at opposite end, lower panel; white-stamped "Rail / Services / T-20172", and logo above toolboxes; handrails and ladder casting matches unpainted black plastic frame; steel axles on truck, with both names on frame. Extremely difficult to find, as is the matching locomotive.   **20   30   40**

(T-20176) 5-8604 SOUTHERN PACIFIC: Uncatalogued; available separately 1976-77; except for the T catalogue number appearing on the carton, the car is exactly the same as 5-8604 SP caboose in U.S. line (see page 45).   **10   15   25**

Note: Verification requested of car existing with Canadian number on its side.

UNNUMBERED CONFEDERATION FLYER CABOOSE: Part of The Confederation Flyer set of 1975-76; the only extended (hack) caboose offered in the Canadian line of HO.

Unpainted white shell, with two ¼" reddish orange stripes across car roof and down side; rear or top stripe continues to rear of shell; white-stamped "THE CONFEDERATION FLYER" on stripe; outline of maple leaf; unpainted black frame with matching smokejack; separate casting of handrails, ladders, and brakewheels; Bachmann name cast into frame, but no other markings present. Extremely difficult to locate in good condition, since the railing extending below the base tends to break when the car is removed from its liner.   **20   30   45**

Note: Reported to exist with painted white shell; verification requested.

Crane Car and Work Caboose

(T-08420) C & O WORK CABOOSE: Same as 5-8404. See page 46.

5-0821: See (T-08421)

(T-08421) 5-0821 C & O CRANE CAR: Same as U.S. model 5-3401 sold on U.S. market; "T-08421" on carton only. See page 46.

(T-08422) UNION PACIFIC CRANE AND 50-FOOT WORK CABOOSES: Uncatalogued in Canada but available with decal of U.S. set 5-8422; "T-08422" on carton only; see page 45 for detailed listing and values.

Flatcars

17326: See (T-20220)

(T-20220) 17326 51-FOOT CONTAINER CAR: Catalogued 1975-76 in set T-10054 and separately; not offered in the U.S. Lionel HO line but offered in Bachmann line of the late 1970s; "T-20220" only on carton.

Light green-painted gray plastic fish-belly body with two separate carriages that were fitted with three small tabs that slipped into the stake pockets cast into the body; white-lettered "PENN CENTRAL" and "17326"; brakes, valves, rivet detail, steps, and wooden-board look cast into place; one vertical brakewheel; "Lionel" and "Made in Taiwan" on frame; plastic trucks with horn hook couplers and steel axles held to car with plastic pin; each carriage has a 20' plastic container painted silver

	Gd	Exc	Mt

and holding black- and red-lettered "SEA LAND". Extremely difficult to find with containers intact. Known to exist with unpainted green body.

(A) Painted body.	15	25	35
(B) Unpainted body.	15	20	25

(T-20221) 42764 GREAT NORTHERN 48-FOOT FLATCAR: Uncatalogued but available in sets and separately 1976-77; same as car in U.S. Lionel HO line, also not seen in a catalogue; only 48' heavy-duty flatcar in Canadian line; "T-20221" only on carton.

Steel-type deck with lots of rivet detail, as on undercarriage also; grabirons and steps cast into body at four corners; two vertical brakewheels; four trucks attached to a swivel arm attached to body with single plastic pin; black plastic couplers and trucks with steel axles; white-stamped road name, data, and "42764"; three hollow brown plastic logs as load, held to car with three copper wires twisted to resemble chain; frame holds "Lionel" and "Made in Taiwan" and has four small metal weights, one at each corner.   **15   20   25**

42764: See (T-20221)

Gondolas and Hoppers

Gondolas

8730: See (T-20126)

T-20125 CANADIAN NATIONAL: Only 40' catalogued gondola, available 1975-76.

Shell painted light brown; white-stamped road name over five of eight side panels, with built date, data, and "T-20125" on other three panels; simulated sand load in one-piece gray plastic casting; talgo-type trucks; one black plastic brakewheel; "Lionel" and "Made in Taiwan" on frame. Difficult to locate.   **10   15   25**

(T-20126) 8730 RIO GRANDE: Uncatalogued; available 1977; same as 5-8730 D & RGW U.S. car with sand load; "T-20126" only on white carton; "8730" on car side. See page 51 for detailed listing.   **6   8   10**

Coil Cars

The coil or cable cars used in the Canadian line are of course the very same Taiwan-manufactured cars sold by Lionel U.S.A., and were offered from 1975 to 1977, with only one new road name added — that being the repainted shell used on the Canadian National, with "T-20210" on its side and carton. In the case of the other two uncatalogued B & LE and P & LE cars, the Canadian catalogue number was on the cartons and non-Lionel numbers on the cars themselves.

T-20210 CANADIAN NATIONAL: Catalogued in sets and separately 1975-76.

Body and doors painted flat brown; white-stamped road name, data, and "T-20210" on three side panels, with a large "CN" on other end; two standing brakewheels, talgo-type truck with special extra-long coupler shaft and separate brakewheel on cover; seven unpainted and unmarked tan plastic coils resembling wooden spools; "Lionel" and "Made in Taiwan" on frame; Canadian catalogue number on carton. Difficult to locate with the spools and with doors unbroken.   **10   15   20**

(T-20211) 31002 B & LE: Uncatalogued; available 1976-77; originally made for U.S. line of HO only.

See (5-8620) on page 52 for description. Few collectors realize this car was part of the Canadian line, since the Canadian number was used on the carton only.   **10   15   20**

Three Canadian-market sets. Together, the top two rows show the T-10067 Confederation Flyer set of 1975, with the four Hong Kong–produced cars on the very top and the five Taiwan-made cars in the second row. The set is headed by a Lionel Alco with a caboose stamped Bachmann. No catalogue number is present. Alco shell is Lionel with Hong Kong drive.

The third row shows the T-10062 GS-4 Daylight Flyer set of 1975. By adding a T-20105 CP Rail car, one would have an uncatalogued Sears Simpson set.

The front two rows combine to show the T-10054 CP Rail Express set of 1975, with its rare container car and repainted CN covered gondola.

Four Canadian-market sets of 1975–1976, Top to bottom: T-10052 Ontario Northland Express set of 1975, T-12013 uncatalogued six-unit freight set of 1975, T-10050 CN Mini Express of 1975–1976, and an uncatalogued four-unit freight set of 1976.

	Gd	Exc	Mt

(T-20212) 42279 P & LE COIL CAR: Uncatalogued; available 1976-77; same car as U.S. 5-8621; see page 52 for detailed listing; "T-20212" on carton only.   **10   15   20**

31002: See (T-20211)
42279: See (T-20212)

Hoppers

The 42-foot hoppers offered were made in Taiwan; no Lionel-made hoppers were ever sold in the Canadian line. Offered in two road names, this car was a steel-sided four-bay hopper with plenty of crisp rivet detail. At each end a black sheet-metal weight is held by the single plastic pin that attaches the separate black plastic frame to the shell. Black plastic talgo-type trucks and NMRA-type couplers are present. Both cars have a simulated coal load held with four corner braces cast into the shell of the car. One black plastic brakewheel is present. Steps and ladders were cast into the body but the steps are thin and break off easily. Both cars are difficult to find in good condition.

T-20130 CP RAIL: Catalogued 1975-76 separately and in sets.

Black shell painted flat black; white-stamped lettering on three of large side panels; red and white logo in first panel on left, with center holding "CP T-20130" and data; road name and additional data in last panel on right; "Lionel" and "Taiwan" on black frame.   **15   20   25**

T-20131 BURLINGTON NORTHERN: Uncatalogued; available 1975-76.

Black shell painted flat light green; white-stamped lettering in two side panels, with first holding road name in two lines and very small "BN" below, with "T-20131" and data below it; large "BN" on last panel; one black brakewheel; simulated coal load; "Lionel" and "Taiwan" on frame. Once again, collectors are generally unaware of this car's existence, with its very small catalogue number. The car is easily missed once out of its carton.   **15   20   25**

Three-Dome Tank Car

T-20150 CGTX: Catalogued separately and in sets 1975-76; only such car offered in the Canadian line of HO; same as car issued in U.S. line except for the decoration.

Car painted flat black; white-stamped CGTX markings on blue background below dome walkway; smaller "CGTX T-20150" at opposite end of tank; great deal of data and built date spread across tank body; tank made of two separate castings with a metal weight hidden inside; talgo-type trucks; one vertical brakewheel; wire handrails and lots of rivet detail on frame and tank body; "Lionel" and "Made in Taiwan" on frame.   **15   20   30**

CANADIAN-MARKET SETS

With only one catalogue issued for the Canadian market, and used in both 1975 and 1976, little information other than the Parker Bros. price lists used in 1975 and 1976 is available to the HO collector interested in sets. The known sets are listed below, followed by the few uncatalogued sets that have been verified. As in Chapter V, on U.S. sets, the letter in parentheses indicates origin: (H) Hong Kong; (L) Lionel; (T) Taiwan. It appears that some of the uncatalogued sets were not assigned numbers, with many cartons simply lettered "4 UNIT FREIGHT", or otherwise

designating number of units.   Verification on any Canadian set, catalogued or not, is requested.

Catalogued Sets

T-10050 CN MINI EXPRESS: $30.
T-12001 Black and white CN Alco FA-1 (L)
T-20102 Blue GT boxcar (T)
T-20125 Brown and white CN gondola (T)
T-20171 Orange CN caboose (T)

T-10052 ONTARIO NORTHLAND EXPRESS: $45.
T-12010 Ontario Northland GP-9 (H)
T-20120 Green BC hi-cube boxcar (T)
T-20130 Black CP Rail hopper (T)
T-20101 Blue ON boxcar (T)
T-20150 Black CGTX tank car (T)
T-20172 Yellow and blue ON caboose (T)

T-10054 CP RAIL EXPRESS: $50.
T-12020 Red CP Rail GP-30 (H)
T-20201 Green BC 50' boxcar (T)
T-20105 Red-orange CP Rail boxcar (T)
T-20210 Brown CN coil car (T)
T-20220 Green 50' flatcar with two SeaLand containers (T)
T-20130 Black CP Rail hopper (T)
T-20140 Brown and white CN stock car (T)
T-20170 Orange CP caboose

T-10062 DAYLIGHT FLYER: $60.
T-12030 SP GS-4, #4454 (H)
T-20130 Black CP Rail hopper (T)
T-20201 Green BC reefer (T)
T-20140 Brown and white CN stock car (T)
T-20176 Red-orange SP caboose (T)

T-10067 CONFEDERATION FLYER: $68.
Unnumbered Confederation Flyer Alco FA-1 (L)
Ten white 50' boxcars: Alberta 1905, British Columbia 1871, Manitoba 1870, New Brunswick 1867, Newfoundland 1949, Nova Scotia 1867, Ontario 1867, Prince Edward Island 1873, Quebec 1867, Saskatchewan 1905
Center cupola caboose (H)

Uncatalogued Sets

6-unit set:
T-12013 Black and white CN GP-9 (H)
T-20120 Green BC hi-cube boxcar (T)
T-20102 Blue GT boxcar (T)
T-20150 Black CGTX tank car (T)
T-20131 Green BN hopper (T)
T-20170 Orange CN caboose (T)

4-unit set:
T-12001 Black and white CN Alco FA-1 (L)
T-20120 Green BC hi-cube boxcar (T)
T-20140 Brown CN stock car (T)
T-20171 Orange CN caboose (T)

CHAPTER VII
Catalogues, Packaging, and Paper

Note that parts lists and instructional sheets appear on pages 92–108.

U.S. AND CANADIAN CATALOGUES

All the catalogues available for these four years measure 9½ by 12 inches.

1974
Eight-page color brochure with blue cover showing nine small inset photos of items offered in sets only. Promoted new features of Lionel HO (illustrated in Chapter I) and offered four sets, including the Chessie featured in the illustration on inside cover.

1975
Twelve-page color brochure with white cover bearing "LIONEL® / 75th ANNIVERSARY" and showing seven inset photos, all having to do with the two bicentennial sets to be made available that year. The observation car is shown with a brass-colored end railing but was only produced in unpainted black. The Lionel 75th anniversary patch is pictured in black, red, and gray.

1976
Twelve-page color brochure with white cover featuring silhouette of the GS-4 and five inset photos showing four power units. Notable for showing the new kit of the coaling tower which was never produced.

1977
Twelve-page color brochure with bluish gray cover showing the GS-4 in daylight colors and the GP-30 in Conrail blue. With the exception of 1976, when the GP-30 in the Burlington Northern road name appeared twice, this is the only year the GP-30 locomotive appeared.

Canadian Market
There was only one catalogue, eight pages, white background with blue "LIONEL HO" and the characteristic red and yellow stripes (see photograph on next page).

The 1974 HO catalogue offered four sets and an invitation to enjoy the new features of the GE motor, increased durability and pulling power, and "new attention to detail".

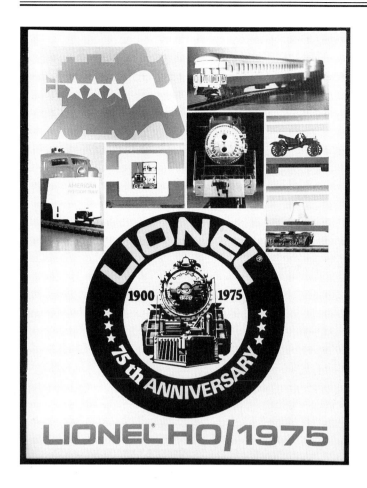

The cover of the Canadian-market catalogue

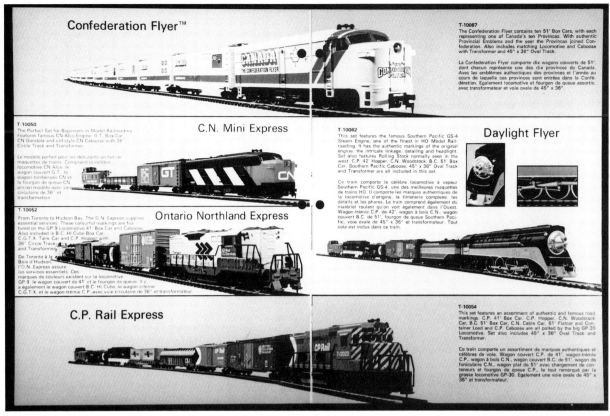

Confederation Flyer™

T-10067
The Confederation Flyer contains ten 51' Box Cars, with each representing one of Canada's ten Provinces. With authentic Provincial Emblems and the year the Provinces joined Confederation. Also includes matching Locomotive and Caboose with Transformer and 45" x 36" Oval Track.

La Confederation Flyer comporte dix wagons couverts de 51', dont chacun représente une des dix provinces du Canada. Avec les emblèmes authentiques des provinces et l'année au cours de laquelle ces provinces sont entrées dans la Confédération. Également locomotive et fourgon de queue assortis, avec transformateur et voie ovale de 45" x 36"

T-10050
The Perfect Set for Beginners in Model Railroading. Features famous CN Alco Engine, G.T. Box Car, CN Gondola and old style CN Caboose with 36" Circle Track and Transformer.

Le modèle parfait pour les débutants en fait de maquettes de trains. Comprend la célèbre locomotive CN Alco, le wagon couvert G.T., le wagon-tombereau CN et le fourgon de queue CN ancien modèle avec voie circulaire de 36" et transformateur.

C.N. Mini Express

T-10062
This set features the famous Southern Pacific GS-4 Steam Engine, one of the finest in HO Model Railroading. It has the authentic markings of the original engine, the intricate linkage, detailing and headlight. Set also features Rolling Stock normally seen in the west. C.P. 42' Hopper, C.N. Woodstock, B.C. 51' Box Car, Southern Pacific Caboose, 45" x 36" Oval Track and Transformer are all included in this set.

Ce train comporte la célèbre locomotive à vapeur Southern Pacific GS-4, une des meilleures maquettes de trains HO. Il comporte les marques authentiques de la locomotive d'origine, la timonerie complexe, les détails et les phares. Le train comprend également du matériel roulant qu'on voit également dans l'Ouest. Wagon-trémie C.P. de 42', wagon à bois C.N., wagon couvert B.C. de 51', fourgon de queue Southern Pacific, voie ovale de 45" x 36" et transformateur. Tout cela est inclus dans ce train.

Daylight Flyer

T-10052
From Toronto to Hudson Bay, The O.N. Express supplies essential services. These colourful markings are featured on the GP-9 Locomotive 41' Box Car and Caboose. Also included is B.C. Hi Cube Box Car, C.G.T.X. Tank Car and C.P. Hopper with 36" Circle Track and Transformer.

De Toronto à la Baie d'Hudson, l'O.N. Express assure les services essentiels. Ces marques de couleurs existent sur la locomotive GP-9, le wagon couvert de 41' et le fourgon de queue. Il y a également le wagon couvert B.C. Hi Cube, le wagon-citerne C.G.T.X. et le wagon-trémie C.P. avec voie circulaire de 36" et transformateur.

Ontario Northland Express

C.P. Rail Express

T-10054
This set features an assortment of authentic and famous road markings. C.P. 41' Box Car, C.P. Hopper, C.N. Woodstock Car, B.C. 51' Box Car, C.N. Cable Car, 51' Flatcar and Container Load and C.P. Caboose are all pulled by the big GP-30 Locomotive. Set also includes 45" x 36" Oval Track and Transformer.

Ce train comporte un assortiment de marques authentiques et célèbres de voie. Wagon couvert C.P. de 41', wagon-trémie C.P., wagon à bois C.N., wagon couvert B.C. de 51', wagon de funiculaire C.N., wagon plat de 51' avec chargement de conteneurs et fourgon de queue C.P., le tout remorqué par la grosse locomotive GP-30. Également une voie ovale de 45" x 36" et transformateur.

A spread from the Canadian catalogue used in 1975–1976

Catalogue Series Numbers, 1974–1977

Items	Series
1974 (no separate items available this first year)	
Power Units	5-5400
Rolling Stock	5-8400
Operating Stock	5-3400
Sets	5-1400
1975	
New Power Units	5-5500
New Rolling Stock	5-8500
New Operating Stock	5-3400;
Crane set used 5-8422	
New Accessories	5-4500
New Building Kits	5-4500
Sets	5-1400; Freedom sets used 5-2586 and 5-2587
1976	
Uncatalogued Power	5-5600
Power Units	5-5500
New U-18-B	5-5500
Steam Locomotives	5-6500
New Rolling Stock	5-8600
(but not catalogued for separate sale)	
Accessories and Building Kits	5-4500
New Kits	5-4600
Sets	5-2600; Diesel Freedom set used 5-3587 and Steam Freedom set used 5-2586
1977	
Power Units	5-5700
Steam Locomotives	5-6500

Rolling Stock	5-8700
Accessories and Building Kits	5-4500
Sets	5-2700

U.S. PACKAGING

The cartons used by Lionel in their 1970s line of HO differed greatly from those used in the 1957–1966 line. In the earlier period the well-known orange carton used in the O Gauge line was used also for HO, with the smaller line almost always having a picture window to display the contents. For the first two years of the later HO, 1974 and 1975, no cartons of any kind were shown in the catalogues. This packaging is described below and shown in the accompanying photographs.

Sets

The cartons used for early sets generally bore the bright orange colors of the earlier HO line. With the appearance in 1974 of the first new Lionel HO sets, the carton changed to a dark blue with red, white, and yellow lettering. Some had picture windows showing the sets while others did not. The set boxes of 1974–1975 were cluttered with pictures of the set, and the power units and catalogue number in black lettering appeared on each end of the carton. The sides were filled with small insert-type photographs showing the motor used and noted the pulling power of the locomotive and the durability and detail of each item offered were promoted.

The punched-out cardboard liner used in the 1960s sets disappeared, to be replaced by styrofoam liners or separate cartons holding each piece in the set box, including transformer and track. None of the arly or late individual cartons ever appeared in the catalogue.

Early 1976 saw the set cartons change to a two-piece white box, with all lettering and stamping remaining red and blue. Most of the sets

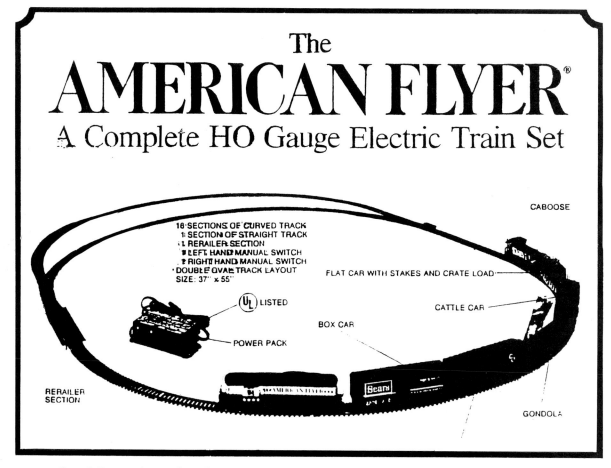

The
AMERICAN FLYER®
A Complete HO Gauge Electric Train Set

CABOOSE

16 SECTIONS OF CURVED TRACK
1 SECTION OF STRAIGHT TRACK
1 RERAILER SECTION
1 LEFT HAND MANUAL SWITCH
1 RIGHT HAND MANUAL SWITCH
DOUBLE OVAL TRACK LAYOUT
SIZE: 37" x 55"

FLAT CAR WITH STAKES AND CRATE LOAD

(UL) LISTED

CATTLE CAR

BOX CAR

POWER PACK

RERAILER
SECTION

GONDOLA

One of the green inserts from the two-piece Sears set, 1975–1976; the picture did not always match set enclosed.

Some of the known set cartons used in the United States. From bottom up: The GS-4 Freedom Train of 1975, the special Sears American Flyer set, an early 1974–1975 Lionel carton, a Sears uncatalogued UP freight set, and the 1976–1977-type carton, the last to be introduced.

were wrapped in clear plastic. The set cartons still showed pictures of the set under the picture window and also on all four side panels. The logo of the power unit's road name always appeared in full color on the lid. The side of the carton carried a notation "imported parts labeled to show country of origin". It was the first reference to the fact that all of the items were not Lionel made. The new freight set

5-2680, with the new Santa Fe Alco power unit, was the first to use the new white cartons that would package all sets until the end of production in 1977.

In 1977 three sets were shown along with their white cartons bearing red and blue stripes. The Lionel name was also in red and blue along with the set name using the road name of the power unit enclosed.

Some of the set cartons used in the Parker Brothers era of Lionel's line and sold in Canada. The top carton was also used for some of the special Sears Simpson department store sets. Note the large numbers on some the cartons: this digit indicated the number of pieces in each set, as many of the cartons will be found without a catalogue number shown.

Some of the individual cartons used in later Lionel HO. From the bottom up: RailScope video unit, the GS-4 steam unit. From next row left up: Rolling stock stamped and unstamped (as found in sets), and the 1974–1975 rolling stock carton. On the right side, the smaller boxes are, bottom up: Canadian unstamped carton found in sets, Canadian clear label, and Canadian black label cartons.

A picture of the set appeared on the front of the carton — a bit strange since a large picture window showed almost every item in the set, whether it was a styrofoam liner or individual cartons holding the contents. Model numbers were stamped on both ends of the set cartons with almost all individual cartons inside having no stamping at all.

The Freedom train sets also used the white set cartons with the liners made of plastic and styrofoam. There were pockets to accept each item, with the GS-4 always packed in a separate liner with a clear plastic cover.

The special Sears sets and many dealer specials are found in plain brown cartons holding the Lionel name in large blue stamping; a white label at the end or side holds the Sears catalogue number as well as the Lionel catalogue number.

Insert pictures are found on the tops of all Sears set cartons, whether the two-piece picture window-type carton or the plain brown carton — both with sytrofoam liners. The green insert picture was part of the color lid when found on the two-piece-type carton, while the plain brown carton always had the insert in a black and white label that was

glued in place. All inserts hold the picture of a freight set, with Sears and Lionel catalogue numbers repeated a second time, along with a safety notice about the 120 volts of electricity needed for operation of the set.

One strange feature of these inserts is that not all showed the set found in the carton, as is the case with the 5-6590 GP-9 American Flyer set; it is known to exist with the UP set 0595 shown on its lid.

It appears that the slogan "Sears American Flyer by Lionel" appears on all set cartons sold by Sears: the two-piece carton shows the slogan as part of the decorated top, and the plain brown cartons have it printed in black lettering on the small label that is glued to the end or side. A large black-printed five-digit number is also present on all the Sears set cartons. This number is the Sears store identification number, applied at the Sears distribution center.

When opened the Sears sets can sometimes be found with a set carton inside and in other cases with just the styrofoam liner. The styrofoam liners used in all the HO sets, whether Sears or other, had formed pockets to accept a particular item. This helps today's collector in that one might find an open set with an incorrect road name but right type of car. The

Individual accessories and building kits, in cartons used in the United States and Canada

pockets would hold the item tightly in place, and only the proper type of car would fit into it.

Separate Items

In 1975, when the models were available separately, these cartons followed the same pattern and colors of the sets introduced in 1974. The early 1975 individual blue cartons showed rolling stock available across the front, below the picture window, with power units and more rolling stock covering the white rear panel. The road name and catalogue number were stamped in black on a white area at each end, while the sides showed wheel sets, car ends, and couplers. Every inch of space was used to relay information to the buyer.

Some of the individual cartons had cardboard inserts to hold the item while others had vacuform plastic trays to hold the car or locomotive. A few of the cartons held sponge rubber liners, but these were only found on the power uits of early 1975.

The separate sale item cartons from 1976 on still showed the rolling stock and locomotives on the rear panel, with the catalogue number in black stamping on the end — sometimes applied on a white label and other times appearing directly on the carton. All of these cartons have the picture window with the sides now showing the building kits offered on one side and the accessories shown on the other. The cartons also carry the country-of-origin notice. Liners of cardboard, plastic, or styrofoam were used in these cartons.

The crane cars, accessories, building kits, and crane car sets used a dark blue box with yellow, red, and white lettering. All showed pictures of other items available on their backs, sides, and ends. The crane car

and the 8422 crane set always come with a cardboard liner, as a few items were. All of these cartons show a very crowded appearance and show once again the many different directions Lionel was moving in their short four years.

The 5509 Southern Pacific Alco power unit will be found in the old blue and red carton with a paper label holding "5509" and the road name. The sticker covers a mistakenly stamped box that read Standard, instead of Southern, Pacific. The white label glued to the carton can be peeled off to verify this. I am quite sure there are many cartons with this type of quick last-minute change by Lionel, and they are yet to be found. The above descriptions were based on examination of items in the collections of K. Armenti, K. Fairchild, and G. Horan. Readers are requested to report any unlisted packaging known to them.

CANADIAN PACKAGING

Lionel Canadian-packaged models appeared as separate-sale items in the same type of white carton with picture window that was used in the United States. However, the cartons held yellow and orange striping, with printing appearing in blue, white, and black as shown on page 81. The cartons were slightly heavier card stock.

Most of them carry a black label with white printing to hold the catalogue number and road name. Some boxes came with a clear label with black printing, while still others had no label, the catalogue number being applied directly to the carton's end. The Lionel name is present on all four sides and both ends of the carton.

The Canadian set boxes followed this same pattern, with the Confederation Flyer set appearing in a three-piece carton with plain cardboard bottom. There was a styrofoam liner and a lift-off top with a large picture window showing a portion of the twelve items belonging to the set. In most cases, the set name with the By/Par Lionel name are shown on all sides and the top of the box. Both the sets and separate-sale items will be found with cardboard or plastic liners.

Another type of set carton is the two-piece box found with the T-10062 Daylight Flyer Set: the box top of white and blue has lighter blue and red stripes along with the set name and "By/Par Lionel" in blue and white. All items in this set are individually boxed in the red and yellow cartons. The carton also carries the information that it was packed in Canada and made in Hong Kong, stamped on the end. This same type and color of carton was used on the special sets sold by the Simpson department stores of Canada.

The second two-piece set carton, with individual cartons inside, all carried the red and yellow stripes on white background. Unlike the U.S. cartons of this type, no set name appeared on the carton except for the notation of its being a four-unit or six-unit Lionel HO train set.

A few rolling stock items will also be found in the white U.S. carton bearing a Canadian catalogue number such as the GN 50-foot flatcar with log load and the Penn Central flatcar with vans. Both of these units were uncatalogued and available in Canada in 1975 and 1976. They were then repackaged in the white U.S. carton in 1977.

All building kits and accessories were packed in the same type of cartons used in the United States. The Parker Brothers name is not found on these boxes.

One thing is sure: Canadian models in their original cartons will surely present the collector with a great challenge. A rule of thumb one can use, when an individual Canadian carton is found having the red and yellow stripes, is that in almost every case the carton will hold an item made just for the Canadian market and only available in Canada.

However, some white cartons made for the U.S. market can also be found containing a Canadian item, but the carton will be stamped with a Canadian T catalogue number. Collectors run into problems when mail order is used to obtain items from Canada and the model shows up in a white carton stamped with the T number while the car itself holds a U.S. number, or no Lionel number of any kind. Some Canadian cars were sold this way.

None of the packaging used in Canada ever appeared in the catalogue, but once you have seen the special carton it is hard to forget. All of them are very eye-catching, which, of course, was their purpose.

PAPER

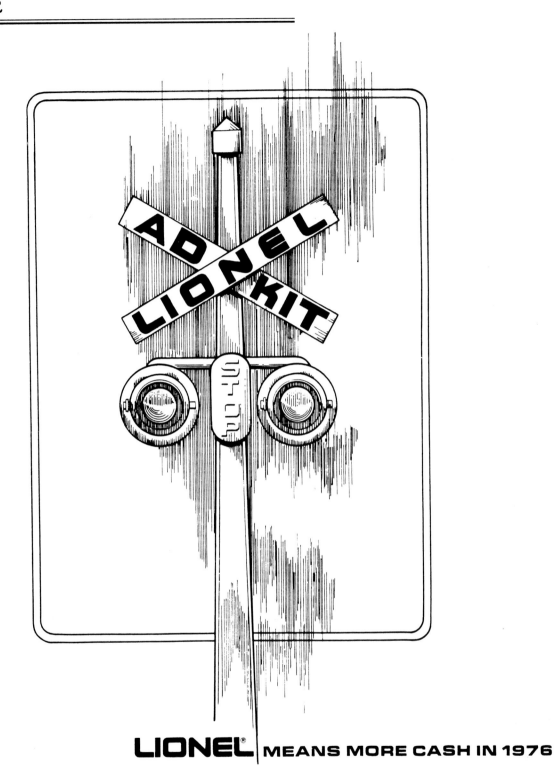

LIONEL® MEANS MORE CASH IN 1976

> Reproduction quality Ads, Headlines, Ad inserts and Artwork to help you establish your store as the place to buy well-known quality Lionel products.

Cover and sample of inside sheet (on next page) of promotional materials supplied to dealers by Lionel; note that no catalogue numbers were included with the illustrations. The packet included statement of the Lionel Warranty Coverage.

CHESSIE — HO

An authentic GP-9 diesel with working headlight and colorful Chessie markings heads this five-unit train set. Every car is authentic in scale and detail. The long cable car has an opening top with cable reels inside.

CHESSIE — HO

An authentic GP-9 diesel with working headlight and color-ful Chessie markings heads this five-unit train set. Every car is authentic in scale and detail. The long cable car has an opening top with cable reels inside.

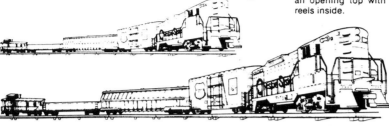

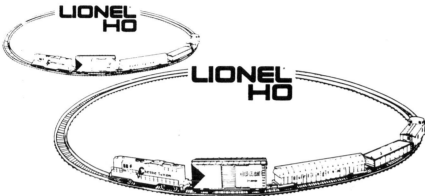

GOLDEN ARROW — HO

Ten different cars with the General Motor' Anniversary gold B&O Chessie at the lead, plus a double oval layout with two switches make for great model railroading with this top of the line set. Included is the Lionel crane car, the finest in HO with a fully operable crane and boom.

GOLDEN ARROW — HO

Ten different cars with the General Motor' Anniversary gold B&O Chessie at the lead, plus a double oval layout with two switches make for great model railroading with this top of the line set. Included is the Lionel crane car, the finest in HO with a fully oper-able crane and boom.

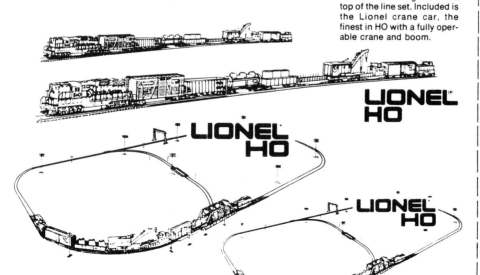

AK76-11

Materials accompanying new sets of 1977 only: cover of an informational booklet shows Southern set 5-2781; below is a large folded map, and an iron-on decal (image reversed) for T-shirt appears on page 86.

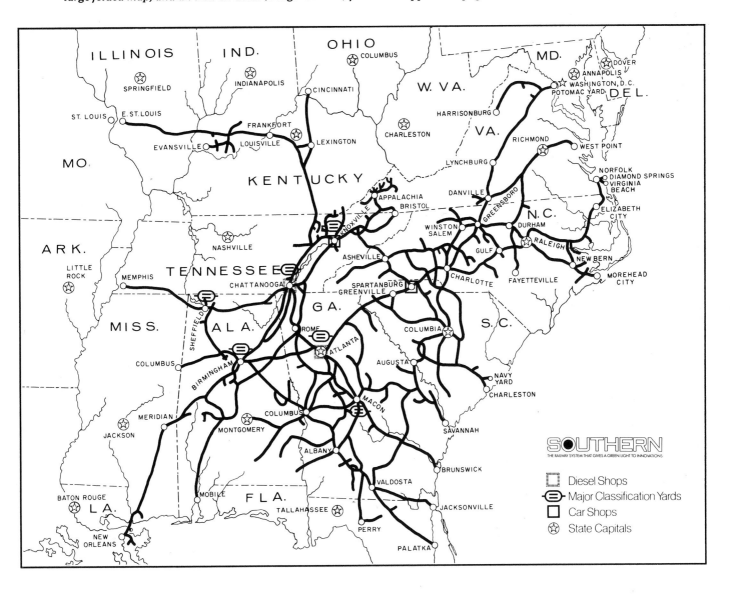

MEMBERSHIP APPLICATION

JOIN NOW! The LIONEL Railroader Club. For only $1.00 you, receive a 1977 LIONEL 027 Catalog, a club patch, a membership card and four "Keep on Trackin'" newsletters per year. You will also be eligible to participate in special offers to club members only.

Print or type your name and address below and send $1.00 to:

    LIONEL Railroader Club
    P. O. Box 1168
    Mt. Clemens, MI 48043

Cash, check or money orders only, NO STAMPS.

Offer expires December 31, 1978. Allow six weeks for delivery.

- -

NAME _____

ADDRESS _____

CITY _____ STATE _____ ZIP _____

                                        70-1760-255

A club similar to the one promoted here was started to encourage kids to grow up as HOers.

CRAFT MASTER • MPC • LIONEL

LIONEL® HO

You will find Lionel sets and accessories at your favorite toy and hobby dealers and we suggest that you see your local dealer for the items you desire. If you are unable to find a dealer who can supply you with our merchandise, you may use this mail order form and we will fill your order.

MAIL TO: **LIONEL/MAIL ORDER**
P.O. BOX 767
Mount Clemens, Michigan 48045

NAME _____ DATE _____

ADDRESS _____

CITY _____ STATE _____ ZIP _____

STOCK NO.	NO. SETS	DESCRIPTION		PRICE
		HO STEAM ENGINES		
5-6500		Southern Pacific Daylight		59.94
5-6501		Freedom Train GS-4		59.94
5-6502		Western Pacific GS-4		59.94
		HO BOX CARS		
5-8701		ConRail	NEW	2.66
5-8702		Southern	NEW	2.66
5-8703		Chessie	NEW	2.66
5-8704		Rail Box	NEW	2.66
		HO REEFER CARS	NEW	
5-8740		Coors	NEW	2.66
5-8741		Budweiser	NEW	2.66
5-8742		Tropicana	NEW	2.66
5-8743		Schlitz	NEW	2.66

STOCK NO.	NO. SETS	DESCRIPTION		PRICE
		HO HI-CUBES		
5-8710		The Rock	NEW	2.66
5-8711		Illinois Central	NEW	2.66
5-8612		Union Pacific		2.66
5-8712		Burlington	NEW	2.66
		HO ACCESSORIES		
5-4501		Rotary Beacon		9.99
5-4530		Trestle Set		6.66
5-4531		Girder Bridge		2.20

STOCK NO.	NO. SETS	DESCRIPTION	PRICE
		HO BUILDING KITS	
5-4551		Pickle Factory	7.55
5-4552		Water Tower	6.88
5-4553		Engine House	7.55
5-4554		Passenger Station	11.99
5-4555		Stockyard w/figures	8.77
5-4556		Boiler House	6.11
5-4557		Rooming House w/figures	6.60
		HO OPERATING ACCESSORIES	
5-8422		Crane Car & Work Caboose	13.88

Prices subject to change without notice. Cash, Check or money order only. Prices include postage.

*Michigan & Ohio residents add 4% sales tax.

NOTE: "New" Items in 1977 catalog may not be ready for shipment until Fall — 1977.
NO C.O.D.

PLEASE ALLOW
6 WEEKS FOR
DELIVERY

ORDER VALUE $_____

SALES TAX* _____

TOTAL $ _____

3-1-77

Customers direct mail order form and catalogue page, featuring new HO items

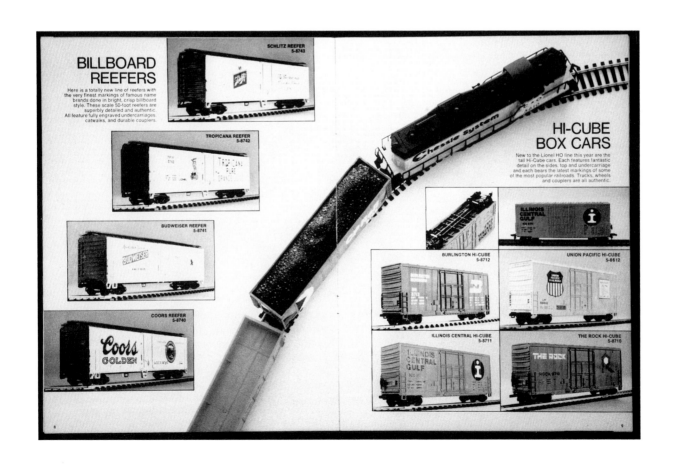

CHAPTER VIII
Motive Components and Couplers, Track, and Frames

MOTIVE COMPONENTS AND COUPLERS

No complete parts list was issued for Lionel HO 1974–1977 (parts for some locomotives are listed on pages 92–97). The following photographs document the components used.

Top row, left to right: Lionel dummy and power truck and Kader dummy and power truck.

Second row, left to right: Components of Lionel power train: housing, sideframe, electric pickup, motor, anchor plate, U clamp, insulation.

Third row, left to right: Wheel sets, worm and drive shaft coupling, clear window material: (a) Hong Kong Alco; (b) Hong Kong Lionel GP-9; (c) U-18-B; (d) Lionel Alco; (e) and (f) are U-18-B number boards; (g) and (h) are Hong Kong light shafts.

Fourth row, left to right shows seven types of trucks, with wheel sets at the far right: (a) GS-4 and crane car six-wheel truck; (b) passenger car four-wheel truck; (c) Kader log car truck; (d) truck used on Taiwan 50-foot cars and cabooses; (e) truck for Taiwan 40-foot cars; (f) truck for all Austrian rolling stock; (g) truck for Lionel rolling stock; (h) wheels sets for, top to bottom, Hong Kong, Austrian, and Lionel cars.

Fifth row: Couplers and trim for, left to right: (a) Taiwan cabooses; (b) Taiwan 40-foot rolling stock; (c) Hong Kong power units; (d) Lionel power units; (e) Lionel rolling stock; (f) Austrian rolling stock; (g) Lionel caboose; (h) Taiwan caboose trim; (i) Lionel caboose trim.

TRACK

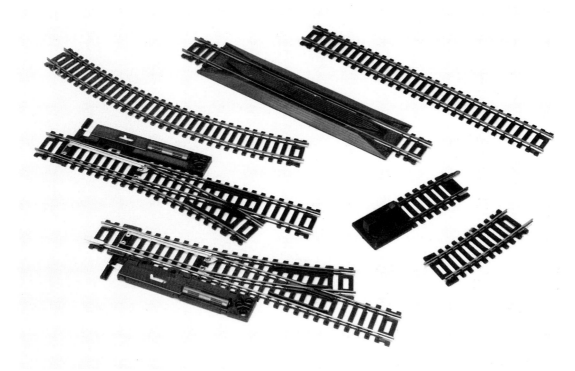

Assortment of Atlas-made track available in early sets of 1974–1975 in U.S. market only. All items are marked Atlas, with no Lionel name present.

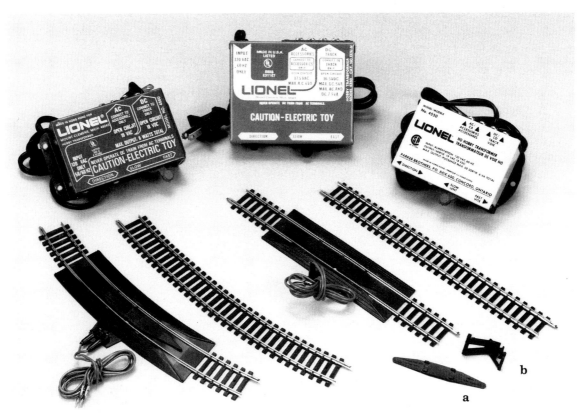

At top, transformers (shown left to right as available in U.S. and Canadian sets, and Canadian sets only); below, track and rerailer stamped Bachmann (a), and bumper (b) used in sets after 1975. All were Kader Hong Kong products and marked as such.

FRAMES

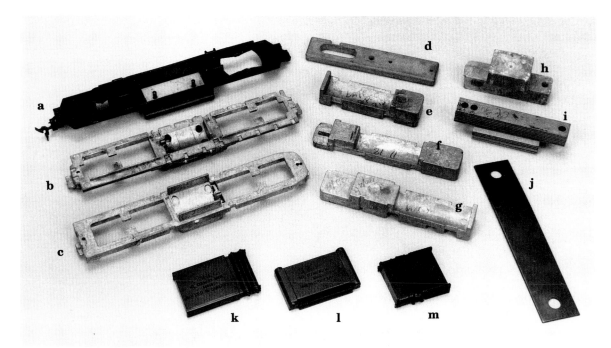

Frames, weights, battery box area used on power units from 1974 to 1977.

Frames: (a) Hong Kong Geeps; (b) Lionel Geeps and U-18-B; (c) Lionel FA-1.

Weights: (d) early 1974 Geeps and Alco Lionel; (e) late 1974 Geep and Alco Lionel; (f) eight-wheel 1976 U-18-B and Alco Lionel; (g) eight-wheel 1975 Geep and Alco Lionel; (h) lead weight for Geeps and Alco, Hong Kong; (i) metal plates for Geeps and Alco, Hong Kong; (j) all rolling stock, Hong Kong.

Battery box area: (k) Lionel GP-9; (l) Lionel U-18-B; (m) Lionel Alcos; none found on Hong Kong–made power units.

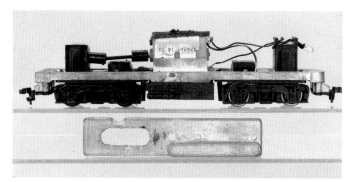

Type I: Early 1974 Alco FA-1

Type III: 1975 Alco FA-1

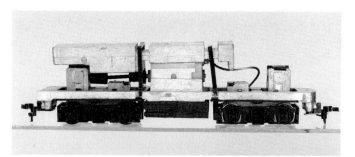

Type II: Late 1974 Alco FA-1 (bulb for headlight missing)

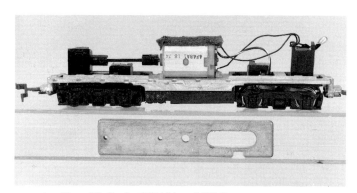

Type IV: Early 1974 Lionel GP-9

Type V: Late 1974 Lionel GP-9

Type IX frame: Hong Kong–made GP-9 drive of 1977, with metal plate weight

Type VI: 1975 Lionel GP-9. Note: rear coupler (left) installed upside down.

Type X frame: Lionel eight-wheel drive for U-18-B of 1976 (couplers have been removed to show cast-on pockets)

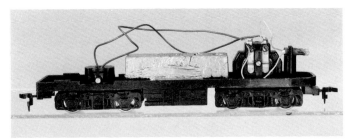

Type VII frame: Hong Kong–made drive; 1976 Alco with Lionel shell. The all-plastic drive was first used on the Kader-made Santa Fe Alco of 1976–1977. Note small pancake-type motor, large lead weight, and metal pin in rear truck. Bulb for headlight is completely hidden by sleeve of insulation at front of frame. There is more detail in the battery box area than in any other Kader-built locomotive.

Type XI frame: Hong Kong drive of 1976 used on first GP-30

Type VIII frame: Hong Kong–made GP-9 drive of 1976, with metal weight. Note that the detail found on Lionel models in the battery box area is missing, with only the air tanks shown.

Type XII: Hong Kong GS-4 drive and frame of 1975 used on all three GS-4 steam locomotives

Lionel HO Locomotive Parts List

HO-6501
PL75

50-6501 GS 4 NORTHERN LOCOMOTIVE

PART NO.	LIST PRICE	DESCRIPTION
50-6501-2	8.50	Boiler & Cab
50-6501-8	1.00	Boilerfront
50-6501-21	.15	Headlight Lens
50-6501-11	.25	Cab Roof
50-6501-7	.05	Cab Screw
50-6501-18	.10	Handrail
50-6501-19	.04	Handrail Post
50-6501-10	.75	Underframe
50-6501-12	.05	Flat Phillips Hd.Sc(Underframe)
50-6501-15	1.00	Steamchest
50-6501-20	1.50	Front End Wheels & Axle W/Washers
50-6501-25	1.50	End Wheels W/Square Center Axle Assem.
50-6501-30	1.50	End Wheels W/Round Center Axle Assem.
50-6501-35	2.00	End Wheels W/Gear & Axle Assem.
50-6501-40	1.00	Front Truck Complete
50-6501-41	.20	Front Truck Frame
50-6501-42	.10	Pivot Screw - Front Truck
50-6501-43	.05	Washer - Front Truck
50-6501-44	.10	Spring - Front Truck
50-6501-45	.25	Wheels & Axle - Front Truck
50-6501-50	1.50	Rear Truck Complete
50-6501-51	.30	Rear Truck Frame
50-6501-52	.30	Wheels W/Axle - Rear Truck
50-6501-43	.05	Washer - Rear Truck
50-6501-55	.10	Spring - Rear Truck
50-6501-42	.10	Pivot Screw - Rear Truck
50-6501-57	.15	Rear Truck & Drawbar Support
50-6501-54	.10	Drawbar
50-6501-56	.05	Washer - Drawbar
50-6501-58	.05	Drawbar Screw
50-6501-60	.75	Brushplate Assem.
50-6501-61	.15	Brush Holder
50-6501-62	3.00	Armature
50-6501-67	.25	Armature Pinion
50-6501-68	.25pr.	Brush
50-6501-69	.10	Brush Spring
50-6501-70	.05	Brush Spring Screw
50-6501-71	.15	Motor Housing Spacer - Round
50-6501-72	.10	Motor Housing Spacer - Square

HO-6501

50-6501 GS 4 NORTHERN LOCOMOTIVE

PART NO.	LIST PRICE	DESCRIPTION
50-6501-73	.05	Motor Housing Screw
50-6501-74	.40	Lamp Assembly
50-6501-75	.05	Lamp Screw
50-6501-76	.50	Drive Gear - Large
50-6501-77	.30	Drive Gear - Small
50-6501-80	.25	Valve Hanger R.H.
50-6501-81	.25	Valve Hanger L.H.
50-6501-82	.10	Rod Support - Valve Hanger
50-6501-83	1.25	Crosshead & Combination Lever Assem. RH
50-6501-84	1.25	Crosshead & Combination Lever Assem.LH
50-6501-85	.75	Eccentric Rod Assem, R.H.
50-6501-86	.75	Eccentric Rod Assem. L.H.
50-6501-87	.10	Side Rod - Front 2 Wheels
50-6501-88	.10	Side Rod - Center Wheels
50-6501-89	.10	Side Rod - Rear Wheels
50-6501-90	.05	Push Pin - Side Rod
50-6501-91	.05	Push Pin - Eccentric Rod
50-6501-92	.05	Spacer - Eccentric Rod

ALCO - SINGLE DRIVE

PART NO.	LIST PRICE	DESCRIPTION
50-5500-450	1.50	Frame
50-5500-22	.15	Coupler
50-5500-20	.07	Coupler Cover
50-5400-105	.40	Headlight Bulb
50-5500-40	.05	Headlight Post
50-5500-42	.20	Truck Retainer
50-5400-4	.35	Frame Skirt
50-5500-510	5.25	Motor
50-5500-32	.30	Female Universal Joint
50-5500-30	.35	Drive Shaft
50-5500-418	.60	Weight Bar
50-5500-150	.15	Insulating Pad (Motor)*
50-5500-44	.10	Strap (Weight Bar)*
50-5500-545	8.00	Power Truck
50-5500-430	1.00	Gear Housing R.H.
50-5500-25	.40	Gear Housing Side Cover R.H.
50-5500-435	.20	Bearing Sleeve
50-5400-116	.30	16T Idler Gear (Small)
50-5400-117	.30	18T Idler Gear (Large)
50-5500-532	1.25	Worm/Shaft & Gear
50-5500-533	.90	Gear & Shaft Assem.
50-5400-135	.15	Thrust Bearing (Square)
50-5500-810	.15	Through Bearing
505400-160	1.25	Wheel Axle - Gear Assem.
50-5400-162	.15	Traction Tire
50-5400-136	.60	Bottom Cover
50-5500-535	5.00	Dummy Truck
50-5500-440	1.00	Gear Housing
50-5500-26	.40	Gear Housing Side Cover
50-5500-435	.20	Bearing Sleeve
50-5500-523	.40	Pick-up Strip Assem.
50-5400-170	1.25	Wheel-Axle-Gear Assem.
50-5400-136	.60	Bottom Cover

Author's Note: Without these two items, this list (1975) would be accurate for 1974; the insulating pad was solid rubber in 1975 and sponge rubber in 1974.

ALCO DUAL DRIVE

PART NO.	LIST PRICE	DESCRIPTION
50-5500-450	1.50	Frame
50-5500-22	.15	Coupler
50-5500-20	.07	Coupler Cover
50-5400-105	.40	Headlight Bulb
50-5500-40	.05	Headlight Post
50-5500-42	.20	Truck Retainer
50-5400-4	.35	Frame Skirt
50-5500-510	5.25	Motor
50-5500-32	.30	Female Universal Joint
50-5500-30	.35	Drive Shaft
50-5500-418	.60	Weight Bar
50-5500-150	.15	Insulating Pad (Motor)
50-5500-44	.10	Strap (Weight Bar)
50-5500-540	8.00	Power Truck R.H.
50-5500-430	1.00	Gear Housing R.H.
50-5500-25	.40	Gear Housing Side Cover R.H.
50-5500-435	.20	Bearing Sleeve
50-5400-116	.30	16T Idler Gear (Small)
50-5400-117	.30	18T Idler Gear (Large)
50-5500-532	1.25	Worm/Shaft & Gear
50-5500-533	.90	Gear & Shaft Assem.
50-5400-135	.15	Thrust Bearing (Square)
50-5500-810	.15	Through Bearing
50-5400-170	1.25	Wheel-Axle-Gear Assem.
50-5400-136	.60	Bottom Cover
50-5500-523	.40	Pick-up Strip Assem.
50-5500-530	8.00	Power Truck L.H.
50-5500-440	1.00	Gear Housing L.H.
50-5500-26	.40	Gear Housing Side Cover L.H.
50-5500-435	.20	Bearing Sleeve
50-5400-116	.30	16T Idler Gear (Small)
50-5400-117	.30	18T Idler Gear (Large)
50-5500-532	1.25	Worm/Shaft & Gear
50-5500-533	.90	Gear & Shaft Assem.
50-5400-135	.15	Thrust Bearing (Square)
50-5500-810	.15	Through Bearing
50-5400-170	1.25	Wheel/Axle & Gear Assem.
50-5400-136	.60	Bottom Cover
50-5500-523	.40	Pick-up Strip Assem.

GP 9 DUAL DRIVE

PART NO.	LIST PRICE	DESCRIPTION
50-5500-460	1.50	Frame
50-5500-23	.15	Coupler
50-5500-21	.07	Coupler
50-5400-105	.40	Headlight Bulb
50-5510-40	.05	Headlight Post
50-5500-42	.20	Truck Retainer
50-5402-4	.35	Frame Skirt
50-5500-510	5.25	Motor
50-5500-32	.30	Femal Universal Joint
50-5500-31	.35	Drive Shaft
50-5500-418	.60	Weight Bar
50-5500-150	.15	Insulating Pad (Motor)
50-5500-41	.10	Strap (Weight Bar)
50-5500-540	8.00	Power Truck R.H.
50-5500-430	1.00	Gear Housing R.H.
50-5500-25	.40	Gear Housing Side Cover RH
50-5500-435	.20	Bearing Sleeve
50-5400-116	.30	16T Idler Gear (Small)
50-5400-117	.30	18T Idler Gear (Large)
50-5500-532	1.25	Worm/Shaft Gear
50-5500-533	.90	Gear & Shaft Assem.
50-5400-135	.15	Thrust Bearing (Square)
50-5500-810	.15	Through Bearing
50-5400-170	1.25	Wheel-Axle-Gear Assem.
50-5400-136	.60	Bottom Cover
50-5500-523	.40	Pick-up Strip Assem.
50-5500-530	8.00	Power Truck L.H.
50-5500-550	1.00	Gear Housing L.H.
50-5500-26	.40	Gear Housing Side Cover L.H.
50-5500-435	.20	Bearing Sleeve
50-5400-116	.30	16T Idler Gear (Small)
50-5400-117	.30	18T Idler Gear (Large)
50-5500-532	1.25	Worm/Shaft & Gear
50-5500-533	.90	Gear & Shaft Assem.
50-5400-135	.15	Thrust Bearing (Square)
50-5500-810	.15	Through Bearing
50-5400-170	1.25	Wheel/Axle & Gear Assem.
50-5400-136	.60	Bottom Cover
50-5500-523	.40	Pick-up Strip Assem.

GP 9 SINGLE DRIVE

PART NO.	LIST PRICE	DESCRIPTION
50-5500-460	1.50	Frame
50-5500-23	.15	Coupler
50-5500-21	.07	Coupler Cover
50-5400-105	.40	Headlight Bulb
50-5510-40	.05	Headlight Post
50-5500-42	.20	Truck Retainer
50-5402-4	.35	Frame Skirt
50-5500-510	5.25	Motor
50-5500-32	.30	Female Universal Joint
50-5500-31	.35	Drive Shaft
50-5500-418	.60	Weight Bar
50-5500-150	.15	Insulating Pad (Motor)
50-5500-41	.10	Strap Weight Bar)
50-5500-545	8.00	Power Truck
50-5500-430	1.00	Gear Housing R.H.
50-5500-25	.20	Gear Housing Side Cover R.H.
50-5500-435	.30	Bearing Sleeve
50-5400-116	.30	16T Idler Gear (Small)
50-5400-117	.30	18T Idler Gear (Large)
50-5500-532	1.25	Worm/Shaft & Gear
50-5500-533	.90	Gear & Shaft Assem.
50-5400-135	.15	Thrust Bearing (Square)
50-5500-810	.15	Through Bearing
50-5400-160	1.25	Wheel-Axle-Gear Assem.
50-5400-162	.15	Traction Tire
50-5400-136	.60	Bottom Cover
50-5500-535	5.00	Dummy Truck
50-5500-440	1.00	Gear Housing
50-5500-26	.40	Gear Housing Side Cover
50-5500-435	.20	Bearing Sleeve
50-5500-523	.40	Pick-up Strip Assem.
50-5400-170	1.25	Wheel-Axle-Gear Assem.
50-5400-136	.60	Bottom Cover

SELECTED INSTRUCTION SHEETS

LIONEL®

OF **fundimensions** DIVISION OF GENERAL MILLS FUN GROUP, INC., MOUNT CLEMENS, MICHIGAN 48043

75-5505-250

HO DIESEL ENGINES

ALCO & GP 9 TROUBLE SHOOTING

LOCOMOTIVE STOPS OR FAILS TO START:

1. Unplug the power pack.
2. Check to see that all locomotive and car wheels are properly on the track.
3. Remove any sort of metal that is across the two rails.
4. Check to see that all rail joints are tight.
5. Check to see that all wiring connections are correct.
6. After locating and correcting the short circuit or loose connection, normal operation can resume.

LOCOMOTIVE RUNS ERRATICALLY:

Clean track rails and metal wheels of the locomotive with track cleaner available from your local hobby dealer. Never use sandpaper or steel wool to clean the track or locomotive wheels.

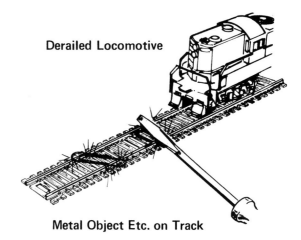

Derailed Locomotive

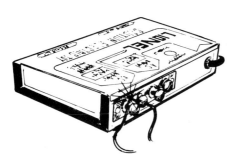

Bare Wires Touching

Metal Object Etc. on Track

GP 9 HANDRAIL ASSEMBLY INSTRUCTIONS

IMPORTANT: READ THROUGH COMPLETELY BEFORE ASSEMBLING

The enclosed handrail assembly is an excellent example of Lionel fine detailing and railroad realism. All model railroaders are aware that excellence in detailing is seldom achieved simply or quickly; rather, it often requires care and is time consuming.

Please follow the following suggestions concerning handrail attachment. Proceed slowly and with caution, to prevent damage to the handrail assembly or locomotive body. Do not rush. Special care will result in an appearance that offers superb authenticity and realism.

ASSEMBLY INSTRUCTIONS

Remove handrails and stanchions from package, being careful not to bend them. Count out correct number of stanchions per railing. Four each for front and rear, eight for each long side railing, two for each short side railing.

(1.) To avoid damaging the locomotive body during assembly, protect the body by inserting a piece of heavy paper or cardboard between the railing and the body. This will prevent nicks or scratches on the body.

(2.) Insert railing ends into appropriate holes as shown. (See Figure A).

(3.) Position and insert stanchions into their proper holes. (See Figure B).

(4.) Using a pair of long nosed pliers, carefully crimp each stanchion around the railing. (See Figure C).

(5.) After all the stanchions have been attached to the railings, it may be necessary to straighten them by sliding them up or back on the railing.

FIGURE A

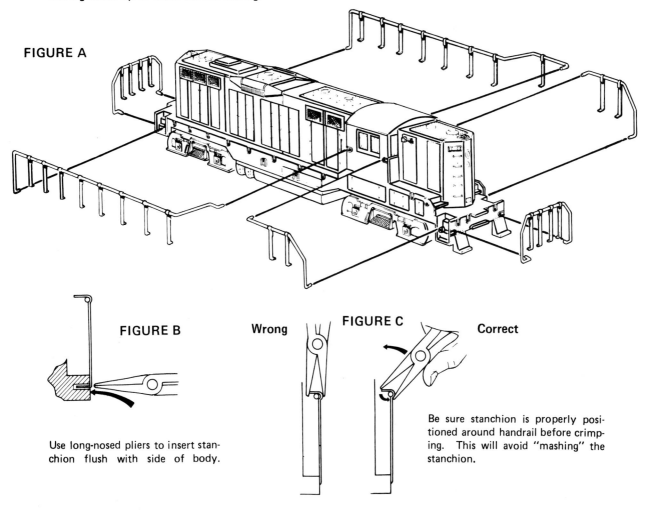

FIGURE B

Use long-nosed pliers to insert stanchion flush with side of body.

FIGURE C

Wrong

Correct

Be sure stanchion is properly positioned around handrail before crimping. This will avoid "mashing" the stanchion.

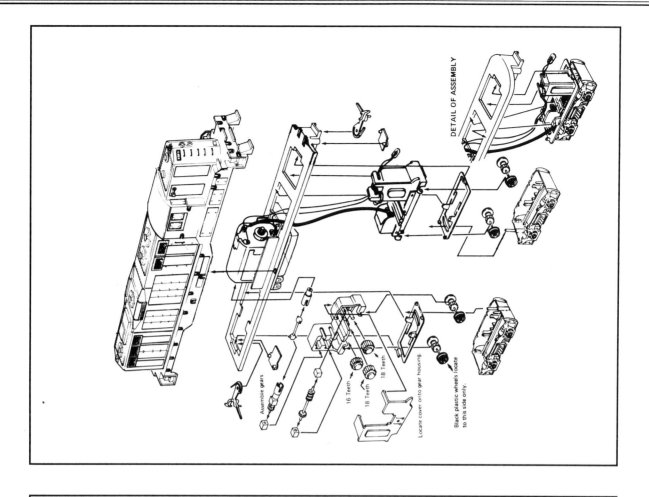

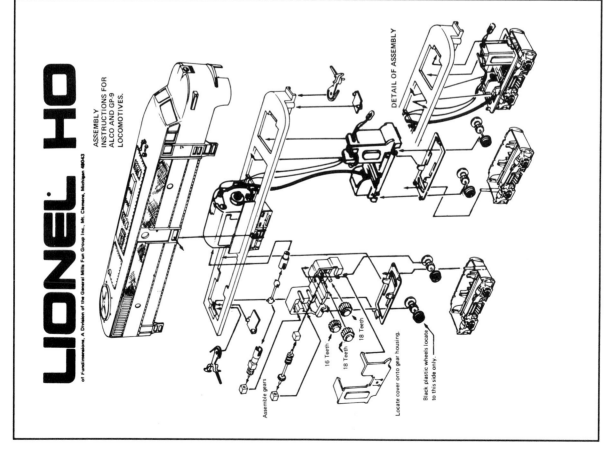

LIONEL® HO

75-2586-250

OPERATING INSTRUCTIONS

OF **fundimensions** DIVISION OF GENERAL MILLS FUN GROUP, INC., MOUNT CLEMENS, MICHIGAN 48043

FOR SETS:

| 5-2586 | 5-2587 | 5-2680 | 5-2681 | 5-2682 |
| 5-2683 | 5-2684 | 5-2686 | 5-2690 | 5-2692 |

Ask an adult to plug in your power pack for you when you are ready to operate your train. Before you attempt to operate the train set read this complete instruction sheet. There are important instructions on train operation and directions on avoiding damage to your train set through misuse.

**Safety
Figure 1**

CAUTION–ELECTRICALLY OPERATED PRODUCT:

NOT RECOMMENDED FOR CHILDREN UNDER EIGHT YEARS OF AGE. AS WITH ALL ELECTRIC PRODUCTS, PRECAUTIONS SHOULD BE OBSERVED DURING HANDLING AND USE TO PREVENT ELECTRIC SHOCK.

Parents should periodically inspect power pack for potential hazard and have repaired it necessary. See Lionel Service Station Listing for information and address of nearest authorized Service Station.

POWER PACK RATINGS – INPUT: 120 VOLTS AC ONLY, 60 HZ. 120 VOLTS AC ONLY, 50/60 HZ. MAX. OUTPUT: 6 WATTS TOTAL.

1 ASSEMBLING TRACK

The small tab on each rail joiner must be pointed toward the rail as illustrated.

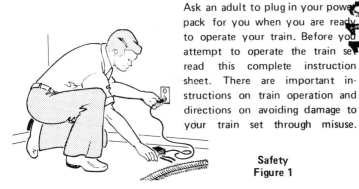

**Installing the Rail Joiners.
Figure 2**

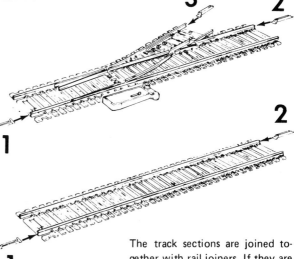

The rail joiners can be inserted on the rails by using a pair of pliers as shown. Carefully push the rail joiners straight onto the rails. Do not twist.

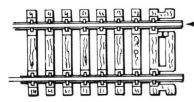

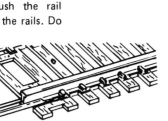

The track sections are joined together with rail joiners. If they are not already installed on the rails, install them in place as shown, two to each track section, three to each switch.

If the rail joiners are loose after insertion, carefully crimp the rail joiners on each side of the rails as illustrated.

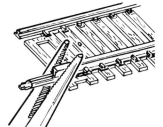

Crimping the Rail Joiners. Figure 3

If there is any flash (excess plastic) over the sides of the rails, have an adult scrap it off with a small knife as shown.

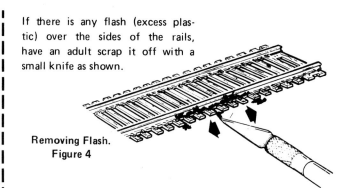

Removing Flash. Figure 4

Install the two rail joiners with lugs and lead wires as shown. These two rail joiners are used to carry power from the power pack to the track. They may be installed between any two sections, preferably close to your power pack.

Installing the Rail Joiners with Lead Wire

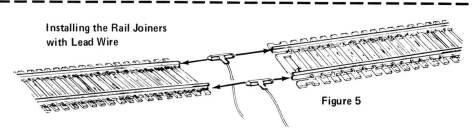

Figure 5

Your completed track layout will match one of those illustrated to the right. Identify yours by stock number and lay out the track pieces on a flat surface in the general shape of the layout. Do not set up your layout on shag carpeting or on soft surfaces. The long threads of shag carpeting may get tangled in the wheels, and soft surfaces do not give the track enough support.

Refer to separate instruction sheet for trestle for trestle set assembly in sets no. 2682, 2686, and 2690.

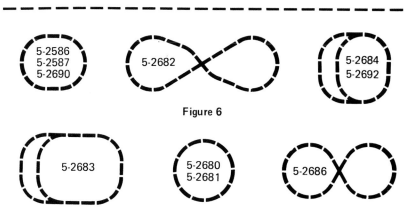

5-2586
5-2587
5-2690

5-2682

5-2684
5-2692

Figure 6

5-2683

5-2680
5-2681

5-2686

Slide the track sections gently together along the flat surface to secure them together. Do not pick up the track during assembly or the rail joiners may bend.

Figure 7

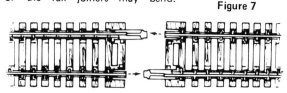

Assembling the Layout

Some sets are equipped with a rerailer track. Other sets have a snap-in rerailer that attaches onto any curved track. The primary function of the rerailer is that in the event of a derailment, the derailed wheels of a car or locomotive are forced to ride back up onto the rails.

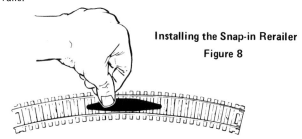

Installing the Snap-in Rerailer
Figure 8

② WIRING LAYOUT TO POWER PACK

Lionel H.O. locomotives run only on Direct Current (d.c.). The power pack included in this set provides sufficient d.c. voltage for locomotive operation. Other transformers should not be used to operate your train unless you are certain they are designed for H.O. trains. Alternating Current (a.c.) transformers will damage the motor of your locomotive.

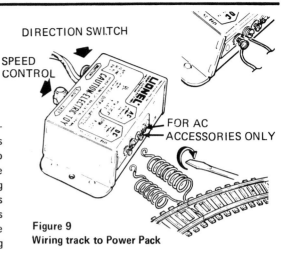

DIRECTION SWITCH

SPEED CONTROL

FOR AC ACCESSORIES ONLY

Figure 9
Wiring track to Power Pack

Lionel power packs have an additional set of binding posts that supply Alternating Current (a.c.). Use the a.c. binding posts ONLY to operate accessories, lights and remote controlled switches. Be sure that the wires from the track are NOT connected to these a.c. binding posts.

Connect the wires from the terminal track to the d.c. binding posts of your power pack. Make a loop with the bare end of wire. Place one loop around each d.c. binding post as shown. Secure the wires by tightening the binding posts with a screwdriver. Be sure the bare loops are not not touching together.

③ OPERATING THE TRAIN

Place only the locomotive on the track, making sure that all the wheels are positioned properly on the track. Move the power pack speed control arm to the slow position and have an adult plug the power pack into a wall outlet. Slowly advance the speed control arm. If the locomotive does not run at all, immediately unplug the power cord and read the instructions regarding Trouble Shooting. All Lionel H.O. locomotives run both forward and reverse. This is controlled by the direction switch on the power pack.

After the locomotive has been running in both directions for a

few minutes the cars may be placed on the track for normal operation. The cars are most easily placed properly on the track by rolling them back and forth over the rerailer until they are rolling smoothly. All Lionel H.O. cars and locomotives are equipped with true-to-life scale couplers manufactured to National Model Railroad Association (NMRA) specifications. The cars will couple when one car is slowly rolled into another car while on any straight section of track. If your set has no straight sections, carefully align the mating car couplers on a curved section to couple them together.

If your set has a manual turnout, the train can be diverted to the spur section by manually operating the controller as shown.

When removing the train from the track, remove the car or locomotive from the right hand end of the train first. Tilt the car toward you at a 45 degree angle and lift the car straight up to disengage

the couplers. ALWAYS UNPLUG THE POWER CORD WHEN YOUR SET IS NOT IN USE OR WHEN REMOVING THE LOCOMOTIVE FROM THE TRACK.

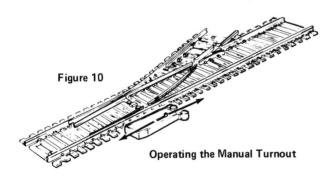

Figure 10

Operating the Manual Turnout

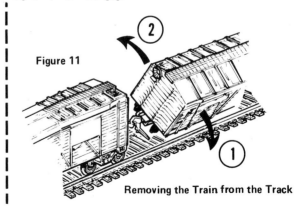

Figure 11

Removing the Train from the Track

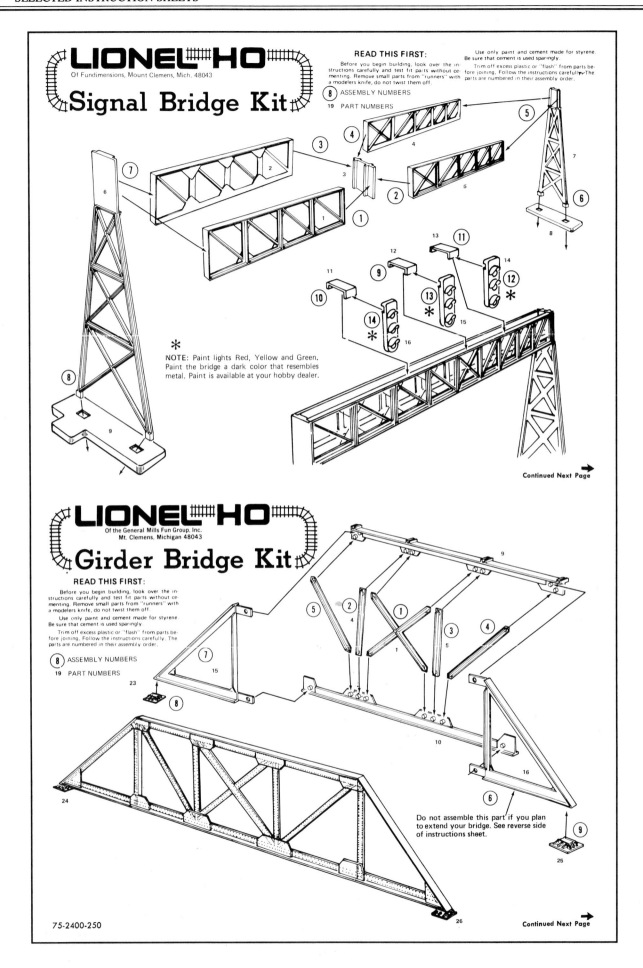

LIONEL HO
Of Fundimensions, Mount Clemens, Mich. 48043

Signal Bridge Kit

READ THIS FIRST:

Before you begin building, look over the instructions carefully and test fit parts without cementing. Remove small parts from "runners" with a modelers knife, do not twist them off.

Use only paint and cement made for styrene. Be sure that cement is used sparingly.

Trim off excess plastic or "flash" from parts before joining. Follow the instructions carefully. The parts are numbered in their assembly order.

8 ASSEMBLY NUMBERS
19 PART NUMBERS

*NOTE: Paint lights Red, Yellow and Green. Paint the bridge a dark color that resembles metal. Paint is available at your hobby dealer.

Continued Next Page

LIONEL HO
Of the General Mills Fun Group, Inc.
Mt. Clemens, Michigan 48043

Girder Bridge Kit

READ THIS FIRST:

Before you begin building, look over the instructions carefully and test fit parts without cementing. Remove small parts from "runners" with a modelers knife, do not twist them off.

Use only paint and cement made for styrene. Be sure that cement is used sparingly.

Trim off excess plastic or "flash" from parts before joining, Follow the instructions carefully. The parts are numbered in their assembly order.

8 ASSEMBLY NUMBERS
19 PART NUMBERS

Do not assemble this part if you plan to extend your bridge. See reverse side of instructions sheet.

75-2400-250

Continued Next Page

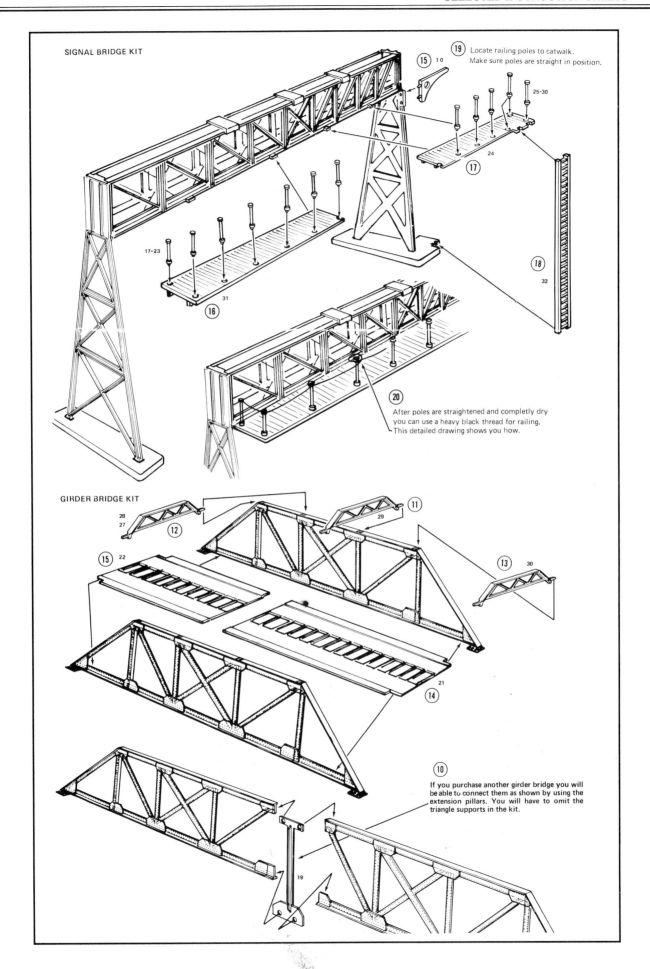

SIGNAL BRIDGE KIT

(19) Locate railing poles to catwalk.
Make sure poles are straight in position.

(15) 10

25-30

(17) 24

17-23

(18) 32

(16) 31

(20) After poles are straightened and completly dry
you can use a heavy black thread for railing.
This detailed drawing shows you how.

GIRDER BRIDGE KIT

28
27
(12)

(11)
29

(15) 22

(13) 30

(14) 21

(10) If you purchase another girder bridge you will
be able to connect them as shown by using the
extension pillars. You will have to omit the
triangle supports in the kit.

19

LIONEL® HO CRANE CAR

of Fundimensions, A Division of the General Mills Fun Group Inc., Mt. Clemens, Michigan 48043

NUMBERED
DECAL 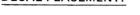 **Road Name Decal**

DECAL IMAGE

DECAL PLACEMENT:

1. See the above illustrations for location of decals.
2. Cut the decals apart close to the images.
3. Dip the decals into water for a few minutes.
4. Remove the decals from the water and slide them from the paper backing onto the car body.
5. Blot out the excess water and air bubbles with a soft, lint-free cloth.
6. Allow time to dry before handling.

Road Name Decal   NUMBERED DECAL

DECAL IMAGE LOCATION

OPERATION:

The fully operable crane swivels 360 degrees into realistic positions for transport or simulated work. The boom and hoist raise and lower independently. They are operated manually by a key inserted in slots on the right side of the cab. The rear slot operates the hoist and the forward slot operates the boom.

Key position for raising and lowering boom.

Key position for raising and lowering hoist.

75-3400-250

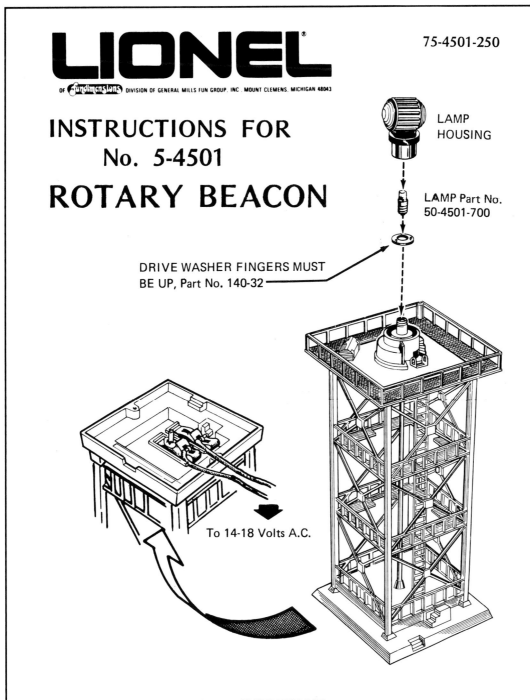

LIONEL®

OF **fundimensions** DIVISION OF GENERAL MILLS FUN GROUP, INC., MOUNT CLEMENS, MICHIGAN 48043

75-4501-250

INSTRUCTIONS FOR
No. 5-4501
ROTARY BEACON

LAMP HOUSING

LAMP Part No. 50-4501-700

DRIVE WASHER FINGERS MUST BE UP, Part No. 140-32

To 14-18 Volts A.C.

IMPORTANT

This Rotary Beacon is designed to operate on 14-18 volts Alternating Current only. This voltage is obtained from power packs which have A.C. terminals, or from transformers. The D.C. power which is used to operate HO locomotives will not operate this beacon and may cause damage.

TROUBLE SHOOTING CHART

PROBLEM / PROBABLE CAUSE	Power pack line cord not plugged into wall outlet	Incorrect wiring between power pack and track	Wires shorted at power pack	Short circuit on track	Dirty engine wheels	Loose wire connections	Dirty track	Track loose, improperly connected or kinked	Car wheels binding	Uncoupler pin too long	Burrs on couplers	Direction switch on power pack
Engine will not run	X	X	X	X	X	X						
Engine hesitates					X	X	X	X				
Engine runs very slowly or overheats					X		X					
Cars constantly derail								X	X	X		
Cars do not stay coupled										X	X	
Engine runs only one direction												X

CORRECTIVE ACTION

- Plug line cord into 120 AC wall outlet See Fig. 1
- Check wiring from track to power pack See Fig. 9
- Check for bare wires touching together at the power pack. See Fig. 15
- Remove metal objects that may be laying across the track. Check to see if engine has derailed. See Fig. 16
- Clean engine wheels with track cleaner available from your local hobby dealer. Do not use sandpaper or steel wool.
- Secure wires at the power pack binding posts by tightening with a screwdriver. See Fig. 9
- Clean track rails with track cleaner available from your local hobby dealer. Do not use sandpaper or steel wool
- Check tightness or track. Make sure rail joiners are properly inserted. Crimp loose rail joiners with a pair of pliers to provide a tight fit. See Fig. 2, 3, 5, 7
- Check wheels and trucks to be sure there is free movement.
- If the coupler pins touch the rerailer or switch, trim them so they just clear all track sections.
- If the couplers have plastic burrs, gently scrape off these tiny bumps with a small knife.
- Operate the direction switch located on side of Power Pack. See Fig. 9

GLOSSARY

Advance catalogue A catalogue sent to dealers prior to release of consumer catalogue for a given year; Lionel used this tool to obtain advance reservations for new items; items which did not receive sufficient interest would be omitted from the consumer catalogue.

Alco FA 1 Type of powered locomotive (prototype) used on main line freight and passenger service.

Body-mounted couplers Couplers housed in a pocket attached to or molded on car floor; opposite of talgo type.

Cast-on detail A detail apparent on a part, such as body shell; opposite of separate detail parts, which are molded or cast individually and added to the main body.

Chemically blackened metal part A part which has been colored black by use of a chemical process rather than painting.

Decorative horn A scale model of the horn found on prototype locomotives; the decorative horn, as distinct from an electrical horn placed inside the unit to produce actual sounds, serves only to enhance the realism of the model.

Die-casting A process which makes smooth and accurate castings by forcing molten metal into a die or hollow steel block.

Direct drive A power truck with the motor being attached to and a part of the truck itself.

Dynamic brakes The fan and tank area found at the middle top of the long hood on GP-9 models.

Fish belly Flatcar of different lengths with a straight deck (or floor) and with the center of the sides depressed following the lines of the frame.

Four-number board door A boxcar door with four flat panels on which numbers or lettering are applied.

Gear drive A tooth gear fixed to the end of the motor shaft to transmit power to a geared axle.

Geep Slang used to identify general purpose power locomotive (GP-9).

GS-4 General service steam loco used for freight and passenger service.

Hobbyline Original owner of diework used to produce most of the Lionel HO models of 1959–1966.

Horn hook coupler The standard coupler used by most manufacturers of HO-scale trains; designated "X2f" by the National Model Railroad Association; also called "NMRA" couplers.

Injection molding A process which shapes plastic by using heat and pressure in molds.

Pancake motor Small three-pole motor of foreign manufacture, usually fixed directly to a power truck.

Phenolic plastic Thermosetting plastics which cannot be heated and remelted once molded; Bakelite is one brand. See **Thermoplastics**.

Plug door Found on insulated type of cars such as reefers or boxcars carrying perishables.

Rigid frame truck A freight or passenger car truck lacking an equalization mechanism, such as a set of springs; generally, a one-piece plastic truck frame with separate wheel sets.

Silkscreened lettering Lettering applied by a painting process, in which a silk screen is employed; the screen serves as a negative to the lettering, thus paint forced through the screen forms the lettering on the model.

Stamped lettering Lettering which is applied directly to item with an inked positive pad, usually rubber.

Talgo truck A freight or passenger car truck with coupler pocket attached.

Thermoplastics Plastics which can be heated and remelted and can be softened to avoid cracking. See **Phenolic plastics**.

Traction tire A rubber belt imbedded in the drive wheels of power units to improve its pulling power and lessen slippage on the track.

Washed-out Term for lettering so thinly applied one can see the basic underlying color of the model coming through.

Worm drive Lionel's power drive used on its diesel units with a worm drive fixed to the motor shaft, transmitting power to geared axles.

INDEX

This index covers Lionel HO 1974–1977 (Volume I covers the earlier era, 1957–1966). It includes both U.S.- and Canadian-market models. Items custom-painted are included and specially designated. Sets and accessories are not included in the following index.

Descriptive listings and illustrations are indexed by catalogue numbers, and side-of-car numbers are included in the one numerical sequence below to direct you to a description of the model bearing that number.

Note that if the only difference between catalogue and car numbers lies in the prefix and/or hyphen, what does not appear on the car is shown in parentheses. If the car number has a different prefix or is an entirely different number, that car number is listed separately, and the entire catalogue number appears in parentheses.

Note: For the purposes of this index, the prefixes are not included in the number sequencing. The page numbers in *italics* below indicate an illustration of the item.

ABOUT THE AUTHOR

GEORGE J. HORAN

George Horan's interest in toy trains started in or about 1946, when a lady-friend of his mother gave him a wooden locomotive. He had already started to build a train layout, but with five brothers and two sisters there was little money for toys. The buildings on George's first layout came from General Mills Cheerios cereal boxes — little did he know that General Mills would later produce the Lionel trains that he came to love. George's first job, working on a dry-cleaning truck, provided the funds to make his train table into an operating layout, and his first electric locomotive was a Hobbyline FM diesel with rubber band drive. George used his earnings to buy a sample of every item in Hobbyline's HO line. Following his graduation from high school, he joined the U.S. Marine Corps and served for four years. Finding that he still had the train bug after he finished his service, he returned to his hobby and as other companies' products caught his eye, George soon became a collector.

Before long, George realized that no reference books had been written on the subject of Lionel HO. Louis Hertz, another toy train historian, indicated that he did not have an interest in the smaller trains, but he provided George with insights into the creation of such a book. On the same day that George had this discussion with Louis Hertz, he also met Ernie Davis, president of LCCA. Ernie suggested that George's experience would be a useful guide in producing such a book. Thus, George found inspiration to undertake a project that continues to provide challenges and discoveries.

His collecting interests have not been limited to Lionel models but also include models from Athearn, Globe, Varney, Revell, and English. He is currently at work on the history of English and Hobbyline models, a logical offshoot because we now know that more than half of the 1957–1966 Lionel HO and one-quarter of the 1974–1977 Lionel HO were made from the original Hobbyline diework purchased by Lionel in 1959.

He is coauthor with Vincent Rosa of a previous volume on Lionel HO, covering the earlier production era. Originally published in 1986, this book has been completely revised and expanded by George and published in 1993 as *Greenberg's Guide to Lionel HO, Volume I: 1957–1966*. His collection was also featured in *Greenberg's Guide to Athearn Trains*.